ROLLS-ROYCE

ROLLS-ROYCE

George Oliver

Acknowledgements

The author is unable to thank by name the great number of individuals whose help over the years has made it possible for this book to be written but he must single out for especial mention and thanks his friend and editorial adviser, Anthony Harding, who launched it and kept it afloat during the writing process, his wife, who has so willingly shared his interest in Bentley and Rolls-Royce cars, and the three people who gave him back his life in 1977 – Doctors A. and A.W. Laughland and Doctor A.J. McGuiness.

His debt of gratitude to his friends at Rolls-Royce, for their help and encouragement over a very long period, is also great.

A FOULIS Motoring Book

First published 1988

© George Oliver and Haynes Publishing Group.

Published by:

Haynes Publishing Group, Sparkford, Nr. Yeovil, Somerset BA22 7JJ, England

Haynes Publications Inc. 861 Lawrence Drive, Newbury Park, California 91320 USA

British Library Cataloguing in Publication Data
Oliver, George A.
Rolls-Royce : the history.
1. Rolls-Royce automobile—History
I. Title
629.2'222   TL215.R6
ISBN 0-85429-663-8

Library of Congress Catalog Card No.
ISBN 0 85429 663 8

Editor: Robert Iles
Page layout: Tim Rose
Printed in England by: J.H. Haynes & Co. Ltd.

*Photograph previous pages: **A Corniche Convertible.***

Contents

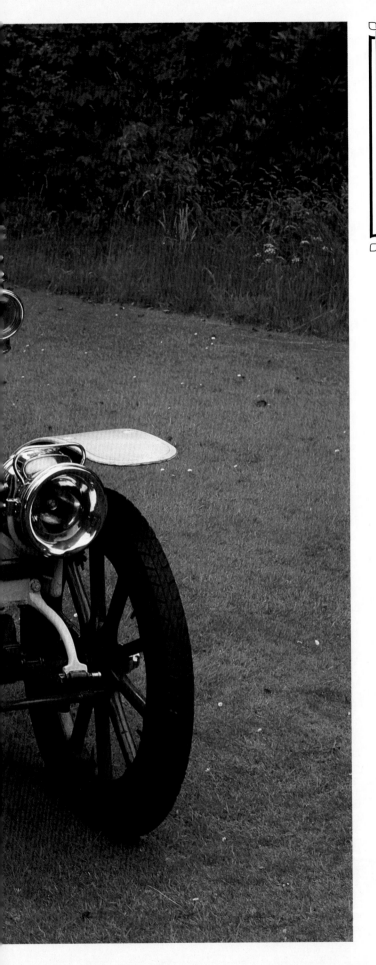

In 1971 there was a very real danger that control of the motor car side of Rolls-Royce Limited might pass into foreign hands. The parent company was in a state of financial collapse (from which it was eventually saved by Government intervention) and the automobile division was open to offer. British ownership was retained, however; Rolls-Royce Limited 1971 was formed, and without apparent delay or hitch of any kind continued to consolidate its position as the world's premier producer of cars of the highest quality, along with a variety of products of other kinds.

Against stronger competition than ever before in the long history of the make and in times of international economic difficulties Rolls-Royce have been able to raise the value of their sales by a significant annual amount and at the time of writing these stand at a higher level than ever before. For several years after 1978 sales were severely affected by the world economic situation. Since then matters have improved steadily. In 1984, 1985 and 1986 production totals were 2,203, 2,377 and 2,603 respectively and by the end of September, 1987 2,009 cars had been sold. Apart from the United States, a market that takes close on 50% of all sales, France & Monaco, Germany, Japan and Spain are very important overseas markets. The Company is properly proud of the fact that it delivered a Bentley Turbo R to the Deputy Prime Minister of Japan, Mr. Shin Kanemaru, in August, 1987. Yearly output has risen well above 3,000 cars: over one-third of

The little 10 hp Rolls-Royce is a model of careful restoration and responsible maintenance.

7

production goes to the United States, export figures, in fact, accounting for more than 50% of total sales. The Company's legendary reputation for the reliability and longevity of its cars, its enduring obsession with excellence of engineering, of execution and of road behaviour, its real concern for long-term customer satisfaction and the maintenance of traditional standards of service are matters of fact and not of fiction.

Idealism is not always a sound proposition, commercially speaking. The men who were primarily responsible for its introduction to the British motor industry in the early years of this century, and their successors, have proved in the most public way possible that it can have sound financial benefits for those involved. Until the First World War Rolls-Royce Limited concerned itself only with the making and marketing of motor cars of the highest possible quality. Profitability increased steadily, year by year. With the addition of aero-engine manufacture from 1915 onwards profits overall continued to rise, and because of wise and careful management the Company was in a sound financial position for much of the span of time covered by this book. Its eventual, involuntary bifurcation in 1971 may have been a disguised blessing for the car side, which regained a freedom of thought and operation that had been restricted to some considerable extent simply because it had become such a relatively small part of a large and complex concern.

Frederick Henry Royce, Charles Stewart Rolls and Claude Goodman Johnson were all Englishmen. Royce was a miller's son and after his father's early death quickly became acquainted with poverty. In almost every sense he was a self-made man, but one who began with certain quite exceptional qualities. He was mentally alert; ingenious – to say the least – mechanically speaking; inventive when necessary but hardly ashamed of the fact that he preferred for much of the time to vastly improve and refine the good ideas of others; eternally curious, a man of wide interests with an all-powerful passion for quality that extended to all that he did. He was a big man, in every way; deceptively benign in appearance, alternately coarse and kind yet always consistent in his search for excellence. For Royce nothing less would do.

Charles Rolls was an aristocrat, whose father, Lord Llangattock, was a rich landowner; unusually for his class he took a sympathetic view as far as his son's strong mechanical interests were concerned and was at all times willing to help him financially and in other ways. Rolls was not afraid of hard physical work on occasion and did not mind dirtying his hands. He was a practical motorist of great experience, a good driver, a splendid demonstrator and an exceptionally able salesman, whose upper-class connections were a most important asset once he entered the motor trade.

Claude Johnson, whose father, an unsuccessful glove manufacturer, eventually joined the staff of

Claude Goodman Johnson, 1864 – 1926

the South Kensington Museum, went to St. Paul's School then, briefly, to the Royal College of Art. Although his aesthetic and sensual awareness were always keen (a fact that may have had much to do with the look and 'feel' of Rolls-Royce cars at a later date) he lacked executive abilities as far as the practice of the visual arts was concerned and took a realistic view of the situation. At the age of nineteen he became a clerk in the Imperial Institute in London, and there he distinguished himself as an organiser of altogether outstanding quality. In 1896, when he was thirty one, he arranged a practical demonstration of "motors and their appliances" at the Institute, at the suggestion of the then Prince of Wales, and a year later he became secretary of the Automobile Club of Great Britain. In 1899 he passengered Charles Rolls in the Paris-Ostend road race and in 1900 he was responsible for the organisation of the important 1,000-mile Trial in England. Three years later he joined Rolls as partner in C.S. Rolls & Co., Motor Agents.

these, however, and the high standards of engineering excellence set by Royce were matched by equally high levels of administration, publicity and salesmanship on the part of Rolls and Johnson backed up, it may be said, by a staff of great competence.

Very quickly the cars established a reputation for quality of construction and running, far above average reliability and low operating costs. Their makers built a reputation for commercial probity and efficiency that few, if any, of their contemporaries could match, and their attention to really effective after-sales service singled them out from most others. There was a Rolls-Royce way of doing things, almost from the start. There still is.

The Hon Charles Stewart Rolls, 1877 – 1910

Frederick Henry Royce (later Sir Henry Royce), 1863 – 1933.

How this trinity met is told later. Despite their very different social backgrounds they shared many common interests and aims, and their pooled practical experience and knowledge was of enormous value in creating the Rolls-Royce car in the first place and, in the second, marketing it in the most effective way possible on strictly limited resources. Imagination was not one of

Well before 1914 the make was recognised internationally as the leading one in the luxury-car class. Its hyphenated name (an inspired choice) became as much a symbol of quality in its field as Bechstein, Zeiss, Purdie, Worth and others had become in theirs – yet the 40/50 hp. model that set Rolls-Royce ahead of all its rivals in those distant, pre-First World War days, was made in comparatively small numbers. Although it was the best of its kind overall it was not the most expensive, and as history has shown early examples are worth many, many times their original cost. What is more depreciation on recent models has been low or non-existent; the make, as they say, is a good investment.

But a present-day Rolls-Royce, or its sister Bentley, is a great deal more than that. In its current forms it is an enormously complex, highly developed automobile that is exceptionally well tailored to its owner's tastes and needs, made in a quite different manner (but to the same unique standards) as all its forebears and likely to be as long lived. Between 1907 and 1925 less than 7,000 40/50 hp. Rolls-Royces of the side-valve type were built – slightly more than twice present-day yearly output from Crewe. A high percentage has survived – visible evidence of the quality of their design and construction and their varied attractions from an owning and driving point of view.

How many of the current range of cars will still be in use fifty, sixty or seventy years from now is a question more easily answered if one had foreknowledge of the state of the world fuel supplies next century. The least that can be said with confidence is that plenty of these cars will still be in existence.

Royce was a successful electrical engineer and manufacturer when he began to tinker with the motor car and Rolls, too, had practical experience with electricity. Each would have been greatly taken with the practical applications of this invisible, inaudible source of energy in the current cars from Crewe. Although these are still propelled by an internal-combustion engine and their suspension, ride height, braking system and power-steering rely on hydraulics for their operation, most other functions are electrically actuated. Windows rise or fall at the touch of switches, doors are electrically locked, changes of gear are signalled to the gearbox by electrical means and even the adjustment of front seats is controlled electrically, by tiny 'levers.' It is hardly surprising to learn that each modern Rolls-Royce or Bentley car carries close on a mile of wiring. Until comparatively recent times Rolls-Royce made most electrical equipment themselves – just as they made the majority of other parts for their cars.

Royce preferred that way to buying-in from specialists, and as long as he was in charge, his policy was followed. After his death in 1933, however, there was a gradual change of attitude, based more and more on realistic financial grounds. The highly efficient and beautifully made Rolls-Royce carburettor, for example, gave way to an S.U. based instrument on later "Phantom II' chassis and on the smaller 20/25 hp. model, Stromberg downdraught carburettors were fitted to the 25/30, the "Wraith" and to the V-12 "Phantom III". Marles steering was a feature of the last 20/25 chassis and of all 25/30s, along with Borg and Beck clutches, for example.

After the Second World War, when the Robotham-inspired policy of rationalisation was finally put into practice, there was even greater dependence on outside suppliers, but with strict controls from Crewe to make certain that close adherence to factory standards was maintained.

In Royce's time the ideas of others were adopted if they were considered good enough, then greatly improved – a case in point being the mechanically-operated brake-servo that Marc Birkigt created in the first place for his 37.2 hp. Hispano-Suiza. Much more recently Rolls-Royce have adopted (and adapted) American-designed automatic transmission systems, for example, and in the suspension of the current "Silver Spirit" and its derivatives Citroen help is freely acknowledged. The independent front-wheel suspension of the pre-war "Phantom III" and "Wraith" models was based on a General Motors design, which is ironical in a way because Maurice Olley, who did so much to develop it in the United States in the nineteen-thirties, was a former Rolls-Royce employee.

Connections with America began in 1906, as will be seen, and continue. During much of the 'thirties W.A. Robotham, who had worked with Ernest Hives in the all-important Experimental Department for ten years or so, made regular visits to the States to maintain contacts with the automobile industry there and was keenly aware of a difference in scale that enabled the volume sales of the cheaper kind of car to subsidise experimental work on a truly lavish scale as well as the production of costly (but possibly unprofitably) cars of real quality.

Reference has been made already to the high

standards of service established early in the history of the Company. By 1906 an inspection system had been put into effect, customers and their cars being visited at regular intervals by highly qualified inspectors, who maintained a valuable link between the owners and the works. They also saw to it that maintenance was carried out to Rolls-Royce recommendations. By 1909 the Company was so confident of the quality of its materials and workmanship that a 3-year guarantee was issued with each chassis. It still is, though nowadays it applies to the whole car.

Physical toughness has always been a feature. Safety margins are high. Early participation in competitive motoring had much to do with this, any component failures being exhaustively investigated and rectified without delay. The cars that

were specially prepared for the 1913 Austrian Alpine Trial, for example, were much modified as a result of experience in the previous year's event, and these improvements were quickly incorporated in production chassis. The margin of strength that they provided was of the greatest practical value during the 1914-18 war, when so many 40/50 Rolls-Royce chassis were adapted for service as armoured cars. The normal peacetime weight limit of $2^{1}/_{2}$ tons was forgotten then; in operational order all-up weight approached five tons and when necessary vehicles were driven at speed over appalling surfaces.

Yet structural failures under such extreme conditions were almost non-existent and along with the light-weight Model "T" Ford the costly 40/50 hp. Rolls-Royce shared honours as the most satisfactory vehicles of their respective types in Allied service. Armoured car squadrons were operationally active in Belgium and France in the

Henry Royce beside one of his side-valve 40/50 hp, cars in the early 'twenties.

early stages of the war, and at a later date were transferred to Libya, to Mesopotamia and to Palestine, where the power and reliability of the cars, plus their great cross-country mobility, were highly regarded. Lawrence of Arabia was a user and admirer who made grateful acknowledgement in his *Seven Pillars of Wisdom* and further references may be found in S.C. Rolls's account of his experiences with the Duke of Westminster's Rolls-Royce armoured car brigade between 1915 and 1917.*

Between the wars some of the survivors remained on active service in the Middle East; indeed many were still operational there during the early stages of the last war. This Services contact was maintained after the introduction of the "B-series" range of engines: the rationalised design evolved in 1938, with overhead-inlet and side-exhaust valves and many common components to reduce costs and simplify servicing and store-keeping procedures. The 4-cylinder B-60, for example, was used in the Austin "Champ" for a time, and the B-80 6-cylinder and the larger 8-cylinder in-line units found many Service vehicle applications, as their present-day counterparts still do. An important feature from a military point of view is their ability to run satisfactorily on a variety of different fuels.

The important aero-engine side of Rolls-Royce activities is largely ignored in this book for the simple reason that it is beyond its scope. That part of Company activities has still to be dealt with at appropriate length and with proper authority. So, too, has its detailed commercial history and the

technical development of cars from 1907, the chance of publication of the second volume of C.W. Morton's *A History of Rolls-Royce Motor Cars* appearing now to be most unlikely.

Although the literature about Rolls-Royce is extensive its quality is not matched by its quality overall; perhaps half a dozen works come up to expectations and reach high levels of accurate reporting, balanced analysis and factual correctness. On the whole it is best to seek out contemporary writings in the specialised motoring journals, in such magazines as *Country Life*, *The Tatler*, and others, and in *The Times* and other newspapers of consequence. Interestingly enough the anonymous writer of *The Times'* reports between the wars often criticised certain Rolls-Royce features quite positively.

More recently the make has had an adverse Press at times. It would be silly to claim that this was never justified: corrosion of standard steel bodies has been a post-war problem for Rolls-Royce as well as for other manufacturers, of course, and the over-sensitive steering of early "Silver Shadows" could not be overlooked by any objective critic. But much of what has been written suffers from a lack of understanding (sometimes, one feels, quite deliberate) of the Company's design intentions. Due account has to be taken of its responsibility to its customers, so many of whom nowadays, as for many years past, demand finger-light control as a matter of course. Familiarity in this respect breeds respect; develops confidence.

The proof of this particular pudding, after all, is in the running. That reaches cordon bleu standards without – dare one say it – a Shadow of doubt.

---

* *Steel Chariots in the Desert* – S.C. Rolls

Chapter 1
The Quiet Ones

Of the individual qualities of the three men who first controlled the design, making, selling and servicing of Rolls-Royce cars a very great deal has already been said. The fact that they got together at all was something of a miracle. That they then got on so well together was another. As important, however, and every bit as wonderful was the way in which the trio were able to assemble such a well-integrated and effective team of the expert and the highly-skilled so soon; one, moreover, that stayed together despite the fact that almost every single member was worked close to the limits of human endurance at times during the earliest years, without special financial inducement or exceptional work conditions as compensation.

In its road test of the 12-cylinder "Phantom III" car that appeared in the issue of October 2, 1936 *The Autocar* said that the braking system achieved prodigies of retardation. Of those who designed, built and marketed earlier Rolls-Royce models it can be simply said that they performed prodigies. Within four years their altogether exceptional efforts and combined abilities raised a new, small and quite unknown concern to the forefront of the world's motor industry.

The earliest advertisements for Rolls-Royce cars appeared in December, 1904, just before their first public showing at the Paris Salon and less than nine months after initial road tests had begun. By 1908, when the number in use was still small, but when manufacture had already been transferred from the little Cooke Street, Manchester works to a spacious new factory at Nightingale Road, Derby, to meet world de-

mand, the make was well-known and well-regarded.

By 1910 its name was beginning to be taken for granted as a synonym for excellence: a state of affairs miraculously maintained ever since despite a tremendous increase in the all-round quality of every kind and class of automobile. Those Edwardians who sought the best, either because they truly appreciated quality or because they felt it necessary to be seen to own it, now went to the fashionable West End of London, to Conduit Street, for their motors.

In 1904, however the position was less clear-cut. Largely because of the patronage of King Edward VII the Daimler, the "Royal Car", was thought by some to be the best available home product: yet the utterly English Lanchester, for example, was very much its mechanical superior. The other major native contender was the rather brutal looking Napier, a make that owed much of its commercial success to the propaganda poured out by Selwyn Francis Edge, that formidable super-salesman and spokesman for the excellent Acton engineers. At that time he had scarcely an equal as a publicist, and his relentless promotion of the 6-cylinder engine (as recently taken up by Napier) was conducted with economy in the correspondence columns of the motoring press. Soon, however, he was to meet his match, there and elsewhere.

The wealthy and well-informed motorist who could resist the attractions of the leading English makes still went to France or to Germany for his cars. Throughout the 'nineties and well into the present century French superiority was more or

The first Royce prototype engine, 1903. It was notably neat in layout and in appearance.

less complete; by producing a vehicle that had its engine front-mounted, with clutch, gearbox and final-drive behind, in 1891, Panhard et Levassor had established a pattern followed subsequently by most other manufacturers, and on the roads of Europe their maintained supremacy, in competition and in daily use, gave them a dominating position.

In the light-car class the special qualities of De Dion, Peugeot and Renault, for example, were unequalled elsewhere for many years, and in the design and manufacture of tyres Michelin already held an international reputation. In fact the value and importance of the successful development of

This, the second of the three prototype Royce cars, was allocated to E.A. Claremont. It was photographed outside the Cooke Street, Manchester premises of Royce Ltd. Production cars had the distinctive radiator.

On his tour of the South Coast defences in 1904 H.R.H. The
Duke of Connaught was driven in one of the Royce
prototypes by Charles Rolls, who was a member of the
recently established Motor Volunteer Corps. The little Royce
car is on the left.

the pneumatic tyre cannot be over-emphasised;
before its introduction there was an absolute limit
to usable performance, and until reasonable levels
of life-expectation and an acceptable degree of
resistance to puncture were reached it remained
not only the most troublesome, least reliable
component of the car but the most costly as well.

Almost the most important thing that the
French did during this period, however, was to
demonstrate beyond all doubt that the new form
of transport had a future, and this they did in the
most effective way then possible by organising
numerous long-distance trials and races, held on
open roads. Although these were stopped abruptly, after the awful carnage of the Paris-
Madrid event of 1903 (cut short at Bordeaux),
their purpose had already been achieved, for the
practicality and the reliability of the horseless-
carriage had been publicly and conclusively
established.

The successes of Panhard, Peugeot and at a
later date, Mors, had beneficial commercial
advantages, and when French leadership was
challenged seriously for the first time it was clear
that their new German rival had noted that
important fact. But the prototype Mercedes of
1901 and subsequent production cars, notably the
great 60 and 90 hp. models, were neither highly
tuned nor temperamental monsters fit only for
fast and furious driving though their competition
success was real enough in fact; the resultant
publicity an excellent stimulus to sales. They were
practical touring cars; reliable, comfortable,
luxurious, even speedy and quiet. The last feature
was becoming more and more important as an aid
to selling; ever-rising standards of all-round
efficiency were effectively subduing mechanical
clamour in ways that added to the attractions of
the horseless-carriage.

Aural and tangible proofs of the production of
power had been all very well at a time when the
average motorist was so carried away by the fact
of newfound mobility that he could overlook the
cacophonies of combustion and fail to notice
vibrations of a visible kind. Towards the end of
the second decade of practical motoring,
however, his sensitivity in such matters was more
acute. There were, after all, many steam- or
electrically-driven vehicles still in use to offer
comparative standards of quiet.

It was at this stage that a new make of car
appeared. It was not large. It was not showy. It
was not at all noisy. It was built to standards of fit
and workmanship far above the average. It was
the work of a mature engineer, Frederick Henry
Royce, a 41-year old Englishman who had been
engaged in the design and manufacture of
electrical equipment since 1884. In that year he
had gone into partnership with E.A. Claremont, a
friend and fellow electrical engineer, on a
combined capital of £70, and between them they

Rolls-Royce: the best car in the World

had built up a successful, though small-scale, business in Hulme, in Manchester.

But if its scope was modest its reputation was not; by the 'nineties the name Royce, whether on bell-set, dynamo, switchgear, instruments, electric-motor or crane, for example, was widely recognised in the electrical industry as an indicator of far above average quality of design, of workmanship and of materials, and of exceptional lasting powers. In 1894 F.H. Royce and Company became Royce Limited, with Claremont and Royce (by now brothers-in-law) as Joint Managing Directors, and its steady progress was maintained.

The products of the prosperous little concern were eagerly sought after by the discerning, and a significant export trade was developed. After the end of the Boer War, however, its affairs were much depressed, the combination of an economic slump in Britain and vicious cost-cutting in the industry (much of it from abroad) seriously affecting current sales and forward prospects.

It was at this time that Royce and Claremont first made direct contact with the motor-car. According to C.W. Morton their practical experience began with De Dion quadricycles, as did that of their mutual friend and doctor, Campbell-Thompson. These rather makeshift-looking machines were fast but fitful, and the single-cylinder engine, mounted 'midships, was scarcely of the unobtrusive kind. The sight and sound of the three Quads in noisome motion must have been a most impressive one.

Royce's next road vehicle was more ambitious, if less conspicuous in aural and visual terms. It too was French: a second-hand Decauville delivered to Manchester by train, then pushed to Cooke Street, we are told, after starting difficulties likely to have roused its new owner to the prodigies of profanity for which he was so famous. But it was not the eternally troublesome, raucous and unreliable contraption of legend; it was, in fact, more advanced in certain details of design and construction than the average car of its type and class. Its engine, clutch and gearbox,

for example, shared a common bedplate (decidely unusual practice at that time), final drive was taken through a torque-tube, instead of the less-costly, more common chains and sprockets, and the rear-axle itself was of the then rare fully-floating type. Another most unusual, almost unique feature was the use of an engine-driven dynamo to generate current for the ignition system and at the same time to maintain the accumulators in a state of charge.

In general, though, the Decauville, like most of its contemporaries, lacked mechanical subtlety and operational refinement. Neither its quality of design nor its comparative coarseness of running could possibly satisfy an engineer whose own standards were set so high, and at some time still unknown he decided that he could do a great deal better. It was by no means a snap or sudden decision; Royce had thought out the matter with his characteristic patient and reasoned attention to every possible detail and from a commercial point of view, moreover, the necessity for diversification of his Company's products and activities then being urgent in his view.

Nor was it the putting into effect of a personal whim. By 1903 Royce was in his fortieth year and in his creative prime, with more than 25 years of accumulated theoretical knowledge and practical experience to sustain him. He foresaw a promising future for the motor-car. Although he was an essentially modest man he was far too intelligent not to be well aware of his personal powers and could have had few real doubts about his ability to engage successfully in the design of cars. Whether or not his firm would ever have the funds necessary to take up their manufacture was a different matter at that stage.

Somehow or other he persuaded his fellow directors to sanction the start of work on three experimental machines at Cooke Street where, by early 1903, spare capacity was available, the main centre of electrical activity having been moved some time before to a new factory at Trafford Park.

Additional staff was taken on to help, and with the 15 hp., 2.09 litre, 2-cylinder Decauville as stripped-down guide, but not exemplar, an operation of the most profound historical significance began. The best documented account of what followed is to be found in C. W. Morton's

book, *A History of Rolls-Royce Motor Cars*, which is the prime source of accurate and detailed information on the early years of this make. By quite exceptional efforts on the part of Royce and his dedicated team the first engine, a 2-cylinder of 1.8 litres capacity and 10 hp., was being bench tested by mid-September, 1903. Towards the end of the following March the second was also running, and on April 1, 1904 a completed car was first tried on public roads. As a consequence of a programme of diligent, and intensive development work it ran well.

Before the month was out it had been driven several hundreds of miles in a matter of days as participant in the "Sideslip Trials" held in Southern England, where its notable reliability attracted favourable attention. In early May it was shown to one of the most knowledgeable motorists in Europe, the Honourable Charles

The oldest known Rolls-Royce – now back in Scottish ownership after a gap of close on 70 years. Mr. Thomas Love's 10 hp., chassis no. 20154, which was rescued and most sympathetically restored by its previous owner, Mr. Oliver Langton, during the early 'fifties, and has been in regular use ever since. It may have been at the 1904 Paris Salon.

Stewart Rolls, who had been persuaded to travel from London to Manchester to meet its designer and to see and try the car itself. This was to some extent against his will because of a long-standing preference for cars of Continental origin, based on many years of road, track and workshop experience, because he had by then no great liking for the 2-cylinder engine, and because he was much preoccupied with the problems of his own retail motor business.

In the event, however, the evident quality of this new machine, not to speak of the equally obvious qualities of its creator, convinced him on

19

What the front seat occupants see in SU 13, the 1905 10 hp. owned by its makers since the early 'twenties. The box on the left conceals the ignition trembler-coil from view but does not altogether quieten its occasional chattering, while the drip-feed lubricator to its right stays silent but demands regular attention as sole provider of oil to the engine.

the spot of its commercial potential, and even at their first meeting (which had been arranged by their mutual friend and business associate, Henry Edmunds) the two men were sufficiently sure of one another's abilities to make tentative plans for the production and sale of an initial batch of cars.

After his return to London, Rolls alerted his partner, Claude Goodman Johnson, to the fact that one of their problems had been solved for he had found an English car comparable with the Panhards, Minervas and other foreign makes then handled by their firm. Higher praise for the newcomer was scarcely possible at that time, coming as it did from one of the best-informed motorists of his day, and it was echoed most emphatically by Johnson after he too had tried the little Royce.

In succeeding months there was much coming and going between South and North as the three individuals and the two concerns they represented became more and more closely involved. From their first meetings Rolls, Royce and Johnson were in accord; differences of

background, of which far more note was taken then than is now the case, were of no account in their shared search for excellence. Administrator, aristocrat and engineer met on terms of absolute equality and with urgent aims in common: to put the new make into production and onto the market at the earliest possible time, and then to establish it as a household name.

In those days action swiftly followed the making of decisions, and while Royce was driving himself and his still-small team to further heights of achievement at Cooke Street, Rolls and Johnson were laying careful plans in London for the promotion of the new car as soon as deliveries began. At an early stage it had been agreed that Royce should increase the number of different models to be built, not simply to widen what is

20

now called market coverage but to anticipate possible shifts in fashion as well. To rely on the 2-cylinder alone, however fine its quality, would be to put all concerned in a vulnerable position if the present popularity of that type were to wane.

By December, 1904, when the first public announcements of Rolls-Royce cars appeared, the range consisted of four distinct models: the original 2-cylinder car (slightly modified in design), a 4-cylinder Twenty and a 6-cylinder

For more than 20 years Adam McGregor Dick's 1905 3-cylinder car stood in the Dick Institute, Kilmarnock, Scotland. It was removed in 1957 and splendidly restored thereafter.

Thirty, the engines of which shared certain dimensions and components in common. There was an odd-man out as well, a 15 hp. 3-cylinder car with the same bore and stroke as the others but cylinders cast singly, not in pairs, that may have been added at the suggestion of Rolls and Johnson to complete market coverage. The type was still quite popular and its inclusion made sound commercial sense.

It was a bold move to exhibit the new English make at the leading European show, and in France, moreover, so long the source of the leading cars of their day. A gesture of this expensive kind was typical of Johnson, of course;

his sense of publicity was of a highly developed and unusually imaginative kind and it was exercised with dash and with a style that Edge and other top-rank automobile propagandists of the time found difficulty in matching. Both he and Rolls were available in Paris to attend in person to the enquiries of potential customers, either on their stand or at the Elysée Palace Hotel.

This effort was well rewarded. C. S. Rolls & Co. received a Diploma and Medal "for the Elegance and Comfort of the Rolls-Royce Cars" and if we are to believe contemporary reports 27 firm orders were taken (with deposits paid, it was emphasised). The majority of buyers must have been British, for of one hundred 2-, 3-, 4- and 6-cylinder cars built, only nine were sold abroad in the first instance. It was not until after the introduction of the 40/50 hp. model two years later that export sales became a significant percentage of production.

Polished power – the result of a magnificent restoration carried out under the direction of the Rolls-Royce historian, C.W. Morton and the owner of the car, Adam McGregor Dick.

The fact remains that Rolls-Royce had made a splendid start. Press coverage had been widespread and universally welcoming, and as soon as cars had been in service for a reasonable time enthusiastic testimonals were carefully collected by the partners, who were in much more direct touch with their customers than was usual then.

A very great deal had been achieved by the beginning of 1905. A close and most amicable working relationship had been established between Royce Limited and C.S. Rolls & Co. (separate concerns still though legally connected by an agreement dated December 23, 1904 that laid down their respective obligations). In brief Royce was to build the cars and C.S. Rolls & Co. to sell them, under an inspired and euphonious-sounding combination of the two names. Buyers, it seemed, were readily found, and this was a rather remarkable thing at a time when the range of options elsewhere, was so enormous and many of the rival makes had 10 or 15 years of development behind them, along with well-founded reputations.

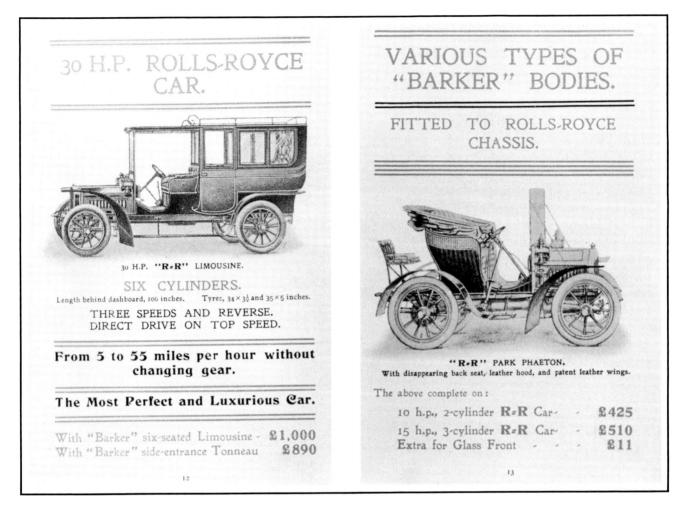

Two pages of the tiny red and black catalogue of Rolls-Royce cars produced in 1905 by S.C. Rolls & Co.

The cars themselves were of fine quality; that was clear. Their promotion and sale were in the hands of two of the most capable men yet to engage in motor-car retailing. Johnson was known as an organiser and administrator of altogether outstanding talents. His involvement with the automobile dated from the 'nineties, and Rolls, with whom he had been in partnership since the end of 1903, had an engineering degree and experience with wheeled vehicles that had begun with a discarded bathchair, so he said. This continued during his time at Cambridge with cycles, then with a second-hand Peugeot purchased in 1896, and widened thereafter as he sampled almost every kind of self-propelled machine, from lurching lorry to roaring race-car. In January, 1902, with the founding of C.S. Rolls & Co., Motor Agents, he entered the retail trade.

In *The Rolls-Royce Motor Car** its co-author, the late Anthony Bird, suggests that Royce's readiness to acquire practical experience may have been a preparation for possible entry into the expanding motor industry as a provider of electrical components. It is a tenable speculation. On the other hand he may have had the idea of eventual manufacture of motor-cars as early as 1902. Whatever the true state of affairs the fact remains that when he did decide he brought to his new set of problems those massive powers of invention, analysis, informed observation, perseverance, concentration and patience that had already gained him so high a reputation in electrical circles. He brought, too, an almost unique concern for quality. He had no time at all for the second-rate, the slipshod, the shoddy; as far as he was concerned there was no point in doing things unless they were done properly, and his standards were of the highest, practically as well as theoretically speaking. He was a master-

* B. T. Batsford Ltd., 1964

craftsman in his own right, trained in early life to handle tools with sympathy and skill.

He had a profound sense of order that is clearly seen from any close study of his work; from the first his motor-cars were neat and tidy in detail and in their general arrangement, and as he gained experience and confidence the standard of their appearance overall was raised to ever-higher levels. The visual, and commercial importance of the famous radiator and bonnet cannot be stressed too highly in this respect; their fine proportions and quite distinctive shape set the car apart from all others. We may never know whose idea it was to adopt the Greek temple pattern (Claude Johnson's inspired imagination comes to mind, inevitably), but it was as brilliant as that of linking the names of Rolls and Royce.

The pitched-roof that occupants of the front seats looked down upon varied in length, of course, with the size of engine it housed. The most impressive was that of the Thirty, the largest, costliest model; in 6-seat limousine form,

in early 1905, it was catalogued at £1,000, for example. Its high price (and a tendency to crankshaft trouble that took some time to trace and cure) did not put buyers off; 37 cars were sold during the two years of production, which was only three less than the total of 40 "Light" and "Heavy" Twenty models built during the same period. These were costly, too; between £650 and £735 in the 1905 catalogue and £735 and £860 in the 1906 edition.

The 2- and 3-cylinder cars were much less successful, numerically speaking, but this was in no way an indication of any qualitative inferiority. Of their kind they were much above the average, a fact the writer can confirm from

Much to look at for the occupants of the 1905 20 hp. car so splendidly rebuilt as a T.T. replica by Mr. Stanley Sears, who has been concerned with the restoration of Rolls-Royces since the 'forties. The ignition distributor of this and the 30 hp. model is set in the 'dashboard' and has a sight-glass through which the action and the condition of the low-tension commutator may be observed.

driving experience of the oldest surviving 10 and of the only known 3-cylinder still in existence. That the larger car is quieter and smoother running is to be experienced, and it is even more flexible. But the smaller Rolls-Royce is neither rough nor noisy, despite its unusual firing arrangements, and in its readiness to accept a very high top gear from the lowest road speeds is impressive, to say the least. For anyone used to later models of the make there are many familiar features: a commanding driving position, for example, an absence of fuss, the same lightness of controls and directness of response and, overall, a look and feel of quality.

Even higher levels were reached in the larger models. Clearly the Light Twenty was a car of

great appeal; quick, quiet, responsive, lively and comfortable; at its very best when fitted with open bodywork; a "flyer", an automobile of eager, effortless performance comparable in many ways with the 3½-litre Bentley built by Rolls-Royce between 1933 and 1936. The Heavy, or Long Twenty weighed 17 cwt.; 1½ cwt. more than its sporting sister and was intended to carry the kind of beautifully made but substantial coachwork that Barker, for example, could build so well. With a wheelbase of 9ft. 6in., a length of almost 7ft. between dashboard and rear axle centre and a frame 3ft. wide it offered a firm and spacious foundation for the exercise of traditional skills.

A similar space was available on the unobtrusive Thirty which was described in the 1905 catalogue as "The most Perfect and Luxurious car". If it was not quite perfect it may be fairly considered as a very good one, good enough, in fact, to challenge Napier, to attract numerous eager buyers and to take its makers into the

The sturdy looking engine of the Sears Light Twenty (chassis no. 26350). The chain-driven magneto (centre foreground) is a later addition and stands above the low-set Royce "carburator', mixture from which passes – reluctantly, in cold weather – to the induction chambers via the shapely branched manifold.

*Above: **This c.1905 20 hp open-drive limousine sits high above the road. Note the subtle and interesting curves of its coach work – probably built by Barker & Co.***

When this photograph was taken, in 1905, the coachbuilder still had work to do; floorboards were missing, as were the cushions of the front seat, and other items had to be secured. The car is a 30 hp, the body of the Roi-des-Belges type.

luxury-car class firmly, squarely and permanently. For their energetic and highly effective sales efforts Rolls and Johnson deserve great credit; they had specialist knowledge and understanding of the tastes of the 'better-off' and maintained quite exceptional standards of service, with dignity but not servility. The fact that Rolls was a member of the English aristocracy was an enormous help of course; he was widely known in the society circles of his time and found a generally sympathetic response when he intro-duced the subject of motor cars.

He was at his best, it would seem, when demonstrating or selling; activities over which he had complete mastery. At other times he was strangely aloof, cold even. Johnson was quite the opposite; warm, kindly, sympathetic, generous, imaginative, far-sighted, aesthetically and

26

1905 3-cylinder 15 hp. Side-entrance Tonneau (replica of original Barker body by J.B. Stevenson, of Glasgow).

Hon. C. S. Rolls   Winner of Tourist Trophy

Opposite page top: **C.S. Rolls and crew pause for a picture on the quayside during their Monte-Carlo to London dash in 1905. Their light Twenty carried much candle-power to deal with driving in the dark across France.**

Above: **The winner of the 1906 T.T. the Hon. C.S. Rolls, was snapped in the shrubbery of his London home, South Lodge, Kensington. The drilling of the frame and brake-drums of his speedy machine was part of a most carefully considered scheme of weight reduction devised by Royce and carried out under his personal supervision.**

sensually aware and active. He had strong interests in the visual arts and in music.

Royce had an aesthetic sense that was innate and intuitive. It found its highest early expression in the design of the first 40/50 hp. car, the look of which is so completely satisfying, in the manner of the best nineteenth century railway locomotives, for example. As a one-time apprentice in the Peterborough workshops of the Great Northern Railway he had become familiar with these at

Percy Northey returns to the pits after the breakage of his offside front spring during the first lap of the 1906 T.T., the dismay on his face matched by that of his riding mechanic, Durlacher. The flared front wings of this racing Rolls-Royce were to feature on later high-performance cars from Derby.

29

close quarters and may well have taken subconscious notice of the honesty and lack of pretension of their appearance. He had an excellent sense of proportion and took as much trouble with the look of the smallest components as with the largest, so that examination of any Rolls-Royce mechanism is visually rewarding to anyone of sensibility in these matters.

The impressive appearance of the Thirty had much to do with its success. The length of its low-set bonnet played an important part, of course, as did the forward-mounted radiator, but there were other significant visual elements as

What the driver of the 1905 15 hp saw! Although they look complicated to the present-day observer the car's controls are quickly comprehended.

With its Cape cart type hood raised the 3-cylinder looks well. Its unusually true-to-period body was built in Glasgow, by J.B. Stevenson.

well, to gratify the eye and reassure the mind with their good and generous proportions. There was also the manner of its going; the quiet, unobtrusive running of its big 6-litre engine (in effect three 2-cylinder units perched along a slender common crankshaft), its top-gear versatility, with a wide spread of speed, good acceleration and much-praised hill-climbing powers.

Although the January 1905 catalogue refers to a 3-speed and reverse gearbox for all models, with direct drive in third, production Twenties and Thirties had the same 4-speed box, the extra ratio being an indirect "only intended to be used for Continental travel or track competitions". With

such a powerful and flexible engine, however, the ambitious, or the merely lazy were encouraged to use this seductive speed, even in the British Isles where an overall limit of 20 mph, prevailed outside built-up areas. Under normal conditions

The controls of the Silver Ghost are laid out neatly and logically.

In November, 1982 the Silver Ghost was at Gleneagles Hotel, Scotland, where specially favoured guests of its makers were able to savour the unique quality of its running.

Rolls-Royce: the best car in the World

it was used to maintain high cruising speeds at low engine rpm, which meant that at no more than a fast tickover 45-50 mph. could be maintained without "auditory sensation", with great fuel economy and with a significant reduction in general wear and tear.

The 10 and 15 hp. cars had three forward gears and the same speed capability in the highest; according to the final-drive ratio specified, which would be determined largely by the type and weight of body to be fitted. This was 32, 36.5 or 39.5 mph. The Light Twenty could reach 44.5, 50 or 54.5 mph., and the Twenty Long and the Thirty, Short or Long, 38, 41.5 or 47 mph. These figures are taken from the 1906 catalogue but the engine speed at which they were reached is not given there. More than likely it was 1,000 rpm., in

which case the maximum attainable speeds of some models would be higher.

From actual experience the writer can speak of the mechanical calm of the 15 hp. car at 40 mph. or so. Mr. Kent Karslake has written memorably of a drive in the Light Twenty so splendidly restored by Mr. Stanley Sears; during its course he found that the car cruised comfortably in the forties in direct top (third gear) and ran with an equal fluency and lack of effort in the fifties on its geared-up, or overdrive, fourth speed, at not much more than a brisk tickover. The extraordinary qualities of this particular car caused Mr. Karslake to declare that it was the best veteran car in its class he had ever driven. From a motoring historian of such very great knowledge, experience and objectivity so positive a statement has to be taken with the most profound respect.

At times during 1905 Light Twenties of similar type were driven faster than any other contemporary Rolls-Royces, but not on English roads of course, where a blanket speed limit of 20 mph.

Apart from its size the 30 hp. Rolls-Royce was immediately recognisable because of its forward mounted radiator and lengthy bonnet. By chance, no doubt, a photographer persuaded C.S. Rolls and his party of French officers to pause during a journey to Windsor in August 1905.

Stanley Sears brought the remains of this 1906 30 hp. car from Australia, where it had been for 40 years or so, and began yet another of his prodigious restorations. Within six years it was on the road again, the only known survivor of its type.

prevailed. Their high velocities were reached in the Isle of Man, where attitudes to the motor car were quite remarkably well balanced and intelligent, and where, because of this, it was possible to organise road racing without passing special Acts of Parliament as was the case in mainland Britain.

This interesting fact had been discovered by the Automobile Club when it was arranging the Eliminating Trials for the Gordon Bennett Race a year or two earlier, and in 1905 it decided to hold a race of its own, over the same course in the Isle of Man. The intention was to encourage the improvement of the touring car, which was a refreshing change from the kind of race then prevalent; the sort of event that stimulated the production of ever-larger, faster and more impractical mammoths. The Club was certainly not interested in encouraging the perpetuation of this breed; its concern was not with many-litred monsters but with "representative tourist cars."

As such its appeal to Rolls and Johnson was strong. The story goes that their attention was drawn to it in the first place by A. H. Briggs, a Heavy Twenty owner much interested in the sporting side of motoring, who suggested to Rolls that a lighter version of this model might do well in the race. Whether or not this is true no time was wasted once the partners had agreed to take part, for the Rolls-Royce entry of two cars

Above: **The fantastic combination of curves and straight lines of this c.1909 40/50 testify to the somewhat eccentric taste of its first owner: Barker & Co. were responsible for its truly remarkable bodywork.**

The late James P. Smith, of Kildrummy, in Scotland, owned and enjoyed this 1907 40/50 – 'The Auld Lady' – for a great many years. Its original body was replaced by this waggonette, taken from a Maudsley car.

(the number allowed each maker) was the first to be received by the Club.

Despite their own long involvement with competitive motoring of many different kinds they were not promoting the Rolls-Royce as a performance car, nor were they encouraging Royce to concentrate on this aspect at the expense of others that all three thought to be of much greater importance. What they were offering was "an unequalled combination of *simplicity, silence, lightness & strength, absolute reliability, ease of management & economy of upkeep."* And successful participation in the forthcoming race would draw attention to this in a very positive way.

The known risks of such public exposure were faced the more readily because at such an early stage in the history of the make there was no commercially valuable reputation to lose; on the other hand success would lead to its establishment and an important and immediate gain in prestige. The race rules were generally straightforward, the most publicised ones laying down weight limits, requiring the provision of a four-seat body and setting a predetermined level of fuel consumption. The latter was an ingenious way of keeping down engine size; each car was to be provided with an amount of petrol sufficient to take it the full race distance of 208 miles as long as it could travel 25 miles at least on each gallon.

The minimum and maximum chassis weights were 1,300 and 1,600 lb. respectively, and a weight of 950 lb. had to be carried – 350 lb. for the body and the balance for driver, passenger and ballast (or driver only and extra ballast). Prototypes were allowed as long as they met the regulations.

Before the end of April, 1905 Rolls was in the Isle of Man with the first Heavy Twenty – "Grey Ghost" – to carry out practical trials to determine the most suitable gear ratios for the course and to find out something about petrol consumption. He passed on his findings and conclusions to Royce, who began work at once on making the few modifications necessary. The chassis was lightened, wherever possible, one engine was prepared with a slightly increased bore, which raised output from the normal 18 bhp. to 20, and most importantly of all, a new gearbox was designed and built. It had four speeds instead of three; third was direct, the most efficient therefore, and the one to be used as *The Autocar"* of August 26 1905 put it, "'for moderate inclines, heavy roads against head winds, and in traffic." The extra gear, the indirect fourth, was to be "called into requisition" only when the car needed little power to drive it, as on the long falling grades of the course, for example. It was a petrol-saver, essentially, but its intelligent use would serve also to lighten the demands made on engine and transmission. Finally, of course, it would greatly increase maximum speed on suitable downhill stretches.

After the by-now customary prodigies of concentrated work at Cooke Street the pair of T.T. cars was ready by the second half of August, and as the race was not to take place until September 14 this gave Rolls and Northey, the drivers, ample time to get to know their

respective mounts and to put in the best part of a week of practice on the course itself. Meanwhile Claude Johnson saw to it that the Thirty he had taken over to the island for the convenience of visiting journalists was fully used by them.

Rolls did not even complete his first lap; in the excitement of the moment he tried to engage gear while coasting with a dead engine soon after the rolling start. In pre-synchromesh days, as Anthony Bird has said, an operation of this kind was not to be tried at anything more than a walking pace, and a simple error of judgement could have disturbing consequences, to say the least.

Percy Northey, who was driving the 18 bhp. car and who had started more than a quarter of an hour after Rolls (the cars were flagged off at one minute intervals), had the tedious task of overtaking those who had left before him. This he did with such skill, such vigour and such enterprise that by the end of the second lap he was in the lead, and there he stayed, completing the 208½ miles at an average speed of 33.6 mph. and a mean petrol consumption of 24.8 mpg. and being first past the finishing line.

But his actual race position was second; John Napier the winner on handicap, who had started much later, covered the distance in 6 hours 9 minutes and 14.6 seconds (2 minutes and 8.4 seconds less than Northey) and averaged 33.9 mph. and 25.4 mpg. It was a triumphant day for the designer of the successful Arrol-Johnston,

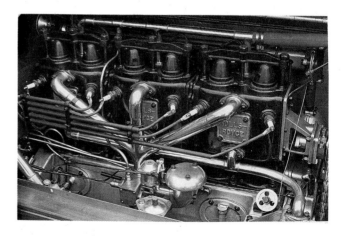

The engine room of the 30 hp. car is a masterpiece of mechanical order and a model of sympathetic maintenance. Distinctive features are the overhead inlet-valve domes, with their substantial bridge pieces, and the three-branch inlet manifold.

whose other entry was fourth. Although the chassis of these Scottish cars were of new design they were fitted with their maker's two-cylinder, horizontally-opposed, four-piston engine – an unconventional unit that had been designed in the eighteen-nineties and previously used for the propulsion of archaic-looking dogcarts.

In spite of the elimination of Rolls so early on it had been a good day for Rolls-Royce also; Northey's spirited driving had shown off the speed and stamina of a largely unknown car to a huge number of spectators and Press coverage afterwards was generous indeed in its references to the fine and regular running of the newcomer. Rolls and Johnson now had the best possible evidence of the soundness of Royce as a designer of motor-cars of all-round merit; already his 2- and 3-cylinder cars had proved their individual qualities in the hands of private owners, and while the number of Heavy Twenties and Thirties

in service by September, 1905 was still small their owners obviously liked them.

But the Tourist Trophy Twenty was rather special, as its race performance had shown. Before the end of 1905 it was in production (as the Light Twenty) with a wheelbase eight inches shorter than that of its sister model called the Heavy Twenty in the first place because it was sturdy enough to carry the weightier type of body. Rolls had not done with the T.T. despite his initial misfortune, and as soon as the list opened for the 1906 event he was first again with his two Rolls-Royce entries.

A new regulation, intended to prevent the continued use of unrealistically high top gears,

This advertisement occupied two pages of The Autocar of March 30 1907, by which time Rolls-Royce Ltd. had set up a selling agency in New York. An interesting non-standard feature of AX192 is the placing of shock absorbers inside the front dumbirons.

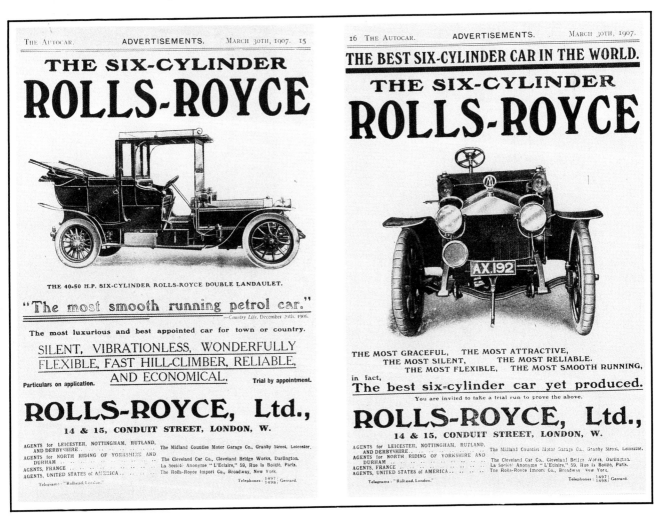

Above: **By 1911, when Barker & Co. built this well-proportioned touring body on a 40/50 chassis for Baron Korff, the opulent curves of the Roi-des-Belges type had given way to simpler overall shapes. Note the complexity of the hood supports and the use of a second windscreen to protect rear-seat passengers.**

Opposite page top: **The driver of this c.1910 Landaulette had only a low windscreen for protection, whereas his passengers could loll in utmost comfort and luxury in its lofty rear compartment. Vertical stripes are a period feature of the body.**

required that competing cars should be able to turn in their highest speed for half a mile at not more than 12 mph., without "clutch manipulation", and that they should also be capable of climbing a gradient of 1 in 6 in first with a specified load.

This gave Claude Johnson a fine chance to show off the performance of the 1905 race cars in public once more, firstly in the Mall, in London, where Rolls's car averaged 8.31 mph. over the distance in its geared-up fourth (at an engine speed below 200 rpm.), and then in Sydenham, where the same car took the 1 in 6 slope of Jasper Road in first gear with six aboard. Needless to say the occasions were fully covered by the Press.

Northey's car was eventually bought by H. J. Swindley, then Editor of *The Autocar*, and this began a friendly connection between its maker and the magazine that has been maintained until the present day. Massac Buist, a Cambridge contemporary and friend of Rolls, who had much

1906 6-cylinder 30 hp. Pullman body by Barker.

At a Vintage Sports Car Club Rally in Buxton, in 1952, Mr. Adrian Garrett handled his big 1908 40/50 with great precision.

experience of Rolls-Royce cars on the road from the Sideslip Trials of 1904 onwards and who wrote *Rolls-Royce Memories* for the Company in the mid-twenties, from first-hand knowledge, was its Editor for a time between the wars. Geoffrey Smith, its Editorial Director for much of the 'thirties and into the fifties also, was one of those specially informed owners from whom advice and ideas were taken, and more recently a former Associate Editor, Warren Allport, has written much about the Company and its cars from the earliest days.

In its Press, as in its public relations, Rolls-Royce have always fared well, a quite splendid foundation having been laid in the first place by Johnson, whose nose for an acceptable news

story was almost infallible. As we have already seen S. F. Edge had a special talent for publicity and must never be under-rated. But whereas he was merely flamboyant Claude Johnson gave repeated proof of an imaginative genius extending to all forms of publicity that was backed up by a Royce-like capacity for dealing with each and every detail, from the smallest to the very largest. While he did not keep in the background to anything like the same extent as Royce (a naturally shy and modest man) he was no limelight seeker on his own account.

In the latter part of 1904 much of his energy went into preliminary promotion of the new car from the North. During 1905 an increasing amount of his time, his effort and his enthusiasm was diverted to the improvement of its position in the British motoring scene, though it must be remembered that C.S. Rolls & Co. were still handling other makes of car. By the beginning of

1906 it was becoming clear to Rolls and Johnson alike that their commercial future lay in whole-hearted concentration on one make only, and by its end it is possible that they were already thinking in terms of a "one make, one model" policy.

But before we take account of the reasons why, there are other matters to discuss. There was the affair of the breaking of the unofficial Monte Carlo to London record time that Charles Jarrott had established in May, 1905 in a 40 hp. Crossley – another Manchester-built car, incidentally. Rolls took delivery of his Twenty for the 1906 T.T. in April of that year and in the following

During the course of the R.A.C. observed trial in 1907, Rolls-Royce Ltd. exploited its publicity value to the utmost, this gallery of portraits being part of the material issued for press use by Claude Johnson.

month he left London in it to see what he could do in a car of half its rival's power, accompanied by H. Massac Buist as navigator, Eric Platford (one of Royce's closest aides) as engineer, and an unnamed expert from Dunlop to deal with any tyre troubles that might arise.

There is no point in repeating a story that C.W. Morton and others have told elsewhere in detail; in brief Rolls achieved his objective, though reducing the time of a journey of so many hundreds of miles by 90 seconds only may not seem a particularly worthy achievement. It should be pointed out, however, that Rolls covered the 771 miles between Monte Carlo and Boulogne in a time that was 3 hours and 21 minutes less than that taken by the spirited Jarrott, and were then held up for 3 hours and 11 minutes before the cross-Channel steamer picked them up. More time was then lost between Dover and London

MR CLAUDE JOHNSON.
COMMERCIAL MANAGING DIRECTOR OF THE Cº WHO ORIGINATED AND ORGANISED THE TRIAL. AND WHO HAS DRIVEN 2635 ⅜ MILES TO DATE.

MR F.H. ROYCE.
THE DESIGNER OF THE CAR AND ENGINEER IN CHIEF OF THE Cº.

THE HON. C.S. ROLLS.
TECHNICAL MANAGING DIRECTOR OF THE Cº.
WHO HAS DRIVEN 1249 ½ MILES TO DATE.

CHIEF TESTOR PLATFORD.
WHO PREPARED THE CAR FOR THE TRIAL. AND WHO HAS DRIVEN 2,629 ¼ MILES TO DATE.

THE "SILVER GHOST".
THE 6 CYLINDER ROLLS-ROYCE CAR WHICH ON FRIDAY LAST COMPLETED 7,214 MILES NON STOP IN AN OFFICIAL ROAD TRIAL UNDER THE ROYAL AUTOMOBILE CLUB AND WHICH IS STILL RUNNING 400 MILES PER DAY BETWEEN LONDON AND GLASGOW.

MECHANICIAN MACREADY.
WHO HAS DRIVEN 1,329 ¼ MILES TO DATE

because Rolls ignored the directions of his navigator and went badly off course. On the part that really mattered Rolls had averaged 27.3 mph. including all stops, an increase of 3.1 mph. over Jarrott. Needless to say Johnson made much of a performance that gave further proof of the speed and exceptional staying power of Rolls-Royce cars.

But he kept quiet when Rolls and Northey took their cars over to the Isle of Man in July to try them out over the T.T. course a clear two months before the race itself. He knew when to stay silent and when to make a noise and after Rolls, who had taken the lead in the second lap, passed the line a clear 27 minutes ahead of Bablot, the next man, on the day of the 1906 Tourist Trophy race Claude Johnson had something to shout about as loudly as he liked. By a strange coincidence half the Rolls-Royce team was eliminated again on the first lap; this time it was Northey's turn; his offside front spring broke and although he was able to get back to the pits there was no spare to take its place.

Northey's telegram to Royce is a classic "Spring broken, heartbroken, Northey". The victor of the previous year had problems too; punctures and tyre trouble generally delayed him greatly and diverted attention from the fact that the combination of Napier and Arrol-Johnston was still a formidable one.

The Rolls-Royce win resulted in extremely good and widespread publicity that was immediately supplemented by press advertisements headlined "The premier and champion tourist cars of the world. Rolls-Royce". The winning car had averaged just under 40 mph. and 25 mpg., and after such a busy and successful season it might have been thought that a rest was due. But by the middle of November it was on its way to New York, along with Rolls and two Thirties. Soon after their arrival the peerless pair took first place in the race for cars of less than 25 hp. at the Empire City Track in Yonkers.

A much-published photograph shows a determined-looking Rolls at the wheel just before the race final. It also shows how thoroughly Royce had gone about weight reduction on his T.T. chassis, largely by drilling the frame side-members from end to end in a way that did not impair their strength. He had persuaded C.S.

Rolls & Co. to part with £40 for a set of lightweight wire wheels that allowed much higher cornering speeds than the standard wood-artillery, type, and these are clearly seen, along with the pierced rear brake drums.

The overall mechanical efficiency of these T.T. cars was high; ball-bearings were used for the wheels and in the gearbox to lessen drag, and even though output was no more than 22 bhp. at 1,000 rpm. it was said that Rolls touched 70 mph, frequently on the way "down the mountain."

That kind of speed was not reached at Yonkers. Rolls raced there as part of a carefully predetermined plan to introduce the Rolls-Royce car to America, the other part being to exhibit one of the Thirties at the annual Automobile Show in New York and to give demonstration runs with the other. As a result of determined and energetic selling he returned with orders for three Thirties, he appointed an American representative, Walter C. Martin, and he acquired a good idea of the state of motoring in the United States. He left behind him the Twenty, which he had sold to a sporting Texan, Captain Hutton; in January, 1907 the latter took one first place and four seconds in a race meeting at Ormond Beach.

The Thirty was well received by Americans and by the local Press, especially by the *New York Herald*, which called it "the absolutely noiseless gasoline car", and the *New York Commercial Advertiser*, which said that "The absence of vibration and noise coincident with the operation of the six-cylinder Rolls-Royce cars is winning many motorists over to this very efficient type of British car." These and other equally favourable quotations were freely used in the first Rolls-Royce catalogue to be specially prepared for the American market in 1907.

December 1906 was a month of critical importance in the history of the make. For some considerable time it had been clear that growing demand was straining production resources to the very limit at Cooke Street, where space was short and there was still some conflict of interest between the electrical and the automotive sides. Although the 3-cylinder car had gone out of production after the completion of the sixth chassis (not because of any lack of quality but simply because the type went out of fashion) and demand for the 2-cylinder had fallen off for a like

"Silver Ghost" in Scotland. The 15,000-mile Trial car, with Claude Johnson at the wheel, swoops effortlessly round a steep turn during the 1907 Scottish Trials. The front-seat passenger was in charge of the extra bulb-horn.

reason the Twenty and the Thirty, Short and Long, were attracting more and more buyers.

At this time Rolls played a leading part in demonstrating and in selling (with growing help from Northey) but it was Johnson who had to persuade Royce to part with the chassis eventually – something he was most reluctant to do because of his obsession with perfection. In this respect Johnson's superb powers of diplomacy were used to the full, not only on his Cooke Street visits but when he was explaining matters to the more impatient kind of customer. In between times he managed to do quite a lot of driving as well . . .

The need to move was vital if the natural expansion of the concern was to continue. Before it could be effected however, further funds were necessary, and at a Board meeting in early November 1906 it was decided to increase the nominal capital of Rolls-Royce Limited (registered in March of that year) from £60,000 to £200,000, and to make a public issue of shares to the value of £100,000.

But investors were slow to respond and it looked as if the issue would be under-subscribed;

a minimum of £50,000 had been specified in the prospectus and as the time limit approached there was a shortfall of some £9,000. A. H. Briggs had been helpful in the past by suggesting participation in the T.T., and it was he who had proposed that Rolls and Johnson should join forces with Royce and concentrate entirely on the promotion of one make of car, the formation of Rolls-Royce Limited being the outcome of that excellent idea.

We are told that at the very last moment the Company's Secretary, De Looze, recalled his close interest in the make and went off to Harrogate for help. This he received at once, to the tune of £10,000, and by his swift and confident action Briggs saved the flotation and almost certainly secured the future of Rolls-Royce Limited. If Edmunds has a place in the history of the Company for assembling the trio in the first place, Briggs has one of equal importance for making it possible for them to stay together.

The other profoundly important thing that happened towards the end of 1906 was the first public showing of Royce's new 6-cylinder car in November, at the Olympia Show in London, where a polished chassis and a most elaborate-looking Barker "Pullman Limousine" shared the C.S. Rolls & Co. stand with a Thirty and the T.T.-winning Twenty. The usual near-miracles at Cooke Street had ensured their presence there,

"White Knave" and "Silver Rogue" (K-83 and K-86 respectively) head a long line of competing cars at a Scottish stop during the International Touring Car Trial in 1908.

and these in turn had been preceded by a spell of the most intensive creative effort on the part of Royce.

That he was able to sustain it at a time when he was already more than busy with a multitude of other matters is a measure of his quite extraordinary capacity for concentrated thought. His physical endurance too, was remarkable, and in an age when daily hours of labour reached double figures as a matter of course Royce worked the same excessive hours as his men, and gained their respect thereby. He handled tools as well as the best, and for that he had their admiration. For the more perceptive his approach to all problems theoretical or practical, and his ways of solving them were a source of great delight, interest and

inspiration that compensated for the long, long hours in an overcrowded factory, the relatively low rates of pay and the uncertainties of employment in the early years of this century.

Royce was a designer of infinite ingenuity and resource who did not believe in the wasting of irrecoverable time on the solution of problems already dealt with by others; quite logically and sensibly he preferred to take their ideas when appropriate and adapt or improve to suit his own especial needs. But if satisfactory solutions did not exist he found his own, and very good ones they were at that. Royce was creative and innovative whenever necessary but not inclined to adopt novelty simply for its own sake. The general design of his early cars is far from unconventional and this had much to do with their appeal, not only to those engineers whose powers of appreciation of the finer points of their construction for example, were highly developed, but to those owners or prospective owners whose practical motoring experience was considerable even when their specialist technical knowledge was not.

The fact that Rolls-Royce engines had overhead inlet-valves and side exhaust mattered little to the latter. What did attract and impress was their quietness of operation, their ready response and their above-average reliability; along with durability features such as these were considered to be of especial importance by Royce, to whom the very thought of design for obsolescence would have been totally unacceptable.

Cars of all the original types except one (the V-8 to which reference will follow shortly) were still in everyday use twenty years or more after they left Cooke Street, and in almost every case this was a matter of expediency. In the early 'twenties there was neither veteran nor vintage movement to serve as conservation agency and

This many-windowed Barker Double Enclosed Limousine, on its maker's stand at the 1909 Olympia Show in London, was developed from a much earlier design and was still being built to order as late as 1912. Claude Johnson used a 1908 car of similar appearance.

elderly motor-cars were retained for work, not for sentimental reasons. To some extent the Rolls-Royce was an exceptional case; by then its reputation was enormously high and there was a certain prestige value in ownership – easily achieved because second-hand prices of any model other than the 40/50 were very low.

It was this particular Rolls-Royce, above all others, that set its maker's standing at such an exalted level. It had been taken from initial idea to the production stage in a matter of months during 1906, and was to be built without major change until the Spring of 1925, at Derby, and until 1926 at the American factory – but with numerous detail improvements and refinements that maintained its high place in the luxury car class in a quite remarkable way. As will be seen in the appropriate place, its lead was largely unchallenged until the post-war period.

The 40/50 was an amazing achievement for a man whose practical experience as an automobile designer and manufacturer was of such brief duration and whose first dealings with the 6-cylinder engine had caused him so much trouble. Although he had resolved his problems

Eric Platford seen here with his newly acquired wife in 1910, when their honeymoon transport was Royce's own 10 hp car, worked on the first Royce engines and cars, and eventually became Chief Tester at Derby.

with the Thirty he was generally unhappy with it, and the chance to start again on a very much larger and more ambitious 6-cylinder car was one that he seized with enormous enthusiasm. Careful analysis had convinced him that a basic cause of his difficulties was the result of his decision to arrange the cylinders in three blocks of two – one of necessity, of course, if the policy of standardisation was to be properly carried out. For his new engine Royce arranged the cylinders in two blocks of three, provided an extremely rigid crankshaft and replaced the drip-feed and splash oiling system of all the earlier models except one with pressure lubrication.

The exception was an extremely interesting 3.5 litre V-8 that Royce had designed the year before for two rather unusual models, a bonnetless,

short wheelbase vehicle to compete with the type of electric carriage then still popular for town work and a more conventional-looking car that was designed to maintain 20 mph. (the legal limit) uphill and down dale without gear changing. Rolls and Johnson were responsible for the idea of the imitation electric, which seemed to them to have commercial possibilities, and the "Legalimit", it appears, was built to the order of Sir Alfred Harmsworth, the wealthy proprietor of the *Daily Mail* newspaper and an experienced motorist.

In spite of intensive publicity neither model attracted custom and as far as is known only one example of each was completed and used. The "R.-R. (8-cylinder) (with invisible V-engine)." as the 1906 catalogue called it, was ingenious in execution and satisfied the design requirements laid down. Its engine was as near as possible noiseless, smell and smoke free, and without vibration. It was placed well away from the passenger space, below the frame, and although it

46

was beneath the driver's footboard in fact its accessibility was remarkably good.

Royce had been asked to make it unobtrusive, physically as well as aurally speaking, and his 90° V-8 was notably compact, its shallowness enabling it to be neatly tucked away below the frame without reducing ground clearance to an unacceptable level. Because its cylinders were arranged in two blocks of four set at 90° it was a short engine, and for the same reason its crankshaft was short and stiff. Pressure-feed lubrication was chosen to eliminate the trails of blue smoke attendant upon cars with badly managed drip-feed systems. Both inlet and exhaust valves were arranged at the side of the engine instead of following the overhead inlet/ side exhaust layout common to the other engines at that time, and special attention had been given to carburation and to the ignition.

Although output was only 18 bhp. the V-8 was lively, and it is a great pity that its natural vivacity was artificially restrained. It is also a matter for regret that its development was not continued, to make it an alternative or, indeed, a replacement for the existing 6-cylinder unit. In the circumstances however, it was wise to concentrate on the production of the multiples-of-two engines, and in any case Royce had learned much from this mechanical digression.

The new 40/50 engine, like the V-8, was "square": that is to say its bore and stroke were of equal dimensions, and it was very much larger than anything Royce had tackled previously. With its original $4\frac{1}{2}''$ bore and stroke the capacity was 7,036 cc. but an increase of $\frac{1}{4}''$ in stroke in 1909 raised this to 7,428 cc. In its early form power output was around 50 bhp. (its rating under the now-obsolete R.A.C. formula was 48.6 hp.) a figure raised to 55 bhp. or so with the 1909 stroke increase and to 65 bhp. by 1914.

Figures such as these may appear ridiculously low to the present day reader who takes 50 bhp. or more per litre as a matter of course. But 7 bhp. per litre was a good figure in 1906 and the 40/50 had an excellent power-to-weight ratio. The chassis weight of the short wheelbase model in 1907 was less than a ton and a typical figure for a completed car, with, say, a Roi-des-Belges touring body, would be around 32 cwt. High torque at low engine speeds is one of the attractions of the large-capacity engine, and when it is coupled with the extreme quietness, smooth-

It might be called an Open-drive landaulette; it might have been built in 1910; it is likely that Barker & Co. were responsible for its vertically striped body. A somewhat similar body was built on a later 40/50 chassis for the Duke of Sutherland.

In 1909 Charles Rolls was in Cannes with a 40/50 hp. Roi des Belges. As was so often the case where he was concerned a camera artist was at the ready while he was demonstrating the excellent steering lock on a sharp curve.

ness and flexibility characteristic of the 40/50 Rolls-Royce the practical result is altogether unforgettable.

Reference has already been made to the exceptional "elasticity" of early Rolls-Royce engines, to their readiness to turn over without fuss from less than 200 rpm. to 1250 rpm. or more, with neither flat-spots nor hesitation. This was due to highly developed and very well-matched systems of carburation and ignition, to control linkages laid out with no lost motion and to standards of fit far above the average. Previous levels were surpassed in the new 40/50 however, and for the fortunate few it is still possible to savour these, the number of surviving cars being as high as it is.

The driver sits high, in a truly commanding position, and all controls "come readily to hand" or to foot in the case of magneto and battery ignition switches on the earliest cars. From his point of view a lasting impression is of the lightness, the directness and the exactitude of

control, the sole exception being the steering at the lowest speeds (below 5 mph. say) when its heaviness does call for some physical exertion. At all other speeds however, its perfect balance, its accuracy and its lightness may make the widely experienced motorist somewhat critical of many present-day power-aided systems.

In spite of very high gearing the car steps away briskly from rest, with little feel or sound of engine (apart from slight air-intake hiss) but with a mellow boom from first and second gears characteristic of all early Rolls-Royce models regardless of size. On chassis previous to the 1,100 series of 1909 a four-speed gearbox with direct drive in third, was fitted. Much has been made of top gear flexibility in connection with Rolls-Royce cars, and rightly so because it was an outstanding feature in pre-automatic days. What is altogether out of the ordinary is the way in which the early 40/50 models would run on their geared-up fourth at well below 20 mph., without snatch or mechanical distress.

It is interesting to look at the gear performance of the 40/50 car (the one and only "Silver Ghost") that was the 13th of its type to be built, in 1907, and is certainly the most famous surviving example, if not quite the oldest. As tested by officials of the Royal Automobile Club in that year it reached speeds of 12.31, 21.78, 37.88 and 47.82 mph. at 1,000 rpm. in first, second, third and fourth gears respectively. Its best speed in second was 42.05 mph. and in third it ran up to 52.94 mph. – the equivalent of 1,400 rpm. At the other end of the scale it was driven for 100 yards in third gear (direct drive) at 3.4 mph. without manipulation of clutch or brakes, at which speed engine revs. were below 100 rpm!

It has been said over and over again that the overdrive gearbox was dropped in favour of one with three speeds simply because its fourth was noisy. There is a certain amount of gear hum it is true, but in the writer's road experience of many early models (including several hundred miles at the wheel of the 1909 four-speed car now in the National Motor Museum at Beaulieu) this is neither loud nor unpleasing. As Anthony Bird has pointed out the main reason for the change was to bring the 40/50 into line with its principal competitors, with their direct drive top gears. When comparisons were being made these tended to be unfair as far as the big Rolls-Royce was concerned, the fact that its direct drive was third speed and not fourth, its highest, being largely overlooked.

There was another contributory cause. Changing gear was by no means easy at that time. It was an operation that demanded concentration, fine judgement, courage, even. It was certainly not the casual matter that it was to become in later years, when the universal spread of synchromesh eased the driver's task so much. The car that spent most of its running time in top gear had strong attractions, and the fewer changes necessary to reach that state the better.

With its high power output at low engine speeds the 40/50 could be moved off in second speed and top engaged long before the speedometer needle had risen to 20 mph., say. The really lazy driver (or the show-off) could get away in top on level roads by a modicum of clutch slipping, and if he were sufficiently skilful remain in that gear for much of a journey.

Pride of possession in 1910 or thereabouts. English chassis and English body (by Barker, need one say . . .) and Scottish chauffeur. Note the window in the scuttle top, behind the A.A. badge.

Rolls-Royce: the best car in the World

Changing gear on this model, it may be said, requires skill and a hyper-sensitive ear, the low level of engine sound and feel making normal judgement difficult. There is a further complication: Royce used retaining notches in the gear-lever gate and before each change the driver has to remember to pull the lever slightly sideways to release it. Then, and only then, is it possible to move it to the required position.

By making use of the governor control on the steering wheel centre (and courageously ignoring the throttle pedal altogether) the specially skilled driver could change speed without shock or sound, as swiftly or as slowly as he wished, and could cope with standing starts on steep gradients without running back or in any way disturbing nervous passengers. And if he felt like resting his right foot he could set the governor lever to the appropriate position on its quadrant and the chosen cruising speed was then maintained at a constant rate, in the manner of modern speed-hold devices.

It may be said that to try an early 40/50 is one of the great experiences available to the mature motorist – especially his first drive of all, when the gear lever is finally drawn back from third to fourth position, with perhaps a mixture of curiosity, excitement and apprehension. Once it is safely secured in its retaining notch however, and the throttle is re-opened, the sensation of speed building up inexorably yet without mechanical effort of any kind, is enormously satisfying. At 60 mph. the big engine is turning over at no more

J. Robertson was the leading coachbuilder in Glasgow before the 1914-18 war and was responsible for many finely finished bodies for the 40/50 Rolls-Royce. This high open-drive limousine (with furled side-curtains on either side of the driving compartment) was built around 1910 and photographed outside its maker's St. Vincent Street premises.

than 1,250 rpm., a rate that it will maintain for hours on end on suitable roads, unchecked by all but the steepest hills, the sharpest bends or other traffic. Its only weak point in present-day use is its braking – very good by contemporary

The Duke of Buccleuch's cars on parade at Dalkeith Palace, in 1911.

standards but inadequate for spirited driving in late twentieth century congestion.

The 40/50 cars shown at Olympia made a highly favourable impression on all who saw them, but it was not until the early summer of 1907, by which time production was satisfactorily under way, that the true quality of the new car was properly demonstrated. With typical boldness Claude Johnson arranged to put it to public test on a scale and in a manner not previously attempted, exhaustive development trials having proved its excellence beyond possible doubt.

To begin with he asked the Royal Automobile Club (formerly the Automobile Club) to observe a long-distance trial between London and Scotland, and back. The car selected was the one to which reference has already been made – the thirteenth production model – and Johnson added to its visual attractions by specifying an aluminium paint finish for its Barker "Roi-des-Belges" touring body and silver-plating for the lamps and other fittings. He also named it "Silver Ghost" – but for some quite unaccountable reason no subsequent side-valve 40/50 car bore this name officially.

The run began on May 3 when the car was driven from London to Bexhill, for speed tests on the track there, and then on to Hatfield. During the next eleven days it was driven as far North as Inverness (and not on main roads only), back South as far as Bexhill and home again, to London. Its longest daily run was 221 miles, its shortest 114, and its total mileage was 2,000$^1/_2$, covered at an average fuel consumption of 17.06 mpg.. On one two-gallon test it averaged 23.25 mpg. – an excellent figure for a large machine that weighed just under two tons laden.

On the road two minutes were spent in adjusting the pressure valve, 30 minutes were spent in replacing packing that had slipped from under the petrol tank and coil adjustment took 30 seconds. Tyre troubles occupied one hour and 58 minutes and repairs and adjustments "in the motor houses" took up another one hour and 28

Routine maintenance on the Duke of Buccleuch's 1907 limousine. The year is 1911.

ROLLS-ROYCE
40-50 HP
CHASSIS - 1912.

Polished perfection. For the 1912 Olympia Show a 40/50 hp. chassis was specially finished. The photograph gives no real idea of the enormously high standard achieved, but it does reveal the long cantilever springs and the railway-carriage frame type of truss evolved by Royce to provide extra beam stiffness without the additional cost and weight of the deeper frame side-members that he had already experimented with.

minutes. After the end of the run the Club's Technical Committee stripped the car and found that the only points calling for attention were the exhaust valves, which were slightly pitted, some of the pinion pins in the differential, which showed play in the case, and the piston rings, which had some end play in their grooves.

Although Johnson set out to drive from London to Glasgow without using any gear lower than third he was forced to drop down on three occasions during the first day – on the test hill in Richmond Park, on Redstone Hill, Bexhill and on the hill out of Bexhill. Thereafter the remaining 518½ miles to Glasgow were covered in third and fourth gears only.

The next test was much more arduous. It began from London on June 21, and its object was to demonstrate the amount of repairs, replacements, and adjustments which would be necessary with proper and reasonable attention, and the cost of running and upkeep over an observed distance of 15,000 miles – this being the maximum permitted by the Club. Distance apart, however, the car was to take part in the 1907

Scottish Automobile Club Reliability Trials during the first part of its marathon run, and this event was far from easy.

On the sixth day the car made its one and only involuntary stop when the petrol cock shook shut and delayed it for a minute. That was at the 629th mile; the remaining 14,371 miles were stop-free apart from 14 hours and 12 minutes spent at a standstill while tyres were removed and replaced and pressures adjusted. The first 430 miles took the car to Glasgow. The next 748 miles took it round the Scottish Trials route and there its performance was good enough to secure a Gold Medal in its class.

From July 1 it ran daily except Sundays, between Glasgow and London via Berwick-on-Tweed and Manchester until the 15,000 miles were completed. Charles Rolls drove 2,707 miles, Claude Johnson who was the Trials organiser as well as its originator, drove 4,093 miles, "mechanician" Macready spent 3,859 miles at the wheel and "Chief Tester" Platford capped all by driving 4,362 miles. This remarkable demonstration of human and mechanical endurance ended on August 8 but it was not until November that the official R.A.C. Certificate of Performance was published. It is a thoroughly detailed and scrupulously fair account, based on continuous observation by Club officials whose names, surely, merited mention at the time.

Some of the figures are of great interest. Petrol

consumption averaged 15.7 mpg. and 955.41 gallons (at 1s 3.7d per gallon) were purchased, for £62/10/od. The cost per mile was one penny. Engine oil consumption was 956 mpg. 15 gallons and 5½ pints were used, costing £2/14/11d, and the cost per mile was .044d. Gear oil was used at the rate of 14,880 mpg.; 1 gallon and 1 ounce cost 2/5d and the cost per mile was .002d.

The cost of repairs, replacements and additions was remarkably low. Labour charges amounted to £4/17/8½d, made up of 40¼ hours at 2/2d per hour and charging accumulators seven times, at 1/6d each time. New material, at retail price, cost £7/16/4d and repairs to the magneto and the coil accounted for another £1/12/6d. At the end

A Rolls-Royce team car for the 1913 Austrian Alpine Trial at Nightingale Road, Derby. Features of interest are the tall steam separator on the radiator (to prevent loss of water under extreme conditions), the well-louvered bonnet side, the circular cutaway in the scuttle side to give the driver's right foot a little more room in what was an extremely narrow body and the high-mounted speedometer and separate distance-recorder.

of the Trial, according to the report, "the car was driven to the Club Motor House in Brick Street, and opened up and was found to be in all respects in perfect running order and in exceptionally good condition when examined by the Technical Committee." After listing parts which showed no wear measurable by micrometer it continued – "Had the car been in the hands of a private owner no replacements would have been considered necessary, but, to bring the car up to a condition indistinguishable from new, the following parts were either repaired or replaced, although the wear was scarcely appreciable:–

Replacing two front wheel pivot pins
one steering tie-rod pin
ball tip of steering lever
magneto driving joint
fan belt
petrol strainer
Refitting sleeve of steering balljoint
Regrinding valves

From the Observers' Reports, confirmed by actual trial by the Technical Committee at the end

of the 15,000 miles, the running of the car was excellent, except for a slight tendency to misfiring at slow speeds during a part of the Trial.

The car as a whole and the engine in particular, were exceptionally quiet (especially the third speed, direct drive) and free from vibration. The springs, however, at the back of the car were scarcely stiff enough for the load carried.

The front footboards became 'uncomfortably warm.'

The cost of parts and repairs necessary to put the car in as-new condition was a mere £2/2/7d. The cost of dismantling, assembling and testing was £14/2/-d and 1½ gallons of oil increased that total by 3/6d. Incidentally the time spent on this most complicated operation was 125½ hours.

By far the greatest expense was that of tyres. It amounted in all to £187/12/6d (3.002d. per car mile) – fractionally more than twice the sum of all other charges, which came to £93/15/10½ d, or 1½d per mile. A front tyre and tube cost £12/0/9d.; those for the rear being of larger size, cost £13/5/9d..

The Trial was a striking demonstration of the real economy of the highest grade of car, but it

Lord Rocksavage was the original owner of this London-Edinburgh model of 1913 and its highly distinctive coachwork was created for him by Barker. The front tyres were steel-studded Dunlops; those at the rear bore the name "Alma Prowodnik", of Riga, Russia.

also proved that there need be no sacrifice of performance or compromise in terms of engine size or load-carrying capacity. From the motorist's point of view it gave a precise idea of the likely expenses involved in running a 48 hp. luxury car over what amounted to two or three years of normal use at that time. In this respect it was a far more realistic (and exacting) test than the 24-hour rush round the newly-opened Brooklands Race Track in a 40/50 h.p. Napier that Edge completed in June of the same year; to maintain 60 mph., as he did, was much more a trial of human than mechanical endurance.

Johnson proved his point; high first cost need not mean high running costs over extended periods, a fact shown over and over again throughout the lengthy production life of the side-valve 40/50, and for countless years after. The Trial car itself is still in full working order, several hundred thousands miles and more than eighty years later, and it has had three owners only since it left Cooke Street in the Spring of 1907 – Rolls-Royce Limited, first and third: A. M. Hanbury, second. The latter acquired it in 1908 and kept it until his death almost 40 years afterwards; since 1948 it has been carefully cherished by its makers but it has been used extensively as well, its mileage over the past 30 years being a surprisingly high one.

The 40/50 chassis was an enlarged and improved version of that of the Thirty; its

The three-car Rolls-Royce team leaving Conduit Street for the 1913 Austrian Alpine Trial. For once the cars were not moving in high society, the onlookers, on the whole, being representative of what were then called "the lower orders."

braking and suspension systems were similar, along with its rear-axle and its general layout. Short and Long versions were marketed (11 ft. 3½ in. or 11 ft. 11½ in.) and provided opportunities for the best coachbuilders of the day that were not ignored. Although the earliest catalogues stated that all Rolls-Royce cars would be fitted with Barker bodies this did not happen in

James Radley's 1913 Austrian Alpine Trial car is still on the road from time to time – a marvellous example of the pre-first war high-performance luxury car at its very best, years ahead of its time in quality of appearance

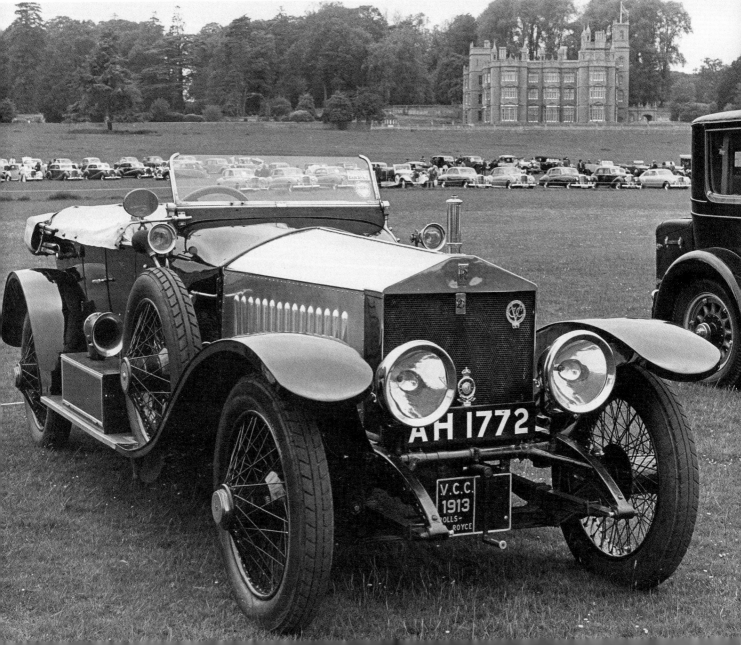

practice; the 10 hp. shown at the Paris Salon was bodied by Cann Ltd., and many other coachbuilders were involved from 1905 onwards. There is little doubt, however, that some of the most striking looking and best made, came from the London works of Barker & Co. "coach makers to His Majesty the King, H.R.H. The Prince of Wales & c.," as the catalogues said.

The chassis of the 40/50 was very well-proportioned and carried much attractive bodywork around 1910-11 and again in 1913 and 1914. This is not to say that bodies built at other times were ugly but standards generally were higher in those years. Until 1912 the parallel-sided, level-topped bonnet was a notable distinguishing feature, along with the superbly proportioned radiator. A change was made when the special London-Edinburgh car was built in 1911, with a taper-bonnet, the top line of which

Don Carlos de Salamanca and Eric Platford took first and third places with 40/50 hp. "Alpine Eagle" tourers in the 1913 Spanish Grand Prix, dust, apparently, being a major hazard.

A puzzle picture taken outside the villa at La Canadel, on the Cote d'Azur in Southern France, where Royce spent his winters from 1912 onwards and where a design office was maintained. The 40/50 has left-hand drive and a narrow body. Is it an experimental model and is its driver Eric Platford?

rose at a slight angle from the radiator and continued through to the foot of the windscreen. In the following year it was adopted as standard, but it must not be taken as a dating feature; many cars of earlier type had their flat-topped bonnets replaced as part of a routine modernisation operation at Derby.

1907 was another highly important year for Rolls-Royce and so was 1908, for then the move from Cooke Street to the new factory in Derby was completed and the Board decided to adopt a one-model policy (urged on by Claude Johnson, whose idea it was). There was a strong case for retaining the successful Light Twenty in the range but from all manner of practical points of view there was more to be said for concentrating the Company's efforts and attention on one type only; as we shall see there was not to be a second car on offer until 1922, when another kind of Twenty altogether materialised.

Finding a suitable place and site for the new

works had been a task largely looked after by Claude Johnson. Bradford, Leicester and Nottingham were seriously considered at one time or another, but it was the enterprise and generosity of Derby Town Council that took the Company there. Royce gave another staggering demonstration of his versatility and apparently insatiable appetite for work by designing and equipping the new plant, and then organising the shifting of existing machinery and of production facilities from Manchester with the least possible disturbance to current manufacture. The change-over lasted from the autumn of 1907 until the following summer, the official opening, superbly organised by Johnson, taking place on July 8, 1908.

In that same month two Rolls-Royces of a new type took part in the International Touring Car Trial, which was organised by the R.A.C. and involved 2,000 miles of varied driving from London to Scotland, then participation in the Scottish Reliability Trial, back down to London and then to the recently opened Brooklands Track for a 200-mile speed event. "White Knave" and "Silver Rogue" were the special cars; their engines were larger than the standard 40/50, they had overhead inlet and side exhaust valves (like their predecessors) and higher compression, and they were known as the Seventies, presumably because their developed horsepower approached that figure. Johnson and Platford were the

The layout of the instrument panel of this 1915 40/50 is exceptionally neat. The needle of the revolution-counter (left) was steady on 300 rpm. at tickover speed when the photograph was taken. The body is only 3 feet wide: it was made by Flewitt, of Birmingham.

drivers; the former had a piston breakage and caught a convenient cold at once; the latter, driving "Silver Rogue", won his class and had so

These Rolls-Royces maintained the secret King's Messenger Service in France during the 1914-18 war with wonderful regularity. The centre car is "Grey Moth", the unconventionally bonneted car on the right is "Silver Rogue", the 1908 70 hp.

Above: **The late W.F. Watson at the wheel of his magnificent 1911 limousine, in Hyde Park, during a Twenty-Ghost Club Rally during the 'fifties.**

Opposite page top: **A 1912 40/50 Shooting-brake from the Sword Collection. Early in its life it was fitted with a vacuum-servo operated four-wheel braking system.**

Below: **The last in the Corgi 'Classics' series was this model of a 1912 Barker Multi-light limousine formerly in the Sword Collection. It was brilliantly realised at ¹/₄₃ scale by Marcel van Cleemput, Corgi's Chief Designer, from drawings made by the author.**

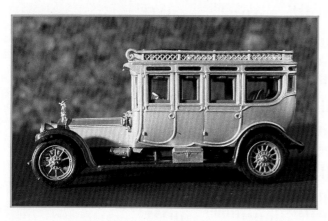

1910 6-cylinder 40/50 hp. Torpedo Tourer by Barker.

much time in hand by the beginning of the speed event that he ambled round Brooklands at an average of only 53.6 mph.. To show what the Seventies could really do he and Johnson (whose cold had been miraculously cured by replacement of the damaged piston) went back to the track some time later and covered 20 laps under R.A.C. observation at 65.9 and 65.84 mph. respectively.

Anthony Bird says that four of these cars were made but the writer has always understood that only three were completed. Their superior performance was achieved at the expense of much of the quietness and smoothness for which the make was now so much admired, and it was to be another three years before Rolls-Royce turned out a high-speed car again. This was the magnificent looking London-Edinburgh model, a slightly modified 40/50 specially prepared to challenge Napier's performance between the capitals under R.A.C. observation. The almost-

"Silver Rogue" ended a varied life as a works truck, fitted with twin rear wheels and used for transport of materials and parts. It was broken up, as an obsolescent model, after the first war.

standard 65 hp. Napier carried out the journey in top gear (2.7 to 1), averaged 19.35 mpg. and reached 76.42 mph. at Brooklands.

The rakish Rolls-Royce, which had a slightly lower top gear ratio (2.9 to 1) also did the trip with R.A.C. observers in attendance. It averaged 24.32 mpg. and was timed at 78.26 mph.

This lively, elegant machine was no mechanical freak; its extra power was gained by an increase in the efficiency of its carburation and a slight rise in compression and its performance was enhanced by very careful attention paid to the reduction of wind resistance. Contemporary photographs show the car without a windscreen: they also show that its body was extremely narrow (frame width, in fact) and of notably simple shape. They also show that its rear springing was non-standard, the usual three-quarter semi-elliptics being replaced by long, reverse-camber cantilevers.

The spirited performance and the altogether exceptional appearance of the prototype London-Edinburgh car were irresistible, and it was soon a catalogued alternative to the standard 40/50 – at no additional charge. It looked its very best when

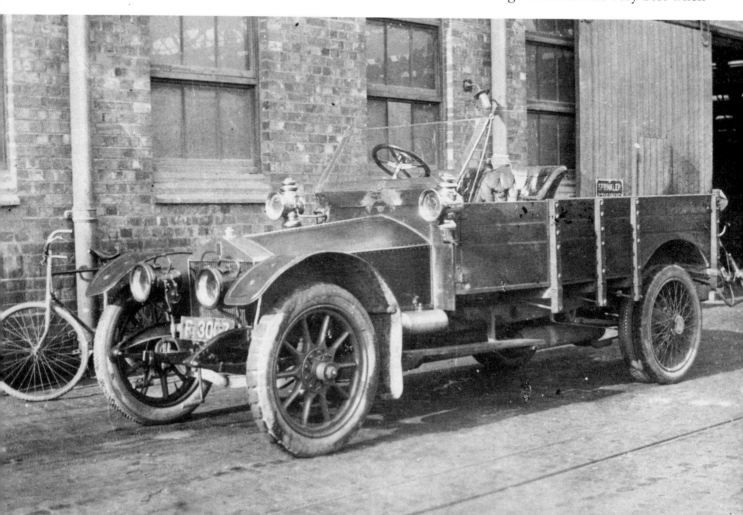

A Rolls-Royce on war service in France during the first world war – perhaps a car in the King's Messenger Service.

fitted with a body closely modelled on the original of 1911, which has a Barker look about it.* This had low, straight sides at the same level as the top of the bonnet sides and carried no spare weight; the mudwings too, were as light as possible with no side valances, and set a fashion not fully exploited for another ten years or so. Indeed the resemblance between the body of 1701E and that of the standard Vanden Plas body fitted to Bentley chassis in the 'twenties is surprisingly close.

This car survives; its chassis discovered in Kent in the early 'sixties and restored and rebodied by its present owner, Mr. Kenneth Neve. Two more high-performance Rolls-Royces survive, and these are of the same type, the "Alpine Eagle" or "Continental" model specially developed for the Austrian Alpine Trials of 1913 and 1914 respectively. The 1913 car is the actual winner of that year's event, driven by James Radley, a private entrant, and the 1914 car is

identical to the machine with which Radley won the event again.

In taking on the motoring might of Europe and America, Radley atoned in full for his failure to climb the Katschberg Pass at his first attempt during the 1912 Alpine. The first gear of the London-Edinburgh car that he was driving was a shade too high for a gradient close to 1 in 3. The altitude also had its effect. Although Radley pulled away after shedding part of his load a weakness had been rather publicly revealed.

In the long run, however, this minor disaster turned out to be of the greatest possible value because it directed attention to the absolute necessity of testing cars by now in world-wide demand under much more exacting conditions than those encountered at home. No time was wasted; soon after the Trial had ended Johnson was abroad to begin a programme of investigation on the road that has continued ever since. Since the death of C.S. Rolls in a flying accident at Bournemouth, in July 1910, and Royce's near-permanent exile to the South of France after his miraculous recovery from a supposedly fatal

It was made by a Derby coachbuilder, in fact.

61

Above: **Millard Newman's 1914 'London-Edinburgh' Tourer** *was one of a number of American owned 40/50 cars that toured Britain in the summer of 1987.*

Compare the elegance and simplicity of appearance of this c.1921 Hooper Landaulette with the clumsiness of the c.1910 car of similar body type. The use of sham-cane is masterly.

HOOPER & CO

Not all the Rolls-Royces ordered in such profusion by Indian rulers were of a showy kind. In 1921 the Grosvenor Carriage Co. built several Tourers of this simple kind for the Nawab of Rampur.

Below: Between the wars it was unusual for a new Rolls-Royce chassis to be used as the basis for a hearse. In the early 'twenties, however, a Paisley coachbuilder made this well-finished body.

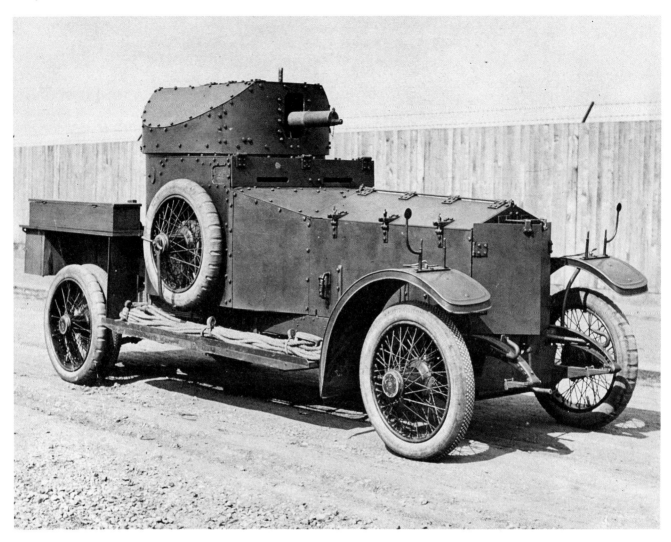

Within their limits Rolls-Royce armoured cars were most effective fighting vehicles – absolutely dependable, fast and manoeuvrable.

illness in 1911, Johnson had been in effective day-by-day control of the Company, and it says much for his powers of delegation as well as of organisation that he was able to leave England to inaugurate continental test routines.

As a result of intensive development work based on the results of these, the three Rolls-Royce cars entered by their makers for the 1913 Alpine Trial had improved cooling, a new four-speed gearbox, with direct drive in fourth, a revised fuel system and carburation modifications. The works cars failed to take the Team Prize only because accident damage to the one driven by Sinclair delayed it so much that far too many marks were lost. It was left to Radley, a driver of great resource, dash, tenacity and superhuman powers of endurance to win, and in the following year (alone this time) he won again.

One further competition success may be mentioned briefly; in 1913 Don Carlos de Salamanca, the Company's Spanish Agent, entered the Spanish Touring Car Grand Prix and won with a three minute lead, and Eric Platford was third. There was no official competition participation after 1913 in fact; its purpose had been achieved and the Rolls-Royce reputation was internationally recognised. In its exclusive way it was as much a universal car as the equally famous (but far less-expensive) contemporary, the Model "T" Ford.

By 1914 the 40/50 Rolls-Royce was positively recognised as the best car of its type then available. Its place in motoring history will never be disturbed. It was – it is – a nonpareil.

Chapter 2
The Twenties

Once the years of senseless slaughter had been stopped, contracts for the construction of killing machines were abruptly cancelled. Suddenly the world found itself at peace, and as is not uncommon at such times there arose a vast and apparently unsilenceable clamour for consumer goods of all kinds.

If they do no more, wars create work, and this in turn creates money, the spending of which continues until immediate needs are satisfied. In some quarters there was plenty to spare and the market for Rolls-Royces was brisk in Britain after the 1918 Armistice, very much more than the original cost of cars being willingly paid. Even as late as November, 1920 a 1914 limousine with dynamo lighting was advertised in *The Autocar* for £2,500 for example, and a 1913 3/4-landaulette for £1,975, and these prices were modest by the levels reached during the previous year or so. As a matter of interest a 40/50 chassis cost £985 in 1914 and a complete car seldom much more than £1,500 – new in each case.

Remember that prices of this magnitude were being paid for vehicles often far from new even before their war service began. It was a measure of their innate quality and sheer toughness that in spite of a work-load that would have worn out lesser cars in a matter of months they were still fit for years of further service. Some indeed, survive to the present day, in full running order.

Within a year or two of the Armistice, however, the boom was over. By late 1920 a serious slump prevailed, post-war problems of many kinds being its source. Labour unease and unrest for example, difficulties over the supply of materials, both raw and processed, unwise investment, inflation and so on, affected the motor industry almost as much as any other.

Yet its immediate and long-term prospects seemed more secure than most because by then there existed a potential market very much larger than ever before. The ownership and use of automobiles in Britain had previously been an indulgence of the well-to-do on the whole, the paid driver being an important and conspicuous figure in the pre-war motoring scene, small as this had been by North American standards.

But because of its almost universal use in wartime the motor vehicle had become familiar to hundreds of thousands of service personnel and civilians of both sexes, for whom "The Caprices of the Petrol Motor" (as C.S. Rolls had described them in a memorable chapter in *Motors & Motor Driving** gradually became yet another fact of life. A high percentage sought further contact on their own account, once the war was over.

For obvious economic reasons small cars had the strongest sales potential as far as Europe was concerned and the appearance here of such simple, ingenious and cheap-to-run machines as the Rover 8 (which could sound at times like a mechanised tin tea-tray) and the later and more refined Austin 7 gave great pleasure and much-appreciated mobility to tens of thousands of "new motorists" and well-merited profit to their makers. So too, did the larger and even more ubiquitous Morris "Cowleys" and "Oxfords" that, in "Bullnose" form, gradually gained the major share of the home market by the mid-twenties.

*The Badminton Library, 1902

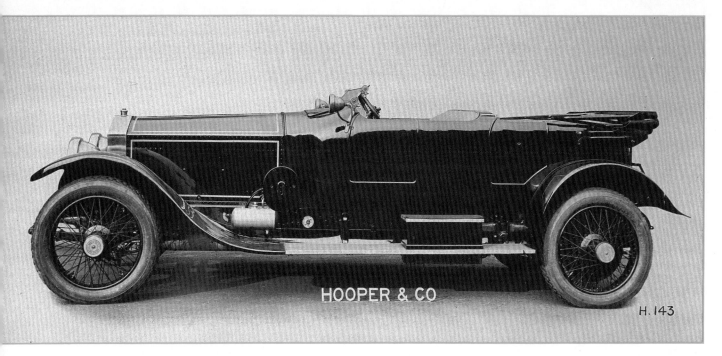

Clearly this c.1922 Hooper Tourer was intended for much spirited motoring. Its windscreen is of the kind more usually found on out-and-out sports cars of the period.

*Opposite page top: **Fine proportions and an effective use of sham-cane, along with the superfine finish for which Hooper & Co. were so deservedly famous, are striking features of this early post-war 40/50.***

Along with cars of this kind, and others of higher cost and social pretensions in the medium-power class, there appeared a number of altogether new models from famous English makers to challenge Rolls-Royce. In theory, at least, one or two had every chance of success, but in practice things were not so simple. None could match the balance of qualities possessed by the

A c.1923 catalogue illustration of a 3-speed Twenty, with All-weather coachwork.

40/50, however well this one or that might excel on individual features.

The new 40/50 Napier bore a greatly-respected name and its excellent engine was of advanced design and construction. Unfortunately its chassis

1923 6-cylinder 20 hp. Doctor's Coupé by Park Ward.

66

was less adventurous in conception; its appearance was stolid, to say the least, and the completed car lacked the dash and distinction of the true luxury car. Less than 200 were built between 1919 and 1924.

Parry Thomas's highly original Leyland "Eight" was masterly, mechanically-speaking, and on that account alone it deserved a long and successful production life. But its makers, the celebrated Lancashire lorry-builders, made less

than 20 "eights" before they decided to get out of the car market; had they stayed a drastic improvement in the appearance of the car would have been an absolute necessity.

In almost every respect the 40 hp. Lanchester was first-class, and its maker's reputation was extremely high, despite a long-standing tendency of its designer George Lanchester, to favour the mechanically unconventional – but for the best of engineering reasons as a rule. It was a car of somewhat inelegant appearance, however, a fact that must have had an adverse effect on sales measured against those of the 40/50 Rolls-Royce. Between 1919 and 1930 about 400 were built.

The other main English rivals to the Rolls-Royce were Daimler and Bentley, the former scoring strongly on the one hand because of its continuing Royal associations, which appealed particularly to the snobbish, and on the other because such a multiplicity of models was available, at prices substantially below those of the Derby cars. Daimlers were well-enough suited to home conditions but outside these islands they were less satisfactory, reliable high-speed, long distance running of the kind and quality taken as a matter of course by Rolls-Royce owners being somewhat beyond their scope.

The lively but audible 3-litre Bentley was never

a serious rival. The 6½-litre might have been had its maker's reputation not been so firmly established in the sporting-car class, even as early as 1925. It rivalled the contemporary 40/50 in some important respects and excelled it in terms of outright speed and acceleration. Its chassis was truly handsome and provided a splendid base for bodies of distinguished appearance. All in all the 6½-litre and its derivative, the even-better "Speed Six", deserved to take a much larger share of the luxury-car market than indeed they did. Between 1925 and 1930 the total number built was just under 550; in the same period Rolls-Royce sold more than 2,200 "New Phantoms" and several hundred 'Phantom IIs".

During the second half of the 'twenties' the only large English car that rivalled the Rolls, aesthetically-speaking, was the Bentley. From 1919, however, its chief continental competitor in this, and in almost every other respect, was the 37.2 hp. Hispano-Suiza, a car that could look every bit as magnificent as its name suggested. Its engine and chassis were thoroughly up-to-date in design and very well-matched, one to the other;

The high mechanical quality and fine performance of the post-war Lanchester "Forty" was not matched by a comparable excellence of appearance.

the big Hispano was a fast car but it was also a most controllable one, its steering and roadholding and braking being exceptionally good by contemporary standards.

Furthermore it was very well made, and its superb overhead-camshaft engine must rank as one of the best-looking ever; if it was not as quiet as a Rolls it must be remembered that it

Not all the Indian Rulers ordered exotically-bodied cars; by normal standards this 40/50, specially supplied to the Maharajah of Kapurthala for use during an early 'twenties visit to India by the then Prince of Wales, was excessively restrained in appearance.

developed practically twice as much brake horsepower. Its splendid appearance almost certainly influenced later Rolls-Royce thinking to some extent – though to be fair the general look and layout of Derby's 6-cylinder engines, large and small, from 1925 until 1939 (from 1922 in the case of the "Twenty") had their origins as early as 1919.

The 37.2 had style. It also had four-wheel brakes that gave it a great advantage, not only in the swift crossing of continents and motoring up and down mountain roads at speed, but in city traffic as well. In this respect its superiority was clear. But by 1924 the 40/50 Rolls-Royce was also available with a four-wheel brake system (based to some extent on that of the Hispano) which had no superior.

In 1918 this was still in the future; just how the motoring scene would develop once the war was over was a matter for guesswork only. One fact was certain, however; everything was going to cost a great deal more. Between 1914 and 1918

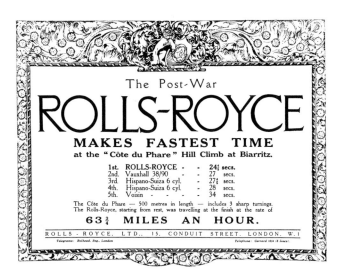

This 1921 advertisement contradicts the generally held belief that Rolls-Royce gave up all official interest in competitive motoring before the First World War.

Opposite page: *A 1924 40/50 Hooper Open-drive limousine of rather austere appearance, with whitewall tyres that give it an intriguing American flavour.*

Left: *The controls of a completely rebuilt 1924 Twenty. Note the centrally-placed gear and handbrake lever and the orderly arrangement of instruments.*

Below: *It is said that the film actor, Jackie Coogan, once owned this remarkably modern-looking American built 40/50. Its roadster body, with open rumble seat (or dickey) is a Brewster production.*

Rolls-Royce engines worked for a living, and after long road service this early 'twenties 40/50 unit continued to serve usefully as a demonstration model. In its original form it was a good deal tidier, much of the poorly arranged pipework, for example, having been added for instructional purposes.

there had been a doubling of prices, and the end of fighting did not bring an end to further increases. In 1919 the 40/50 chassis cost £1,450 and a year later it had risen to £1,865. Coachbuilding costs showed comparable increases, so that a completed car could reach £3,000, or more, which was an enormous figure even when contemporary levels of inflation are taken into account. It bought something very special, however. Rolls-Royce standards were still of the highest. They were maintained, what is more, and in time prices were stabilised, along with the state of the economy.

Whether or not the market for costly cars of this kind would survive in a world wearied and financially weakened by years of war was a question almost impossible to answer. The Board of Rolls-Royce Limited did its own bit of guessing – very intelligently as it happened.

It was decided to develop a smaller car to sell alongside but not directly against the existing model. The new car was to be aimed at the same kind of discriminating motorist, but at the less affluent one, relatively speaking. At the same time it was realised that not everyone might still want a car as large and as powerful as the 40/50, even when considerations of cost were quite unimportant.

But the main appeal of the "Goshawk", as it became known inside the Company,* was to be to those whose means were ample by all normal standards but no longer sufficient to make the purchase and extended operation of the largest, most expensive type of car quite so easy a matter as it once had been.

While post-war production of the 40/50 gained

*At first it was known as "Cinderella"

pace, to catch up with current demand, Royce and his team of designers concentrated on the creation of a smaller car of comparable quality but very much lower first cost, that was more up-to-date in its general design. Meanwhile Claude Johnson ingeniously denied rumours that his Company had anything new in mind.

For policy reasons, no doubt, the name "Goshawk" was not used publicly; when the new model was introduced in the autumn of 1922 it was as the Twenty, which made much sense because it gave an immediate indication of its size relative to that of the larger 40/50. The latter, it should be said, was still not officially known as the "Silver Ghost".

By Derby standards the Twenty was a comparatively small and mechanically simple motor-car. Its engine was an in-line, monobloc six of 3,127 cc, capacity, with push-rod operated overhead-valves and a 7-bearing crankshaft, Royce carburettor and coil ignition, the latter supplemented by a standby magneto (an optional extra at first), timed and ready to couple up in the unlikely event of battery failure. It was in unit with a centre-change, 3-speed and reverse gearbox. The adoption of the latter was a controversial feature that incensed the diehards, as did the adoption of Hotchkiss drive – a widespread and perfectly acceptable method of transmitting power to the rear wheels without using the costly and rather weighty torque-tube fitted to the 40/50 chassis. Less fuss was made because the new model lacked four-wheel brakes; although these had been in fairly general use on the Continent since the end of the war (and in one or two cases since very much earlier than that) their universal adoption in this country was not to begin seriously for another year or two. In any case the Twenty's two-wheel brake system was a most effective one in its day – and its use was another of the factors that held the chassis price down to such a reasonable level, taking into account the sheer quality of its materials and workmanship. In this respect there was absolutely no compromise.

From late 1925 onwards the Twenty had its maker's highly-developed and exceptionally efficient servo-operated four-wheel braking system. At first, when it was optional, it cost £85 extra; shortly afterwards it became standard equipment and the chassis price rose to £1,185, a figure held

until the end of production in 1929, incidentally. Along with a splendid four-speed, right-hand change gearbox that was introduced in the same year, this gave the Twenty an improved cross-country, average-speed performance and made its conduct in town or country even more agreeable than before.

A good example is still notable for its suavity of movement, for the lightness, precision and quickness of response of all controls, for the directness and sensitivity of its high-geared steering and for a braking system that combines an immediate, but very subtle reaction to the lightest of pedal pressures with quite astonishing powers of progressive retardation. Time and time again in contemporary reports reference is made to the quality of Rolls-Royce brakes – to their delicacy of operation, which was relatively uncommon at that stage of motor-car development, and to their ability to pull up a heavy vehicle from speed with the utmost smoothness and lack of effort. The principle of the mechanical-servo operated system was not at all unique; in different forms it was used by Hispano-Suiza and by Renault for example, to regulate the movement of their large and lively 37.2 and 45 hp. models.

Royce preferred the Hispano system, which was the work of Marc Birkigt, its maker's brilliant designer, and arranged for a 37.2 to be acquired for detailed and critical analysis and trial. It would be interesting to know if the compliment was returned once the 40/50 was available with servo-assisted four-wheel braking.

Royce's adaptation, improvement and development was carried through with typical thoroughness, and as already mentioned his design had no superior; indeed a mid-twenties Rolls with its brakes in proper adjustment is at no disadvantage whatsoever in modern traffic. With only minor changes the system evolved by Royce and his design team more than forty years before, remained in use until the mid-sixties on all Rolls-Royce and Bentley cars.

The servo motor is a small disc-clutch at the side of the gearbox that rotates at a rate proportional to the speed of the car, its drive being effected by the rear wheels as long as the car is moving. Initial pressure on the brake pedal begins direct application of the rear brake-shoes

Production lines at Derby circa 1923. Two rows of 3-speed Twenty chassis, left and centre, and three 40/50 chassis on the right.

and draws together the friction discs of the servo. Through a system of very carefully proportioned levers, secured to the backplate of the latter, the momentum (or stored-up energy) of the moving car is then used to engage both front and rear brakes, its driver's effort, of course, being greatly amplified as far as rear-shoe engagement is concerned. The overall effect is distributed, front and rear, in a ratio of roughly one-third to two-thirds, to allow for weight transfer under deceleration. The system is just as light and effective in reverse, which the Hispano system is not.

Rolls-Royce paid royalties to their most effective rival, without demur, and it is more than probable that the irony and the humour of the situation were appreciated by both sides. Some space has been given to the matter because its braking system has been one of the most outstanding features of the Rolls-Royce since 1924. In pre-war days its first cost may well have exceeded that of a complete small car.

The critics condemned the Twenty as being too American, but conveniently forgot to acknowledge the quality and originality of so many of that country's cars. Royce himself took the closest interest in their design and the manner of their manufacture; indeed, he had stationed a namesake, a cousin, in Detroit some years before the war to make regular reports on the North American automobile industry. His mind was always very open and receptive; excellence, whatever its kind, attracted his respect and his admiration was often expressed in most generous terms.

In North America, of course, attitudes towards the motor-car had been much more down-to-earth, almost since its beginnings in the 'nineties; it had always been looked upon there as a utility and not as a luxury, and practicality was taken with great seriousness.

The Twenty was of practical design as well, while routine maintenance, for example, was on a scale daunting by latter-day standards it was in no way comparable with that of the 40/50, and it was far from difficult to carry out. Ease of access and the general simplicity of its layout helped to keep down labour charges for servicing or repair, and

74

replacement parts were not at all expensive. Nevertheless the weekly or 500-mile service required attention to 26 oiling points, the fortnightly or 1,000-mile one to just twice that number, and once a month (or at 2,000-mile intervals) eleven main tasks had to be attended to, along with numerous less important ones.

All this may sound tedious to a present-day motorist accustomed to vehicles that may have no lubrication points and require oil changes at six- or twelve-monthly intervals only. An important practical advantage, however, lay in the fact that the person responsible became intimately acquainted with the state of the chassis in his charge

It is difficult to believe that this Brewster body was built in 1924 for its lines would have seemed up-to-date ten years later. The drum-shaped lamps are typical of American taste of the time.

and was able to attend immediately to any incipient mechanical or structural malfunction. Even when Rolls-Royce fitted their cars with a centralised, "one-shot" lubrication system (from 1926 in America and from 1929 in England) the prudent chauffeur or service-engineer still took a regular look at each of the points it served.

Properly cared for and sympathetically driven the Twenty was a quite exceptionally economical car to operate, in the long term as well as in the short. The driver who knew his car and knew how to manipulate the mixture control with true finesse could achieve 20 mpg. or more and oil consumption was low; and both tyres and brake linings could last for an almost unbelievably long time. This was the case also with cylinder bores and main bearings, upwards of 100,000 miles being possible before attention was necessary – though to be fair it should be said that such

After the First World War Royce spent his summers in the south of England, at West Wittering, in Sussex, where a design group worked close to his house. Tea there might be in the garden for his experts – but pistons and magnetos were as likely to be on the table as pancakes and muffins. Royce, with beard, has Evernden on his right and Elliott (later Chief Designer) on his left.

near-immortality was most often achieved on cars used for fast continental driving. A bore life as short as 15,000 miles could be the result of intensive London traffic work, on the other hand.

In its original form the engine of the Twenty developed about 50 bhp. at 3,000 rpm., the main emphasis being placed on smooth and quiet running, strong pulling-power (or torque) at low and medium speeds, and extreme flexibility. As long as it was not overburdened, bodily speaking, in terms of weight and frontal area, the Twenty was a lively car, pulling effortlessly from a crawl in top gear or stepping off in the gears in brisk fashion from a standstill. Most of its running could be carried out in top, of course, despite the fact that the final-drive ratio was quite high, and this is one reason for the maintained quietness of intermediate gears on these cars. Extensive experience of Twenties in taxi service in Edinburgh in the late 'forties and throughout most of the 'fifties provided aural evidence that even after years and years of the hardest kind of useage however, Twenty gearboxes retained their original reticence, along with the rest of the transmission. This applied to engines as well, and as much

to the earliest, three-speed cars as to the latest 1929 models.

For what it had to do the Twenty had sufficient power but there was no real reserve unless it were fitted with one of those appealing barrel-sided touring bodies that Messrs Barker, Hooper and Park Ward designed and made so well, or in the second half of the 'twenties, a closed body built on the Weymann system, which united strength and freedom from rattling with lightness of construction. Until the end of production in 1929, maximum speed was still between 63 and 65 mph. and it is unlikely that bhp. was much above its 1922 level. Chassis weight then was a mere $18\frac{1}{2}$ cwt. A tourer tested by *The Autocar* in January 1926 weighed just over $28\frac{1}{4}$ cwt. (it had four-wheel brakes) and a Weymann saloon tried by the same magazine 3 years later was 5 cwt. heavier. The actual limit for guarantee purposes was 39 cwt., which covered "chassis, body, passengers and all else therein or thereon."

It is easy enough now to say that this was too high; Royce and his colleagues were well aware of the fact but all the time they were up against the combined strength of the coachbuilders, who behaved on the whole as if they were still catering for the horse-drawn vehicle and allowed far too high a margin of safety in their structures. The Company exercised strict control in one way by issuing highly detailed bodybuilder's drawings and making certain, through a most rigorous pre-delivery inspection system, that its instructions were correctly followed. Its trump card was the three-year guarantee; by threatening to withhold this it could discipline the errant bodybuilder or perhaps his wilful client.

All this was of course, in the best interests of the owner; Rolls-Royce had an immense store of experiences to draw upon and tended to know what was best for their customers, the majority of whom sought unobtrusive, mobile luxury. A minority (in the main they favoured the 40/50 chassis, with its high performance potential) took an extremely active interest in the creation of their cars, mechanically and bodily speaking, and might even suggest design improvements or modifications at times. As they tended to be men of great motoring experience, they were listened to and action taken, if appropriate; owners in this rather rare and exclusive category at different times included Rudyard Kipling, the first Lord Northcliffe (a close friend of Claude Johnson), G.R.N. Minchin, Captain Kruse and Geoffrey Smith (one-time Managing Editor of *The Autocar*).

Although this kind of relationship between customer and manufacturer has been at no time unique to Rolls-Royce it has perhaps been more thoroughly cultivated by them than by any of their contemporaries during the last 70 years or so. Claude Johnson was largely responsible; he was actively engaged in the stimulation of what is nowadays called 'feedback', and while there is no doubt that he exploited publicity aspects to the full, whenever this was practical, his chief concern always was the improvement of the product for the greater good of its owner. Nor was this a matter of short-term satisfaction only; Rolls-Royce have always maintained their interest in each and every car built, not simply while it was in the hands of its original owner but for many, many years after.

During the 'twenties, for example, many of the earliest models were still in use and owners were able to obtain parts from Derby, upwards of 20 years after their cars had gone out of production. Until recently many spares for the 1907-1925 40/50 chassis were still readily available, and so many elderly Rolls-Royces have remained in regular use that the world demand for replacements such as clutch- and brake-linings (and tyres, of course) is a sizeable one. A state of affairs of this kind would be pleasing to Johnson and to Royce, who believed in the building of ever-lasting motor-cars, and made it happen.

Because their Twenty was a smaller, lighter and cheaper car than their 40/50 it might be reasonable to assume that its life-expectation would be of shorter duration. In practice this has not been so, the smaller car having proved beyond all doubt that its toughness, its inbuilt resistance of mechanical and structural deterioration is on the same exalted level as that of its larger contemporary. Examples of both types survive in first-class working order after hundreds of thousands of miles of intensive use, whereas a handful only of their former rivals has remained. In the long run Rolls-Royce won their battles of the early 'twenties, fought against strong competition from firms that took advan-

Royce at West Wittering with two of his design staff and an early Twenty.

tage of wartime advances in engine design, for example, and produced new models with up-to-date power units – Lanchester, Leyland and Napier chief among the English makers and Hispano-Suiza (a Franco-Spanish concern whose designer was Swiss) by far the most important from the Continent. With the exception of Leyland, for whom Parry Thomas had created a straight-8, the former favoured efficient, overhead-camshaft, 6-cylinder engines that developed around 80 bhp., reliably and quietly. Hispano were in an altogether different class, with their 135 bhp. 37.2 model and the later 45 hp. "Boulogne" – motor-cars magnificent by any standards.

The American approach was a different one; side-valves were still popular there, as were multi-cylinder motors, of which their makers had such enormous production and operational experience. As early as 1914 Cadillac had introduced their fine 90° V-8, a quiet, refined and reliable 70 bhp. engine that remained in production almost without change for 12 years, no less. The number built was high – 13,000 in 1915 for example, and over 20,000 in 1918.

Between 1917 and 1922, when it was rescued from collapse by the Ford Motor Company, Lincoln made about 3,000 examples of a fine car designed by Henry Leedland, the engine of which was a 90 bhp. 60° V-8. Sales so poor by American standards may have been the result of a low level of body appearance design; at any rate styling changes were made so swiftly and effectively by Ford that from March to December, 1922 over 5,500 new-look Lincolns were sold. The least costly standard touring model at that time was $3,300 (£650 or so in our money; here however, it would have sold for around £1,200 because of import duty and other charges) though cars with high-grade custom-built bodies were $6,000 or more.

The 1915 Packard 60° V-12 – the splendid Twin-Six – produced 85 bhp. at 3,000 rpm. (high figures, both, for their time) without fuss and took its makers into the aero-engine building business a year or two later. In 1916 over 4,000 Twin-Sixes were sold. In 1923 its V12 engine was replaced by an 84 bhp. straight-8, installed in a four-wheel brake chassis. The tourer cost $3,750. Cadillac first fitted four-wheel brakes in that year but they were not seen on production Lincolns until 1927.

Against such competition Rolls-Royce still offered a 7,410 cc. side-valve engine designed in 1906 and world-famous as the quietest, most flexible and most reliable 6-cylinder in production, set in a chassis of equal design antiquity so to speak. This combination was unsurpassed, however, for quality of running, materials and workmanship, for balanced performance, for operating economy, for comfort, for driver and passenger satisfaction and for durability.

The post-war 40/50 differed little from the 1914 model. Aluminium pistons helped to raise output to 75 bhp. or so, and an electric starter and lighting set appeared at long last as standard equipment. Top speed depended to some extent on the type of coachwork fitted; over 70 mph. was possible with a tourer and even the tallest limousine, laden to the limit, could exceed 65. On continental roads maintained speeds of 60 mph., surface permitting, were perfectly practical, but potentially dangerous as far as the structural security of bodywork was concerned.

To the conservatism of coachbuilders reference has already been made. Had all chassis-builders worked on the lines laid down by Dr. Lanchester this might not have mattered quite so much, but his emphasis on the extreme importance of a rigid foundation was largely unheeded. Frame flexing and twisting were inevitable accompaniments to the passage of large, lively and weighty motor-cars over poor road surfaces (the thought of three tons of laden Rolls-Royce dashing down France at 60 mph, under post-war conditions must have been a case of constant concern at Conduit Street and Derby) and often led to the partial disintegration of bodywork, it being far from uncommon for doors to fly open or for panels to become detached from their framework.

The coachbuilders – the main culprits here – had to be educated, persuaded to abandon traditional attitudes and methods for an up-to-date engineering approach to the problems of producing structures strong and flexible enough to cope with the stresses of such use over extended periods.

Ivan Evernden, a member of the small design team based at West Wittering, was the engineer-diplomat chosen by Royce for this task. To take on a long-established craft-based industry and to try to convert it to more modern ways was no sinecure, even for someone of Evernden's engineering stature, backed by a concern of such high repute as Rolls-Royce. Scores of accredited coach-builders had to be dealt with, throughout the British Isles, and there were foreign ones to be tackled also. They were given every kind of help, advice and encouragement. Very gradually and very reluctantly in many cases they adopted a more realistic approach, became body engineers as well as bodybuilders, and gave their productions a structural quality that fitted them for years of service of the most demanding kind.

The introduction of the Weymann system in the early 'twenties showed what could be done in the way of weight saving and noise reduction. The framework of a Weymann body consisted of wooden members that could not touch but were joined by light metal strips (to allow a limited amount of flexibility) and it was covered with a special type of leathercloth, tightly stretched. Lightness was combined with exceptional freedom from self-induced noise: the latter a particularly important feature in bodies mounted on chassis as inherently quiet as those of Rolls-Royce, for example.

In 1927 Park Ward & Company (established in Willesden, London, in 1919) built a 6-light saloon

These 1923 Rolls-Royce Twenties were still in everyday service in Edinburgh until the late 'fifties, along with not quite so ancient tramcars.

body for a Twenty that weighed a little under 7 cwt. – about the same as a Weymann of similar type and size. This small concern had shown considerable initiative in adopting new methods and materials and from quite early in its history there was a good deal of active collaboration with Rolls-Royce on a production as well as an experimental basis. Eventually Park Ward was taken over and survives to this day as part of the H. J. Mulliner Park Ward group now responsible for all specialist bodybuilding projects for Rolls-Royce Motor Cars Ltd. The conjunction of two of the most famous names in motor-car bodybuilding is a happy one.

The success of the Twenty was immediate, the market for its maker's products greatly widened by its introduction. Relatively speaking it was excellent value, a tourer costing £1,590 at a time when the price of a similarly bodied 40/50 was £2,400. For the first time since its earliest days the Company made some attempt at standardisation of body design, a tourer, a landaulette and an all-weather of restrained appearance being among the types listed. Ivan Evernden had a good deal to

do with their evolution and Park Ward with their production. When standard bodies were next offered in 1931 (when for the first time they were shown on the Rolls-Royce stand at Olympia), this coachbuilder was again much involved.

In the difficult economic conditions that followed the boom years of 1919 and 1920, and against stronger competition than ever before, it was not surprising that sales of the larger car began to drop. Design and development work on its replacement (the factory code name of which was Eastern Armoured Car) was intensified as soon as the Twenty was in production, but it was not until May, 1925 that the New Phantom – more commonly known as the Phantom I – was introduced. On the outside it looked little different from the model it replaced; below its impressive bonnet, however, there was an altogether new engine – a handsome 6-cylinder overhead-valve unit of about 100 bhp. It had a longer stroke than the side-valve unit and a narrower bore; its capacity was 7,668 cc. and its RAC rating was 43.3 hp. It was a good deal tidier in appearance, its new colour scheme of black stove-enamel and unpolished aluminium looked well and it was much easier to keep clean and decent.

The new engine was an enlarged version of the

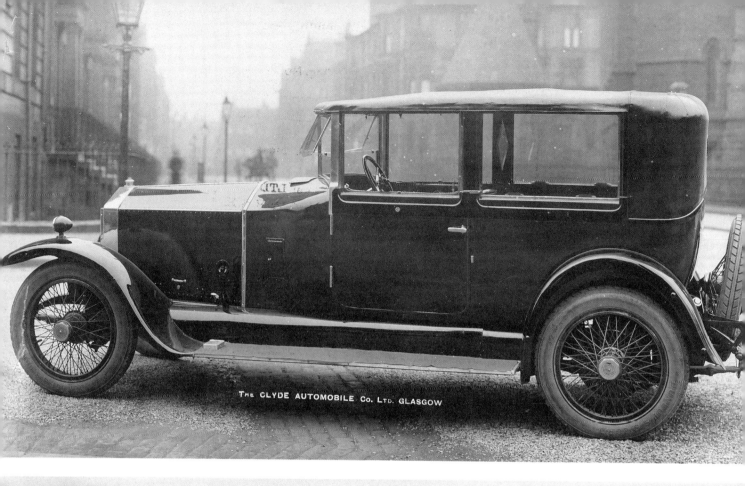

THE CLYDE AUTOMOBILE Co. Ltd. GLASGOW

Opposite page top: **The lines of this 1923 3-speed, 2-wheel brake Twenty All-weather are simple but not severe. Its chassis number was 5552, its body was almost certainly made for the Clyde Automobile Company by J. Robertson, it was blue with black wings and it was supplied to George Urie Scott.**

Above: **The Twenty was at its very best in two-seat form, when its lightness gave it added litheness of movement. Claude Hamilton & Co., of Aberdeen, built this lovely tourer on a 1926 chassis.**

Twenty, but fitted with the versatile and highly sensitive governor-controlled throttle of its predecessor, which held speed steady at any pre-selected setting, downhill, uphill or on the level. A new feature was now introduced, a hydraulically-operated device that automatically regulated the separate coil- and magneto-ignition systems, advancing or retarding them at the differing rates necessary through a most ingenious and beautifully constructed mechanism. Precise synchronisation of the two ignition

"So smooth, so sweet", wrote Herrick; had he lived at a later date he might have written excellent advertising copy for the Rolls-Royce Twenty. Hooper built this most stylish body in the mid-twenties – and from the fact that it had a louvered bonnet it is reasonable to assume that the car was intended for use in hot climates.

81

The instruments of Alec Hird's 1929 Twenty saloon are scattered across a panel shaped to follow the vigorous curve of the windscreen rail. Uniformity of arrangement began with the Phantom II in 1929 and was extended to the 20/25 model a year or two later.

systems was thus achieved whether the driver left the governor to cope on its own or used the hand control on the steering wheel centre to override it under extreme conditions.

The maximum of the New Phantom was around 75 mph. (with an extra 3 or 4 mph. if the exhaust cut-out was opened) and cruising at 60 mph. or more was quite effortless. In spite of a power increase of 25%, flexibility was altogether exceptional; with the ignition fully retarded and the throttle closed the big car could crawl at 4 or 5 mph. in top gear with neither sound nor snatch – a characteristic of all subsequent manual gearbox cars from Derby and Crewe, along with quietness of running throughout the whole speed range.

Contemporary reports all referred to the increased liveliness, to the power of the brakes (and their delicacy of application), the lightness of control and the riding comfort of the new car. The fact that the chassis remained unaltered, except in minor details, meant that handling showed little real difference from that of the previous 40/50. During production, however, hydraulic shock-absorbers replaced the friction type first fitted and later chassis had improved comfort and roadholding.

In 1928 the original cast-iron cylinder-head was replaced by a new aluminium one and the compression-ratio raised a fraction, from 4 to 1 to 4.2 to 1. Presumably there was a slight increase in power as a result.

Although it was such a costly machine the New Phantom sold extremely well, over 2,200 being built at Derby between 1925 and late 1929. During that period, it is true, the British economy was comparatively buoyant, but an annual average sale of 440 expensive motor-cars was rather remarkable. That was not all; between late 1922 and late 1929 an average of 412 Twenties was sold each year as well. By American luxury-car standards such figures were derisory. In 1927 alone for example, Packard sold over 32,000 of its Single Eight model, which cost around $4,000 on the home market. As the price of a New Phantom in the United States at that time was at least four times as much it is scarcely surprising that so many Americans preferred the local product, especially as it was of such high quality.

In terms of absolute quality, however, the Rolls-Royces large and small, held their lead. Home sales were strong throughout this period but they were not the only ones; the 40/50 had sold well in India since its first appearance there in 1908. The Princes, Maharajahs, Nabobs and others who had bought it on such an ostentatious scale over the years were at least as enthusiastic about the Twenty. Sales in North and South America had not been negligible either, and in the Antipodes they increased to such an extent that by 1928 there were service facilities in Adelaide, Brisbane, Melbourne and Sydney, and sales outlets in New Zealand at Auckland, Christchurch and Wellington.

Nor was that all. Service was provided all over Europe in Belgium, Denmark, France, Germany, Holland, Italy, Portugal, Spain, Sweden, and Switzerland. Apart from the facilities available throughout the year at Automobiles Rolls-Royce (France) Ltd., in Paris, others were offered at Easter, and from July to October, in Biarritz, and in Nice during the winter months. In Spain there were two depots; in Germany, rather surprisingly, there were five.

Elsewhere – in the United States, in the Argentine, Brazil and Peru; in Egypt and the

Cape Province; in the Straits Settlements and in India and Ceylon – specialist services were also available. There had even been representation in China, in Japan, (the Emperor purchased two 40/50 limousines in 1920) and in Canada. One of the most important centres, not only for Austria herself but for Czechoslovakia, Hungary and Yugoslavia as well, had been Vienna. To some extent the locations of the rich and their seasonal movements could be plotted by reference to the siting of Rolls-Royce service facilities round the world.

Along with the Model "T" Ford the Rolls was one of the most widely travelled of all cars and the likelihood of its use almost anywhere on the earth's surface was taken seriously by its makers. Instruction books and tool-kits were far more comprehensive than most so that the owner or chauffeur who found it necessary to carry out a decarbonisation for instance (a 10,000-mile service requirement in the 'twenties) far from home or from his home country, was enabled to do so by following the clearly written, well illustrated directions provided and using the appropriate tools, each of which had been designed for its specific purpose by Royce.

But in those days it was not particularly expensive to have such work carried out in the workshops of an official retailer (as long as one was handy); parts were moderately priced and the charging-out rate for labour – in this country at any rate – cannot have been much more than two old shillings, or 10p., an hour. The life-expectation of these cars has already been mentioned. With proper care of the kind laid down in detail by their makers, it was more or less indefinite, and even when there was abuse or neglect their capacity to keep going was far beyond the average. It is a recognised fact that their latter-day counterparts are somewhat more vulnerable unless recommended schedules of maintenance are closely and conscientiously followed.

Servicing in the United States was something of a problem simply because of the size of that country. Until 1921 it was comparatively unimportant because the main concentration of Rolls-Royce cars was in the East, in the New York area. When deliveries of the American-built 40/50 began early that year, however, and

The offside of the engine of Mr. Alec Hird's 1929 Twenty. Despite the apparent untidiness of its layout accessibility to all parts is first class. The nearside, with its distinctive finned exhaust manifold and eminently polishable aluminium inlet manifold, dynamo and stand-by magneto in tandem, and firewall-mounted Autovac, is completely original.

ownership spread more widely over the Union, it became obvious that the initial idea of producing chassis identical in every respect to those from Derby would have to be swiftly modified.

Apart from batteries, magnetos, sparking-plugs and wiring, Rolls-Royce had always made their own electrical equipment and, of course, it required specialist attention on occasion. It was

The body of this 1929 Twenty was designed by its doctor owner and built by H.J. Mulliner and the immaculate chocolate coloured car was a familiar sight in the New Town of Edinburgh until the late 'fifties.

most certainly not of a type familiar across the Atlantic; moreover it was based on the 12-volt system. To overcome this problem quick action had to be taken; American magnetos, dynamos (or generators), coils and starter-motors replaced those English components previously used, and from then on servicing of the electrical side – now 6-volt, to put it in line with standard American practice, was possible anywhere in the States.

Another essential change was from right- to left-hand-drive but that took much longer to carry out because of the number of chassis modifications that had to be made. As each and every one had to be seen and passed by Derby before it could go into production there were inevitable delays while the paper-work sailed to and fro across the Atlantic; in those days there was no regular air service between Europe and America and the one-way crossing by steam-ship took the greater part of a week. Eventually, however, all the alterations were approved, and

the l.h.d. chassis went into production with a centre-change, three-speed gearbox, four speeds being out of favour at that time in American automobile circles.

This changeover was an extremely important sales aid in a country so completely committed to the left-hand way of motoring life but it was not introduced until 1925, just before the New Phantom was announced in England. During the following year, manufacture of the new model began at the Springfield plant of Rolls-Royce of America Inc., the time lag caused by the solving of the problems of adapting its altogether new engine to fit satisfactorily into l.h.d. chassis having been a rather lengthy one. It took even longer to modify the design of the gearbox to accommodate the brake servo-motor, and as a result the first 60 or so of the American Phantoms

Hooper & Co. designed and built some superb looking bodies on Rolls-Royce chassis during the mid- and late-twenties and without doubt this beautifully proportioned Coupé was one of their supreme achievements. Note its distinctive headlamps – and the fact that its bonnet and scuttle are of unpainted, highly polished aluminium.

were built without four-wheel brakes. In time, however, they went back to the factory for what Rolls-Royce called "retrospective embodiment of improvements", emerging eventually with the modified gearbox (a four-speed again, automobile fashions having changed once more) and braking on each wheel.

Because of American attitudes towards the purchase of motor-cars home-produced Rolls-Royces were offered from the beginning complete with bodywork, the latter "custom-built" and of standardised pattern, more often than not and subtly different in line from their English contemporaries but comparable in quality. It was one of the triumphs of the American operation that the cars built there could meet their English counterparts on such level terms. It has been suggested, in fact, that the later Springfield New Phantoms were superior in some respects.

From the start of production in 1920 until its end in January 1931, 1,303 chassis of the 40/50 Silver Ghost type and 1,241 New Phantoms were made. These are impressive totals for cars of high

Another Hooper masterpiece, circa 1926, with crests on each door, ship-type scuttle ventilators, Colonial-type louvered bonnet and special steering-wheel (perhaps of ivory). Obviously built for an owner of exalted rank.

first cost, marketed during a period of economic unease. Prices varied according to the kind of "Rolls-Royce Custom Coachwork" ordered and to the number of extras added. They were never less than $12,000 and rose to $20,000 or more on occasion, several times as much as the cost of an average top-quality American car.

Sales, which had reached a peak of 400 in 1928, were mortally affected in the awful aftermath of the 1929 Wall Street crash. In the same year another major problem arose; Derby announced a successor to the New Phantom so thoroughly up-to-date in specification, in looks and in performance that it made the older model obsolete immediately. Moreover the fact that it was shortly to be available from England with left-hand drive meant that there was no point in developing an American version.

Under such circumstances it was decided to end production at Springfield, once current orders had been satisfied. From February, 1931 until the closing of the factory in 1936 a repair and maintenance service only was provided by Rolls-Royce of America. The operation had been defeated by economics, but it was not the rather shameful failure that so many writers have

suggested. To sell almost 3,000 extremely expensive motor-cars of alien type during such a difficult time and against such worthy competition was a major achievement, surely.

Claude Johnson had willingly supported the idea of setting up a separate American concern when it was first proposed. His Company's cars had always sold well in the States, and he felt that there was a better chance of long term market stability than in post-war Europe. By manufacturing there, high import duties, high shipping costs and other charges would be avoided and prices could be more competitive.

Towards the end of the war Rolls-Royce aero-engines had been built in quantity in the East; as a result there was a readily available supply of craftsmen accustomed to Derby methods and Derby standards of construction and workmanship. There was also a sizeable team of supervisory staff, sent across from Derby during the war to guide and advise, and accustomed by them to transatlantic ways of life.

Although J.B. Duke, the tobacco tycoon to whom the first Lord Beaverbrook (then Sir Max Aitken) sold his controlling shares in Rolls-Royce Limited during an Atlantic crossing just before the war, was not at all excited by the project. Others were, and Rolls-Royce of America Inc. was established in 1919 with a major American investment (though the parent company had the controlling share). The former American Wire

Wheel factory at Springfield, Massachusetts, was acquired, production began during 1920 and first deliveries were made early in 1921.

Mention has already been made of the fact that complete cars were offered from the beginning, and as early as 1922 body design was being

Claude Johnson initiated the idea of a high-performance Phantom I before his death in 1926 and Evernden eventually realised it, with encouragement from Royce. This is one of the four special cars made between 1927 and 1928 (known at the works as "C.J.'s Sports Cars"). Careful reduction of weight and wind resistance and the raising of the final-drive ratio gave it a top speed around 90 mph.

carried out at Springfield. In 1926 Brewster & Co., of New York, the leading American coachbuilding concern of the day, was taken over. It had been responsible for most of the custom-built bodywork on Springfield chassis anyway, and the main result of the union was that Rolls-Royce were able to supply complete cars "off the showroom floor" when necessary. It nearly always was; impatient buyers could choose a car and drive it away almost immediately. Others could place their order, after much highly enjoyable deliberation on type, looks and specification, and – in the European manner – wait for months while chassis and body were built with quite exceptional care and craftsmanship, then united, tested and delivered.

That was the way it happened here, and there are still buyers quite content to pay more and wait longer for a specially bodied Rolls-Royce (or Bentley). To this day, however, most automobiles in America are bought on sight, the average

A 1928 advertisement. The big Phantom is still a tall car but its good proportions and general neatness of appearance, along with a strong horizontal emphasis, combine to give it a sleeker look than most of its forerunners.

customer preferring to look, and if he likes, to be able to leave in the car of his choice.

The original 40/50 was in production from 1906 until 1925 in England and from 1920 until 1926 in America. The New Phantom was built here from 1925 until 1929, there from 1926 to 1931. "Phantom II" had a longer run; it was announced in September, 1929 and made until 1935, but at Derby only.

It was the last of the really big 6-cylinder Rolls-Royces and the most vigorous; and although it was more powerful and had a wider range of engine speed it was as flexible as any of its forebears. It could be driven in two ways; "on the gearbox", for maximum acceleration and all-round performance, or in traditional manner, second or third being used to get away from rest and top engaged at 15 to 20 mph.. Most of a day's

In theory, at least, the Hispano-Suiza was the most formidable competitor Rolls-Royce faced in the European Market. In practice, however, the splendid French car sold in much smaller numbers between 1919 and the mid-thirties. This is a 1929 45 hp. 6-cylinder.

motoring could be carried out in the highest gear for in it the car could crawl through dense traffic at tick-over speed, climb practically any main road hill in the British Isles and cruise wherever possible at an easy 70 mph. At the latter speed its engine was turning over at much less than 3,000 rpm.

Whereas the usable maximum of the New Phantom in third was little more than 45 mph., its successor could sweep up to 70, if its driver felt ferocious, and more than 40 was possible in second. The gear-change of the Phantom II was splendid; easier, even lighter and very much

Phantom II H.J. Mulliner limousine.

swifter than that of the previous 40/50 models, and the best drivers (who had perhaps, attended the Company's School of Instruction) were able to shift from one speed to another without their passengers being conscious of the fact. Intelligent and confident manipulation of the throttle governor made it possible for example, to move from top to third, or third to top at 60 mph. or more, without clash of any kind and as quickly or as slowly as required. The degree of control that could be exercised was onc demonstrated to the writer by C.W. Morton, that best-informed of all Rolls-Royce historians who played the gearbox with the artistry of an Ashkenazy and the same lack of show.

Inexperienced drivers of the smaller Rolls-

Royce sometimes had trouble changing gear simply because the smoothness and quietness of the engine made it so difficult to judge its speed. For them the introduction of synchromesh in 1932 was most welcome. Drivers of the Phantom II, on the other hand, had sufficient sound and feel of its engine to guide them, not that this was noisy or rough by any normal standards but under hard acceleration, for example, the push of its six large pistons was palpable. It was also rather exhilarating. At steady speeds quietness and smoothness reached impressive levels.

Before the appearance of the Phantom II there had been the usual rumours, one of which was to the effect that Rolls-Royce had a sports-car in preparation. In fact its works' code-name was "Sports Car" and this was apt, for its performance far excelled that of any previous standard

*Above: **A 1925 Phantom I with Park Ward All-weather bodywork and the steel artillery wheels that were an alternative to wire wheels.***

*Opposite page top: **A splendid Springfield 40/50 with Brewster Sedanca-de-Ville coachwork of extra-fine quality, and now in Scottish ownership.***

1927 6-cylinder 40/50 hp. Phantom I Brougham by Clark, of Wolverhampton.

Derby car in terms of speed, acceleration and hill-climbing powers. Its quality of control, its steering, its braking and its roadholding all reached even higher standards. It was a very comfortable car, a very restful car to drive or to travel in, a very quick one on occasion. Early models were good for more than 80 mph. and in standard short-wheelbase form or in the special "Continental" type to which reference is made in the next chapter, 90 mph. or so was possible. Acceleration was powerful, particularly so for such a large and weighty vehicle, yet absolutely regular because of the quality of the carburation and ignition systems and unusually precise control linkages.

Its chassis was based on that of the Twenty; it was carried on extremely long, flat semi-elliptical springs and was much closer to the ground than its predecessors.

91

The torque-tube was dropped along with the cantilever springs previously used at the rear; it was replaced by an open propeller-shaft, and the latter part of the transmission was of the Hotchkiss type. The gearbox was in unit with the engine for the first time on a 40/50 chassis and its ratios were quite closely spaced. Gear noise was at an exceptionally low level, which was to be expected.

The engine closely resembled that of the New Phantom; its capacity was the same but because of its new "crossflow" cylinder head, raised compression and other modifications, it could turn at well over 3,000 rpm. and produce far more power than any of its predecessors. Yet it was no less economical – 10 to 14 mpg, according to the type of use and speed maintained – and at least as durable; and it was set into a much lighter chassis, of exceptionally fine proportions and appearance.

The Phantom II was large enough to accommodate spacious, luxuriously equipped coachwork and powerful enough to cope with an all-up weight that could be as high as 58 cwt. (the guarantee limit). On the better roads of its time it could maintain high average speeds quietly, reliably and without effort.

A present-day stranger to the make and model might find its sheer bulk somewhat intimidating at first. Once at the wheel and on the move, however, he would probably be astonished at the lightness of its steering at any speed over 4 mph., and especially when he discovered that less than three turns of the wheel took the car from one lock to the other. The immediacy of response to movement of any of the controls (and the lightness of their operation, too) would impress at once, and while acceleration that was considered swift almost 60 years ago might not impress so much, the manner of its delivery most certainly would.

The smaller Rolls-Royce was a good deal less vigorous on the move, even in its new form for 1930. At long last its engine capacity had been increased, from 3,127 cc. to 3,699 cc.; its R.A.C. rating rose to 25.3 hp (from 21.6), and its developed power was up by 20% to somewhere in the region of 65 bhp. As its final-drive ratio was unchanged and the maximum speed of its engine differed little from that of the Twenty, it was no faster at first. But it was a livelier car; one far better suited to the denser, faster-moving traffic of its day or to long-distance, cross-country journeys.

Apart from its larger capacity the 20/25 differed in no significant way from its predecessor; even its "one-shot", or centralised lubrication scheme had been fitted to the last two series of Twenty chassis and there were no dimensional changes until 1930, when the wheelbase was lengthened by 3 inches.

During production however, between late 1929 and the Spring of 1936, numerous detail alterations were made, largely to ensure that increased performance was matched by corresponding improvements in braking, roadholding, suspension and refinement of running. In recent years there has been an inclination on the part of some not very well-informed critics to label the 20/25 as a dull machine. By present-day standards it may well be so, as long as comparisons are being made in terms of speed and acceleration. During the 'thirties matters were somewhat different. Few cars in its class were faster than the 20/25 (and in any case this was a matter of academic interest to the majority of owners, who were after other more important qualities) and none, perhaps, excelled in lightness, exactness and responsiveness of control, or, for that matter, in quietness, in reliability, in economy and in durability.

Chapter 3
Rolls-Royce
in the Nineteen Thirties

After the complexities of making pressed-steel bodies in quantity had been sufficiently mastered, their designers began to prove their hitherto latent powers by creating coachwork that positively pleased the eyes. By 1930 even Fords were good to look at.

Their maker may not have bothered overmuch about the look of his Tin Lizzie until near the end of its over-extended production run, by which time the sales success of such appearance-conscious competitors as Chevrolet had given him the commercial fright of a lengthy lifetime. After that, however, he saw to it that the new Model "A" and its successors for nearly 20 years were kept properly up-to-date in style, in a distinctively Dearborn sort of way. An early Ford high point was reached in 1931-32 – not surprisingly perhaps, because car appearance and design in general had reached agreeably high standards by that time. If it had been somewhat self-conscious for a while that was understandable; industrial design as such was a comparatively young profession and its practitioners still had much to learn.

But those concerned with the look of automobiles, like other creators of fashion goods, scarcely needed to be taught the importance of keeping the closest watch on what their competitors were doing. Seldom during the past 40 years or so have they ever been slow to adapt or adopt the commercially successful ideas of others. Nevertheless the original thinkers – the real pacesetters, so to speak – have usually managed to stay sufficiently far ahead to gain commercial benefit, especially in the mass-production field,

where the interval between drawing-board and final assembly line has always been such a very long one.

In the luxury-car class the situation is a little different. For various reasons the majority of owners favour the car of conservative appearance, and they have always been well catered for. A minority is more adventurous, aesthetically speaking, and for them too demand has always been well matched by supply. The designer of the bespoke or custom-built body is after all, involved in the field of high fashion and here change is swift.

During the 'twenties one could drive to work or play just as efficiently in a jitney as in a Rolls-Royce, but the difference in quality between the two kinds of car was about as wide as the gap between the incomes of their respective owners. Ford had his market and so had Royce, and at that time there was no doubt as to which was the cheap car and which the dear.

A little later, when the Ford V-8 literally leaped into the motoring scene in 1932, signs of change were clear; the mass-produced article *par excellence* had caught up in terms of measurable performance (and to some extent in refinement of running) and was to challenge the luxury car on other counts as well within the decade. In 1930 and for some long time after, the superiority of the high-grade automobile in terms of all-round quality was more or less absolute.

Yet in those days it was a brave manufacturer who carried on turning out products of high first cost that were not prime necessities of life. The Wall Street crash of 1929 tumbled the United

Opposite page top: **An early Phantom I, with a polished, unpainted bonnet (or hood) and a curvaceous Close-coupled coupé body, complete with skylight.**

Opposite page bottom: **The Barrel-sided tourer was a body type especially well suited to the Rolls-Royce This is a 1927 example, by Park Ward, on a 1927 Phantom I chassis.**

Below: **Claude Hamilton, of Aberdeen, built this elegant body on a 1926 Twenty chassis. Until recently it shared quarters with 'The Auld Lady'.**

States into a state of acute economic decline that persisted almost to the outbreak of war and seriously affected her automobile industry at every level. Here in Britain, although the worst effects of a financial crisis soon to become worldwide were not fully experienced until the late summer of 1931, they were almost as persistent and pernicious.

By then the 20/25 and 40/50 Rolls-Royces had

A 1930 20/25 with Hooper close-coupled Foursome Coupe – a highly attractive combination. Note the wide 3-hinged door and the lockable tool compartment housed behind the front mudwing valance.

been selling remarkably well for almost two years, in spite of the deteriorating economic situation and in spite of powerful competition from the top American makes, chief among them being Cadillac, Lincoln (ironically enough a Ford product) and Packard. Nearer home Hispano-Suiza, an old and much respected rival, was still in the running and Daimler's recently-adopted fluid-flywheel and preselector gearbox were strong selling points before the general introduction of easy gear-changing systems.

But the strongest challenge came from Bentley, whose 8-litre car was as much a "sensation" of the 1930 Olympia Motor Show in London as the Phantom II had been in 1929.

Its designer's reputation had been somewhat audibly established in the first place by his excellent four-cylinder 3-litre car, in the second (and more quietly) by his six-cylinder 6½-litre, and in the third by another thunder-maker, the four-cylinder 4½. The 6½ and a later, much improved version known as the Speed Six, were

in direct competition with the 40/50 Rolls-Royces between 1925 and 1930, but in spite of high standards of design and construction, comparable quietness of operation and a generally superior performance they were outsold about six to one.

It is unlikely, to say the least, that the 4½-litre strained the allegiance of many Rolls owners either; the decibel output of its eager engine was just too much to stand for any length of time in a closed body, even if that body were of the Weymann type and the silencing system of the special closed-car pattern.

The new model, however, was another matter. Its 7,983 cc. engine developed around 220 bhp. at 3,500 rpm. with ease, with quietness and with reliability. It was set behind an extremely handsome and imposing radiator and into a low-set frame of fine appearance and massive construction that was available in 12 ft. or 13 ft. wheelbase lengths. With so much latent power on demand there were no tiresome weight restrictions to hinder customer or coachbuilder. Even when the largest and most completely furnished body was fitted a maximum speed of around 100 mph. was easily attainable, though not often in the British Isles.

On paper, at least, the Phantom II made a

96

less-impressive showing. Its top speed was between 85 and 90 mph. according to body type and weight and the final-drive ratio chosen. 90 – 95 mph. was possible with the short-chassis model in "Continental" form or when suitably bodied in other ways that eased its passage through the air.

A 12 ft. chassis "Continental" tested by *The Autocar* in August 1933 covered a timed half-mile at Brooklands Race Track at 92.31 mph., accelerated from a standstill to 70 mph. in 28 seconds and averaged between 10 and 14 miles to the Imperial gallon. It weighed 49 cwt.

In its road test of an 8-litre that appeared in

The author's first Rolls-Royce – a 1930 20/25 semi-Weymann sport saloon (bodybuilder unknown) at Pittenweem, Fife, Scotland in 1950. In over 8 years and 50,000 miles of use the cost of repairs and replacements was no more than £50.

December 1930 *The Motor* reported that top speed was 104 mph. and that it went from rest to 70 mph. in 25 seconds. Its weight was about 50 cwt. and its petrol consumption around 10 mpg.

If these figures are compared, it will be seen that the big Rolls showed up rather well, in fact. Its very lively performance was achieved on 140 bhp. at most, which suggests that its overall mechanical efficiency was remarkably high; to have to find an extra 80 bhp. or more for a speed increase of 10 mph. or so smacks a little of wastefulness surely. The fact remains that almost from scratch, as it were, the 8-litre was able to tackle the Phantom II on level terms, take away a sizeable number of potential buyers and seriously worry its makers.

Between October 1930 and the following summer when Bentley Motors Ltd. went into

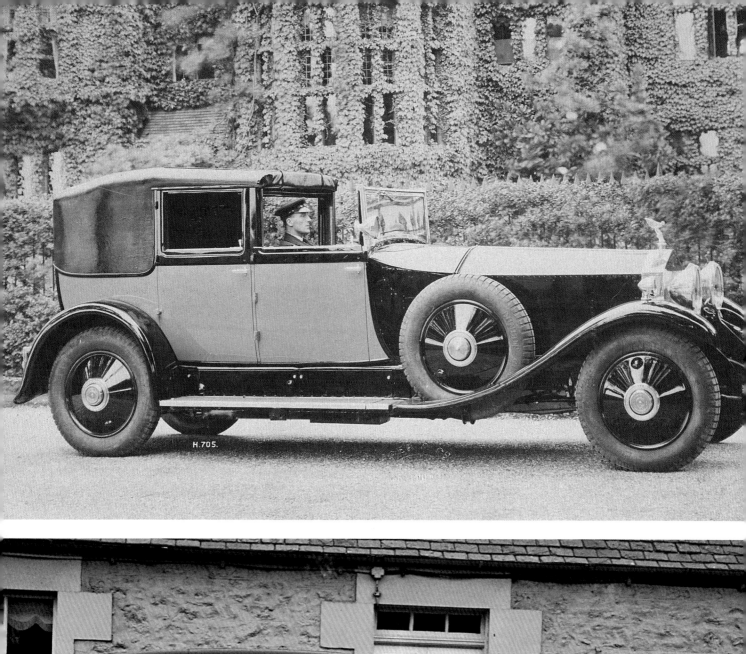

*Left, top: **During the 'twenties Hooper & Co. designed and built many outstandingly handsome bodies for Rolls-Royce owners. The proportions, the finish, the very 'presence' of this c.1928 Phantom I Sedanca-de-Ville are truly classic.***

*Left, bottom: **The lightweight, noiseless Weymann type of body was particularly suitable for the Twenty chassis. In the sympathetic hands of its owner, Alex Hird, this H.J. Mulliner four-light saloon was a familiar sight in Aberdeenshire for a great number of years.***

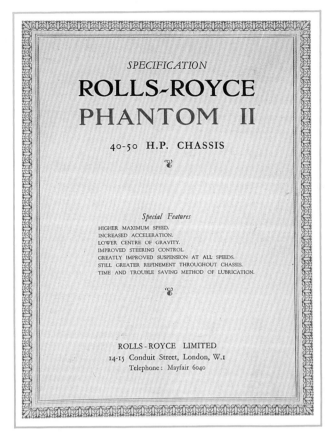

SPECIFICATION

ROLLS-ROYCE PHANTOM II

40-50 H.P. CHASSIS

Special Features

HIGHER MAXIMUM SPEED.
INCREASED ACCELERATION.
LOWER CENTRE OF GRAVITY.
IMPROVED STEERING CONTROL.
GREATLY IMPROVED SUSPENSION AT ALL SPEEDS.
STILL GREATER REFINEMENT THROUGHOUT CHASSIS.
TIME AND TROUBLE SAVING METHOD OF LUBRICATION.

ROLLS-ROYCE LIMITED
14-15 Conduit Street, London, W.1
Telephone : Mayfair 6040

The first Phantom II catalogue lacked illustrations but was well provided with facts. It marked a change of attitude towards design on the part of Rolls-Royce and is in itself an example of distinctive typography.

liquidation, 63 8-litre cars were built, bodied and disposed of, and a further 37 were completed and sold later on. When the main circumstances are considered – the awful state of the British economy by late 1930, the high cost of its chassis (£1,850) and bodywork (as much as another £1,000, perhaps), the fact that it was a new and still untried model of a make highly regarded internationally for its racing successes but not taken too seriously by the carriage trade, so called, the decidedly unstable state of its maker's affairs and the sheer strength of competition, not simply from Rolls-Royce but from some of other makes as well – it is astonishing and altogether admirable that the 8-litre did so well in such a short space of time.

It did so well that when Bentley Motors was put up for sale by the liquidator in November, 1931, Rolls-Royce (disguised as the British Central Equitable Trust) whipped it away from Napier, a former rival in the automobile business

An unusually sleek barrel-sided tourer (by Barker?) on what looks like a 20/25 chassis.

and a still-active one in aero-engine manufacture, with a slightly higher bid. By so doing they removed potentially powerful competition from the scene at one go; whether or not the projected

Rolls-Royce: the best car in the World

6¼-litre Napier-Bentley – or Bentley-Napier – would have been such an invincible rival as their action suggests they thought it might be, is something no-one will ever know.

Bentley's other challenge to Rolls-Royce in 1931, the 4-litre, was designed to compete with the 20/25. Although its engine developed 120 bhp., which was far above the 65-70 bhp. produced by the smaller Rolls at that time, it lacked low-speed torque and the liveliness normally associated with the name Bentley. The fact that surplus short-wheelbase 8-litre chassis were used was a main reason for the lethargy of the 4-litre, a model wished upon W.O. Bentley at the most unpropitious of times.

Total production was only 50. Enthusiasts for the make tend to treat the 4-litre as a kind of mechanical skeleton in the cupboard, to be talked about, if at all, in whispers.

Meanwhile the 20/25 sold strongly. Between 1929 and 1934 many exceptionally handsome bodies were created for it; indeed the highest standards of a decade were reached during that period, not only on the smaller chassis but on that of the 40/50 as well. After 1934 a sort of visual

decline began; curves became over-exaggerated (a tendency at its worst among American cars on the whole) and the earlier subtlety of line, of proportion and of form was lost for the next 15 years or more.

An important factor in the widespread improvement in automobile appearance was the reduction in height that became noticeable towards the end of the 'twenties. Until then closed bodies, especially on the larger chassis, tended to be clumsy-looking, ill-proportioned, staid and static. Gradually the upright look gave way to something lower, sleeker and decidedly smart, and a feeling of movement was implicit in many of the new designs even when the car in question was at rest.

Although the chassis of the 20/25 was no lower than that of the Twenty the visual ingenuity of the best bodymakers and designers (the latter anonymous almost to a man, for no good reason) made sure that the coachwork they created for it was always abreast or ahead of contemporary fashion until 1938, when it was replaced by the completely new and different Wraith.

Quite the highest standards of design were maintained by the leading London concerns – Barker, Hooper, H.J. Mulliner and Park Ward. The level of their best work was so high, in fact, that when a body in bad taste was produced by any one of them it is almost certain that it came

AX 148, the 1905 10 hp. Rolls-Royce that is now in the London Science Museum collection, took part in the 1930 London to Brighton Commemoration Run. The photograph is an evocative period piece.

about because a customer thought he knew better.

In the 'twenties and 'thirties the number of coachbuilders officially approved by Rolls-Royce was a large one but apart from the top four, only Freestone & Webb and Gurney Nutting produced much work of consistently good appearance, that of the others being decidedly uneven in quality. Although Rolls-Royce supplied highly detailed coachbuilders' drawings and laid down stringent rules to make certain that essential mechanical functions were not interfered with, for example, that the movement of controls was unimpeded and that ready access for maintenance or repair was provided, the company had no real say over appearance.

Because bonnet and scuttle were supplied with each chassis, however, its makers were able to ensure that the driver was placed in the best possible position for seeing forward; he always looked down and along the bonnet – and he still does in the present day Silver Spur, Corniche, Camargue and Phantom VI. Even when the bonnets of most other makes rose to such heights (by fashion's stupid decree) that nothing of the road surface immediately in front of the car could be seen for as much as 50 feet, perhaps, the driver of a contemporary Rolls-Royce always enjoyed a commanding view, the safety aspects of which should not be overlooked. After all the company view on accidents was that if you had one in a Rolls-Royce it was your fault!

Attitudes towards automobile safety were much less strongly emphasised between the wars though public demonstrations of the inherent strength and safety of pressed-steel saloons under staged collision conditions took place during the late 'thirties. Generally speaking, however, the fact that steady improvements in braking, steering and roadholding, for example, automatically raised standards of safety tended to be played down.

For a time during the 'twenties some owners of cars fitted with four-wheel braking systems provided warning signals to that effect, presumably to reduce the risk of being rammed from behind under panic-stop conditions. More recently, it may be remembered, similar warnings about disc-brake equipped cars were commonly seen.

John Bolster, the motoring writer and connoisseur once called this "The noblest prospect in motoring". Driver's view from a 1934 20/25 on the road from Forfar to Aberdeen, in 1953.

Braking of the highest possible standard has always been an outstanding feature of Rolls-Royce cars and the mechanical-servo operated system first used on late Silver Ghost chassis from 1924 onwards was unchanged, except in detail, until 1939. During the early 'thirties its effectiveness was increased to keep pace with improved performance yet its legendary lightness and delicacy of operation were in no way impaired.

Precision was a characteristic of all controls, of course, and had a great deal to do with the sheer sensual pleasure of driving these cars. There was an immediate response to any movement made by the driver, without delay and without lost motion of any kind, and this applied to all – to the hand-throttle, ignition advance-retard and mixture-setting levers located on the steering-wheel centre, to the steering itself (requiring fewer-than-average turns from lock to lock yet retaining exceptional lightness by contemporary standards), to the gear-change lever and the hand- and foot-brakes. Indeed the movement of the hand-throttle from one notch to the next in its quadrant – a matter of a millimetre or so – altered the tick-over speed of the engine by a slight but discernible degree.

Such concern for adding to the pleasures of driving was no new thing; it had been characteristic of the earliest cars as well, reaching its pre-first war zenith with the 40/50 model. If the excellence of steering of the best examples was

Barker & Co. built this striking Drophead on a 1931 Phantom II Continental chassis for Captain Kruse, of the Continental Daily Mail, *a* Northcliffe *publication.*

never quite equalled again, according to connoisseurs of the greatest experience and discrimination, the reasons were physical and unavoidable and had almost everything to do with weight, that ancient enemy of the designer.

When narrow-section beaded-edge tyres were used and front axles were without brakes, precision and lightness of steering followed so long as its design and quality of construction were satisfactory. The addition of brake drums and control mechanism to front axles inevitably increased weight, as did the change over to wide-section balloon tyres, which also presented a larger area of rubber to the ground at any given time. Weight distribution was another factor to be taken into account, variations in the percentage loading of front and rear axles having their effect on the relative lightness of steering effort.

This was something taken very seriously by

This Barker Sports saloon, on a Phantom II Continental chassis, was exhibited at the 1931 Berlin Show. Distinctive period features are its two-colour finish, its helmet-type mudwings, the decorative use of louvers and the steps that replaced the more usual running-board.

Rolls-Royce, its influence extending as well to suspension, to roadholding and to braking, and before the building of a chassis began some essential information was obtained from its owner-to-be. The type and weight of body had to be known, of course. So, too, had the number of occupants to be carried normally and the maximum as well as the average weight of luggage – and the kind of use to which the car would be put as well as the level of speed at which it would be driven.

Such concentration on detail was typical, part of a philosophy that considered the production of the best possible of the utmost importance. At

1928 6-cylinder 40/50 hp. Springfield Phantom I Sport Touring by Brewster.

Miniature "Continental"? Freestone and Webb made this sleek-lined body for a specially tuned and equipped 20/25 in 1934. The chassis has driver-controlled friction shock-absorbers over and above its normal hydraulics and its main instruments are of the 6 in. diameter, "soup-plate" type.

this preliminary stage, for example, the customer was consulted about the kind of suspension he preferred; obviously "soft" springing could be provided for low-speed town running, while a firmer system would be specified for a car intended for high-speed touring.

To strike the correct balance between riding comfort and high standards of roadholding was a problem common to all manufacturers of large, fast cars in those inter-war years. Few, if any, went to the lengths taken by Rolls-Royce. But in the early 'thirties both Cadillac and Packard for example, fitted different forms of driver-operated ride control, largely to compensate for the wide differences in weight and in its distribution between a fully-laden car and one almost empty. A tank full of petrol could weigh anything from

two to three hundredweight, according to its capacity.

In 1933 Rolls-Royce introduced a most ingenious system of automatic ride control, with driver over-ride, for the Phantom II, and in the following year it was added to the specification of the 20/25 and the new Derby-built 3½-litre Bentley. Its use was only discontinued with the introduction of self-levelling suspension for the Silver Shadow in 1965.

Particular attention was paid to weight distribution in the design of the Continental model of the Phantom II early in 1930. According to Ivan Evernden, who was largely responsible for its realisation, it was inspired to some extent by Royce himself, who had been greatly attracted by the compact arrangement of the Riley Nine Monaco saloon and wanted something like it – ostensibly for himself – on the 40/50 chassis. A Monaco was acquired surreptitiously for reference purposes and Evernden began work in the Spring of 1930. His design for a close-coupled sports-saloon was based on bodies of the same type built on the first production Phantom II and on at least one of the pre-production experimental cars of this model.

As he had also been responsible for their design Evernden was on familiar ground. Without drastic changes of any kind he effected a quite remarkable improvement in the appearance of his earlier design and the completed car – a true "classic" of its time – took the Grand Prix d'Honneur at the 1930 Biarritz Concours d'Elegance on its very first public showing.

It was – it still is – a car of most striking appearance, its proportions close to the ideal, its contrast of straight lines and curves most subtly contrived. Even the tread patterns of its big Dunlop 'Fort' tyres play an important part, as do its radiator shutters and the close-spaced bonnet louvres. The long flared front mud-wings give the car a rakish, sporting look, shield the body most effectively from flying spray and effectively reduce wind resistance, their shape having been carefully determined by Evernden during experiments with sports Phantom I referred to in the previous chapter.

Barker & Co. built Evernden's earliest sports saloons and his prototype Continental, and along with Hooper, H.J. Mulliner, Park Ward and one

New Bond Street, London in 1951. No-one heeded the sight of an elderly 20/25 "come whispering by" – but the expert might have been a shade perturbed at the out-of-proportion P-100 headlamps.

This 1935 20/25 has a Gurney Nutting body of clumsy shape and the fitting of spats over the rear wheels adds to its heaviness of appearance. Its pillarless construction would cause problems in time with such a wide and heavy door.

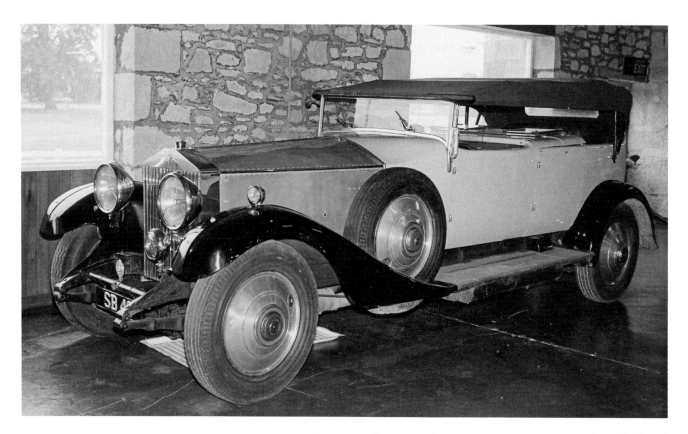

18-EX, the very first prototype Phantom II, was completed in December 1928 and began endurance tests in France later that month. It was rebodied after an accident in the mid-thirties and stayed in the possession of the Noble family for a very long time.

or two others were responsible for many subtle variations on the basic shape of the latter between late 1930 and 1932, more or less. Thereafter the very real beauty of the original and many of its derivatives was gradually lost as the cult of the compound curve became more and more widespread.

Although many of the later bodies in this style were handsome enough in their own way none reached the standards of the best of the earlier models: apart from anything else the amplitude of their curves gave them a heavy appearance that contrasted unfavourably with the elegance of the latter. Everything had been in precisely the right place before, from the big P-100 headlamps flanking the deep and splendidly-proportioned radiator at the front to the twin spare wheels mounted on a specially-designed carrier at the rear to equalise weight distribution as effectively as possible.

Because the rear seat was mounted well ahead of the axle, in front of the upsweep of the frame, and because footwells were provided in the back compartment its occupants sat well down inside the body, yet had ample headroom even though the roofline itself was appreciably lower than normal.

When the Continental was officially announced in October 1930, its makers claimed that they had "experienced a definite demand for a model capable of maintaining high speeds on Continental roads." Its chassis was that of the standard Phantom II (the short wheelbase version, which is to say the 12 ft.), "with a few modifications", these consisting in the main of "specially selected springs of a type which permit continuous high speeds over bad roads", controlled by Rolls-Royce hydraulic shock-dampers supplemented by adjustable Hartford friction-type shock-absorbers of the kind normally found on sports-cars at that time. Whether or not the engine was tuned (even if only to the extent of a higher-than-normal compression ratio) is one of the minor Rolls-Royce mysteries.

The Continental type of close-coupled body was perfectly suited to the chassis of the 20/25, upon which numbers of very fine examples were built during the early 'thirties. The fact that its wheelbase was a foot shorter did not seriously reduce internal accommodation for the bonnet of the smaller car was much shorter than that of the Phantom II.

Few Weymann bodies were made for Rolls-Royces after 1930, (though H.J. Mulliner – who else – did build one on a 3½-litre Bentley chassis as late as 1935), but especially attractive four-light saloons along the same lines were a highly acceptable alternative, Croall of Edinburgh (the parent company of Mulliner, incidentally) and Park Ward producing many excellent examples.

The Phantom II was up against formidable competition in 1930 – the impressive looking 8-litre Bentley. This example was once in the Sword Collection in Scotland.

Touring bodies were quite out of fashion by this time except for sports-cars, yet several were built on the large and small Rolls-Royce chassis. Convertibles were rather more popular but had to be very well made in the first place if their tendency to develop rattles were to be checked successfully.

In this respect the drophead coupé could be a prime offender. Because it normally accommodated four people, access to both front and rear seats had to be provided by one necessarily wide door on each side; these doors were heavy, and unless particular care was taken over their hinging, extended service led to sagging and rattling, draughts and leaks. In extreme cases the use of dropheads was only tolerable in dry spells between showers; in rain they leaked and in extended dry periods they rattled!

Motoring masterpiece. Ivan Evernden's 1930 prototype Phantom II Continental, with Barker body, at Englefield in May, 1974.

A practical answer to these problems was the fixed-head version. Its head was made of metal and not of, duck or mohair, and it was a permanent fixture, only the front part being movable, to cover or uncover the driving compartment below. Perhaps the best-looking of all were those marketed by H.R. Owen Ltd., and usually made by Gurney Nutting. Owen's original design for "a motor-car, the predominating material being metal" was registered in December 1932 and subsequently appeared, with variations, on many Rolls-Royce and Bentley chassis.

Early examples were really three-position dropheads; the head could be folded back completely; it could be raised but the front part rolled back, the effect being that of a large-area sunshine roof fully opened; or it could be raised and the front part closed, in which case everything was as snug as in a saloon. Distinguishing features of the original were its high waist line, its very deep doors and its prominent boot, the capacity of which was unusually large for its day.

The Owen Sedanca-Coupé and its numerous variants had the style once associated with the smartest kinds of "owner-driver" horse-drawn vehicles; they were very English in overall aspect yet they could stand critical comparison with the best work from their Continental contemporaries. Of these the French firms of Binder and Kellner deserve special mention. Their designs had the expected chic without going to extremes unacceptable to the English majority taste, which has always inclined towards the conservative.

The drophead looked its very best on the 20/25 and Bentley chassis. On the 40/50 it could look magnificent as long as its design was absolutely right; if it was not, if the disposition of its three main visual components – bonnet, passenger space and boot – was in any way an awkward one, an out-of-scale effect resulted.

Another type that was more difficult to handle – and much less rewarding for its designer in the end, in strictly visual terms – was the formal, six-light limousine. H.J. Mulliner managed it with more success than most of their contemporaries, their traditional restraint being exercised to best advantage on both chassis. Some others triumphed with bodies of different kinds that they handled with individuality of style at times; for example Barker, Hooper and Thrupp & Maberley all coped well with the Coupé-de-Ville, the Cabriolet-de-Ville, the Limousine-de-Ville and the Sedanca-de-Ville (differences between these types were not great, in practice; fancy names sometimes helped sales . . .).

Towards the middle-thirties car appearance and design at all levels began to deteriorate. For some years previously it had been notably restrained; the period was one of good visual manners, historical precedents in this country being the Georgian and late-Regency periods, when architecture and furniture, respectively, also reached standards of consistently high quality.

Along with the short skirt of the flapper, however, the clean-lined, well-proportioned, sweetly-curved motor-car gradually disappeared. As ever-lengthening skirts and dresses covered more and more of the female shape there was a corresponding increase in the amount of automobile anatomy hidden from sight by the greater areas of sheet metal considered fashionable.

Apart from the fact that many interesting and attractive chassis details were now concealed from view, access to parts requiring regular lubrication, for example, became less and less convenient. Indeed, the practical difficulties in this respect encouraged neglect. The gradual hiding away of such splendid mechanical prospects as the front axle and front suspension and braking systems of a Rolls-Royce was regretted

The Barker Close-coupled Cabriolet body of this 1930 Phantom II Continental sits well between the wheels. The size of the car is well concealed by the excellence of its proportions.

by a minority only and the other matter was of little concern, semi-automatic (one-shot) lubrication having been a feature of both chassis since 1929. It had been standard on the American-built Phantom I since its introduction in 1926 but was not fitted to the Derby-built chassis of this type.

Towards the end of the 'twenties attitudes had changed considerably as regards reducing the cleaning and maintaining of motor-cars. The introduction of chromium plating (which gradually replaced nickel from 1928 onwards) greatly simplified the task of keeping bright-work clean, and the new cellulose paints that took the place of the traditional paint and varnish from 1926, on all but the most expensive bodies, were far less difficult to maintain in decent condition.

Cleaning the radiators of Twenties, of Phantom Is, of early 20/25s and of early Phantom IIs was a devilish job; the area to be dealt with was by no means inconsiderable and the task was greatly complicated and lengthened, by the presence of movable shutters that had to be individually treated. For all its practical advantages chromium was not quite the right thing for Rolls-Royce, however fine its quality, and the decision to offer an "untarnishable finish" at extra cost, in 1930, was a wise one, (on compassionate grounds, if none other . . .).

In fact it was soon adopted as standard and the "Staybrite" stainless-steel radiators of Rolls-Royces from 1931 onwards not only enhanced their front-end appearance in the subtlest of ways but greatly lightened the work of those responsible for their upkeep. The black-and-white scheme of six-cylinder engines built since the introduction of the Twenty, in 1922 – with the exception of the Silver Ghost, of course – was based on the use of stove enamelling, aluminium, and cadmium plating, and it was relatively easy to maintain them in a smart and clean condition (as far as the V-12 engine of the Phantom III was concerned, however, qualification of the latter remark might have to be made . . .).

Until 1935 Rolls-Royce concentrated on the production of six-cylinder engines and chassis of generally conventional design, made in the best way possible, of the best materials available. Their reluctance to wear out was already legendary, and the number of pre-first war cars still in use was remarkably high. The life-expectancy of a chassis was so long, indeed, that it often paid to update it by a change of body (a

Instead of the usual wood facia this particular Phantom II, (ALF 222, the car shown in the accompanying plate) had a turned aluminium panel and 6 inch "Soup-plate" speedometer and rev. counter. It was a Continental model.

relatively inexpensive business between the wars).

Two enterprising London concerns reconditioned Twenty and Phantom I chassis and offered them for sale in the late 'thirties with up-to-date looking coachwork at extremely reasonable prices . . . For example, a Twenty "Replica" saloon of highly respectable appearance, inside as well as out, cost around £450, and drophead coupés of considerable smartness were available at prices that ranged as high as £695 for post-1932 20/25 models with synchromesh. The fact that many of these cars are still in use is an

1933 Phantom II with Thrupp and Maberly Drophead Coupé – again owing something to the H.R. Owen patented design for this type of body. When photographed in London in 1970 or '71 it had just been extensively and expensively restored.

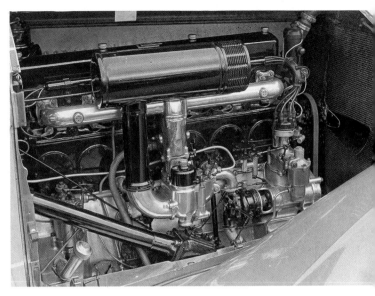

Ergonomics was a word that no one used in the 'thirties, even if it existed then. Rolls-Royce knew all about the subject, however, as any examination of the way they located controls and instruments quickly proves. The car is a 1935 late-series Phantom II with Gurney Nutting All-weather body.

1934 Phantom II – offside of the 7.6-litre engine. The carburettor and its big air-cleaner and silencer dominate the scene.

indication of the quality of both body and chassis.

In terms of performance the big Rolls-Royce was outclassed by very few of its contemporaries. It had powerful acceleration, a high maximum and its safe *continuous* cruising speed was 75 mph.. Top gear flexibility was quite remarkable, in spite of high gearing; from 4 or 5 mph. the car could pick up speed without hesitation or flat spot of any kind and without fuss. It was an extremely economical car to own and operate because of its reliability, its relatively low fuel consumption and its quite exceptional longevity, and because of its straight-forward design maintenance and repairs could be carried out with an ease that was reflected in comparatively modest charges.

But its engine was outclassed in certain respects by American contemporaries which had more cylinders, more power, superior smoothness and even higher standards of relative quietness of running. There were practical limitations as far as increasing the effective speed range and power of such a large 6-cylinder engine was concerned and to attempt its further development could only lead its makers into a technical and commercial dead-end. In any case most competitors were committed to 8- or 12-cylinder

motors by the early 'thirties; the big 'six' was going out of fashion even then, and Conduit Street was well aware of this.

It was entirely logical of Rolls-Royce to adopt the V-12 format for the engine ultimately intended to replace that of the Phantom II. Their aero-engine experience in this respect was very great and there were practical advantages to be considered. A V-12 would be shorter in length for one thing; for another its speed range would be a great deal wider and its smoothness and silence of running would be enhanced.

Within three years of the introduction of the Phantom II, work on its successor was under way. Two years later, in 1934, an experimental car was on the road and in October, 1935 Phantom III was announced. Deliveries began in 1936 and by the time production ceased, in 1939, over 700 cars had been built. An annual rate of 236 compares favourably with that of 294 for its predecessor, but neither shows up well in comparison with the Derby-made Phantom I, the average annual production rate of which was 553.

If there had been any doubts at all about Rolls-Royce leadership in the luxury-car class the behaviour of the new car on the road immediately dispelled them. Although at first it was little faster than its predecessor, quietness and smoothness of running showed significant advances on

previous standards, good as these had been, and acceleration was even more rapid than before. The big car would leap from 10 to 30 mph. in top gear in little more than 7 seconds and in second take little more than half that time. It could cruise safely all day at 80 mph. when and where road conditions allowed; because of its independent front wheel suspension (based on a General Motors design, incidentally) it was far more comfortable over really rough surfaces, and far faster too. Its roadholding was also much improved.

The wheelbase of the new model was 11 ft. 10 in. (for the Phantom II it was either 12 ft. or 12 ft. 6 in.) yet its body length was the same as before; the shorter engine was set further forward in the frame, along with the radiator, which was now a much more dominant feature.

There has been much criticism in recent years of the appearance of the Phantom III, as if it were entirely the fault of its designers and makers. It

The forward-mounted radiator of the 12-cylinder Phantom III was a most impressive sight.

The Phantom III 12-cylinder engine was compact but it was not the easiest of units to service or repair when installed.

The large-diameter speedometer and much-less lethal steering wheel boss were characteristic of all Phantom III and Wraith models. The latter was suggested to Rolls-Royce as a safety feature by Geoffrey Smith. The photograph is of a Phantom III.

was the fashion of the day that was really to blame; when fluency of line and correctness of proportion were combined successfully, as in the case of the James Young razor-edge sports-saloon, its appearance was little, if at all, inferior to that of a good Phantom II. There were bound to be differences between them and it must be emphasised that the earlier car was current during one of the best periods ever in car appearance-design. Nevertheless it attracted more than its share of downright ugly bodies during its production life of six years – but perhaps not so many, relatively speaking, as the V-12.

A feature of the Phantom III that gave some trouble in service was the automatic regulation of its valve clearances at the correct figure by

hydraulically-actuated rams, or plungers, that were totally dependent on a regular provision of spotlessly clean oil for their continued and accurate functioning. As long as the servicing procedures laid down were scrupulously followed the system was trouble-free, but the human element being what it is there were cases of neglect followed by complaints.

The solution was simple; the hydraulic system was dropped and "solid" tappets introduced instead. Most of the early engines were converted before the war but for those somewhat tardy in attending to the matter it was still possible in recent years to obtain the necessary parts.

Too much has been made of the fact that Rolls-Royce have always been reluctant to discuss the power output of their engines. The observant enthusiast for the make will have noticed that over the years actual figures have often been published, and from time to time percentage increases have been quoted that enable very

113

reasonably accurate estimates to be made as to the potential of this engine or that. According to *The Motor* description of the Phantom III that appeared in its issue of October 8 1935, there was an overall weight reduction of 8% and a power increase of 12%.

In its road test of January 15 1937, *The Times* quoted the output of the V-12 engine as 165 bhp. at 3,000 rpm. Presumably this figure was provided by its makers. In 1938 a four-port cylinder head raised maximum power to something like 180 bhp., which was useful when an overdrive gearbox was fitted to the last batch of DL-series chassis. It is known that even higher outputs have been obtained from this engine.

The updating of the design of the 40/50 enabled it to hold its own until the outbreak of war in Europe ended automobile production here. During its brief production very few changes were made to its specification whereas its predecessor was extensively modified in detail over the years, the main purpose being to increase power and improve standards of smoothness and quietness. At the same time braking efficiency

was raised, to take care of extra performance, ride control was introduced to further improve suspension and roadholding at all speeds, and the changing of gear was eased even more by the addition of synchromesh to second.

The smaller model was also subjected to this process of continuous improvement, with a power increase for the 1931 season cars and another for 1932 models. Although the early 20/25 engine was 20% more powerful than that of the Twenty (which meant that it developed about 65 bhp.) its safe maximum speed was little higher. Its acceleration and hill-climbing powers benefited most from the increase in cubic capacity.

When the compression-ratio was increased in 1930, however, the range of engine speed was extended and top road speed was raised above 70 mph. The second increase in compression-ratio, in 1932, was accompanied by yet another speed increase, so that 75 mph, or more could be readily achieved. In the absence of definite

This very well-balanced sports saloon was built by Hooper. Its razor-edged treatment is especially successful.

information it is reasonable to assume that 20/25 cars from 1932 onwards had an output of around 80 bhp. If we work backwards from the percentage increase of the V-12 engine quoted by *The Motor* in 1935 we can take it that late-production Phantom II engines developed something like 145 bhp.

The 20/25 was never a "flyer" in the way that the Phantom II was. It was not intended to be so, of course; it was the town-carriage *par excellence*, with its extremely smooth and quiet and flexible engine – yet it had much low-speed torque and could step away swiftly from a standstill, so that it could more than hold its own in 'thirties town traffic. After 1930 its cruising speed could be as high as 65 mph. (this was its maker's recommended safe continuous limit) and because it had very good steering, springing and roadholding, as well as splendid brakes, it could be a fast car cross-country and a most enjoyable one to drive.

By far the most appealing type, of course, was the lightweight sports-saloon that reached such a pinnacle of near-perfection in the early 'thirties. The best examples were marvellous to look at for one thing, and for another they went about their business in a quiet yet sprightly manner that was highly attractive to those temperamentally in tune with their maker's intentions.

If it is thought that Rolls-Royce took rather long to change over to i.f.s. it must be remembered that the ride quality of their cars was remarkably high overall, sheer size having a lot to do with this in the case of the 40/50 chassis. Yet it was the larger model that had i.f.s. first.

It was a major feature of the new Wraith model that replaced the 25/30 in 1938, along with a cruciform-braced frame and an engine somewhat simpler in some aspects of its design than its forerunner. The 25/30, incidentally, was a bored-out version of the 20/25, offered as an alternative at first, in 1936, for owners who would insist on adding luxuries (and weight, therefore) yet who complained when performance was reduced. It was even quieter than the 20/25, despite its increased power, and could manage 80 mph. under the right conditions.

Some of its components were no longer made by Rolls-Royce but were bought in. The clutch was a Borg and Beck, the carburettor a downdraught Stromberg and the steering was by Marles (it required more turning of the wheel than before but was lighter in operation). Derby dependence on outside suppliers was still small and increased in no significant way until the post-war cars went into production.

The Wraith was a good deal more comfortable than the 25/30, at least as quiet and fast, and somewhat roomier from the passenger's point of view, its wheelbase being 4 inches longer. Also its engine and radiator were mounted further forward in the frame, which was now of the all-welded type.

In what cannot have been more than a year, at most, almost 500 Wraiths were built; a high figure when its price and the imminence of war are taken into account. Along with the Phantom III it is popular nowadays with enthusiasts in the United States, a fact related perhaps to the relative

During 1937 H.R. Owen Ltd. indulged in some costly and extremely effective colour advertising in selected "quality" magazines.

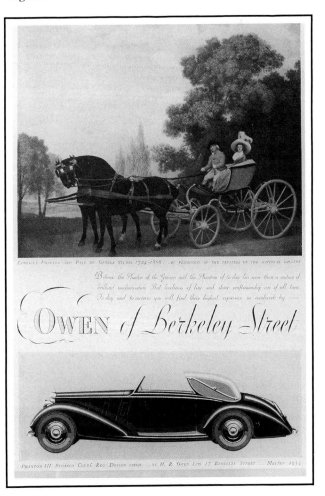

Left, top: **A Phantom III Sports Saloon at Compton Winyates just before the second war. Photographs of this kind were much used in Company advertising during the 'thirties, with the minimum of copy.**

Left, bottom: **A very special Windover Cabriolet built to the order of Prince Berar in 1937 on 3-CP-116, a Phantom III chassis. The extra lamps recessed in the front wings anticipated post-war practice. The Lalique mascot is a little after its time, perhaps. A gramophone was housed in the boot.**

softness of ride and extreme lightness of control of these models. Their predecessors certainly made few concessions to American preferences for the "boulevard" kind of ride, tending towards firmness unless the first owner decreed otherwise.

Rolls-Royce suspension was not simply a matter of four springs, four shock-dampers and ride-control; it extended to the seating of the car as well and by careful attention to the phasing of seat springs, for example, the overall standard of comfort was enhanced. This was particularly noticeable on cars with firm suspension (the Derby Bentleys were a case in point, with their 'thirties-style sports-car stiffness of springing).

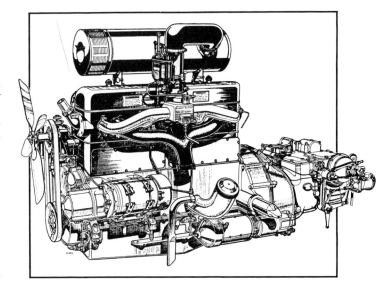

The engine of the 25/30 hp. Rolls-Royce had much in common with that of the Twenty, but it produced close on twice as much power and was of somewhat tidier appearance. A worrying design feature was the placing of the carburettor immediately above the exhaust manifold.

The advisory editor once enjoyed open-air motoring in the 1937 Freestone and Webb Drophead Sedanca Coupé – the body a rarity on the 25/30 chassis.

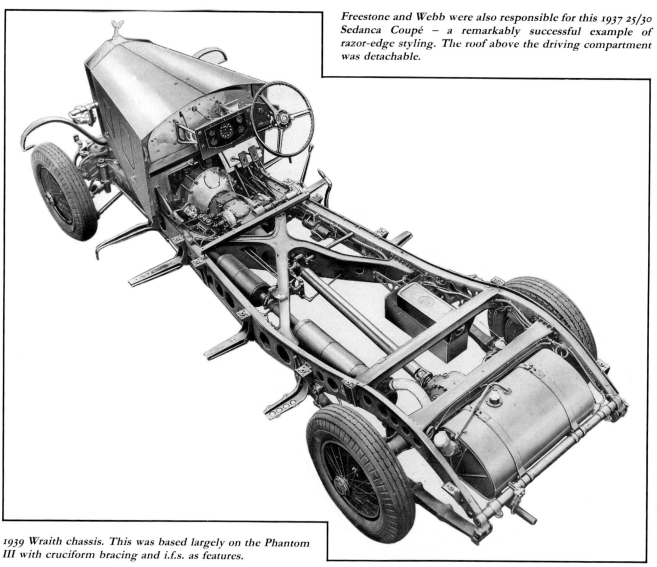

Freestone and Webb were also responsible for this 1937 25/30 Sedanca Coupé – a remarkably successful example of razor-edge styling. The roof above the driving compartment was detachable.

1939 Wraith chassis. This was based largely on the Phantom III with cruciform bracing and i.f.s. as features.

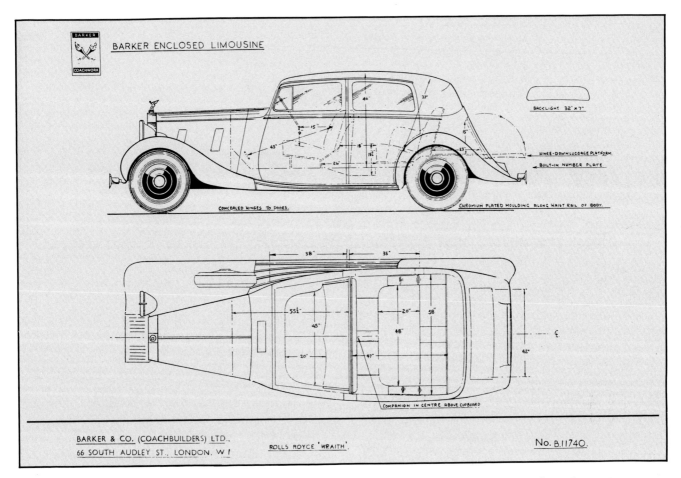

BARKER ENCLOSED LIMOUSINE

BACKLIGHT 32" x 7"

HINGE-DOWN LUGGAGE PLATFORM
BUILT-IN NUMBER PLATE

CONCEALED HINGES TO DOORS.

CHROMIUM PLATED MOULDING ALONG WAIST RAIL OF BODY.

COMPANION IN CENTRE ABOVE CUPBOARD

BARKER & CO. (COACHBUILDERS) LTD.,
66 SOUTH AUDLEY ST., LONDON. W.1

ROLLS ROYCE 'WRAITH'.

No. B.11740.

Barker design scheme for an Enclosed Limousine, 1938. The swept-back type of body had a limited run of popularity.

The car might move about on rough surfaces taken fast but little of its motion was transmitted to the occupants. There was usually more than a set of coil springs inside the seats of these cars, of course; swansdown was an exotic, and luxuriously effective, supplement at one time, replaced in more recent times by foam rubber cunningly shaped, and nowadays by even more versatile materials.

Such attention to detail was possible because the customer could pay for it – as he could for bodywork made of the best and most appropriate materials by some of the most highly-skilled craftsmen in the country, and mounted on chassis individually assembled, checked and tested in a manner simply impossible on a quantity production basis.

During the 'thirties the cheaper cars caught up very significantly with the high-priced ones in terms of performance and in many aspects of road

behaviour. Indeed most American cars, regardless of first cost, were a match for the smaller Rolls-Royce (or its superior, even) in respect of speed and acceleration and those fitted with i.f.s. were better sprung until the advent of the Wraith.

The Rolls-Royce margin of superiority might have been even greater than it was, had there not been the growing distraction of rearmament in this country in the second half of the decade, which hindered design thinking and forward planning to a significant extent. Even so work was already under way in 1939 on a range of new engines of simplified design, to be marketed eventually in 6- and 8-cylinder versions for motor-car propulsion.

At that time W.O. Bentley was back in competition with his former employers (for he had been taken over with Bentley Motors and had to stay with the new Rolls-Royce-owned company until his service contract expired in 1935) – this time with the 4½-litre V-12 that he had designed for Lagonda. Like the Phantom III it did not survive the war.

119

Chapter 4
The Derby Bentleys

In 1924 D. Napier & Son Ltd., gave up the manufacture of their only post-war car, the 40/50, to concentrate on the development of the aero-engine side of their business, which was in direct competition with that of Rolls-Royce Limited. In 1931, however, when Bentley Motors Limited was in liquidation, they were seriously interested in acquiring its assets and the services of its founder and principal designer, W.O. Bentley, so that they could re-enter the motor industry. Their projected new car was to be a modified and somewhat smaller version of the 8-litre Bentley which had sold so unusually well during a brief production life that began and ended in a time of extreme economic difficulties, worldwide, and it was intended to compete with the Rolls-Royce, their oldest and strongest rival.

But nothing came of a scheme that might be considered foolhardy at such a time; established manufacturers were finding it hard enough to sell sufficient motor-cars to stay solvent and competition was fierce, to say the least. It is not surprising, therefore, that Rolls-Royce Limited were also interested in Bentley goodwill and assets; their offer was substantially higher than the Napier one and it was successful. Ever since they have been adversely criticised by many motoring writers for what was in fact a straightforward commercial transaction.

Almost two years later Bentley Motors (1931) Ltd. announced their new car. It looked like a Bentley, with its well-proportioned radiator (a scaled-down version of that fitted to the 8- and 4-litre models from Cricklewood), long, well-louvered bonnet, almost vertical steering-wheel,

wire wheels and sporting coachwork. It was much lower than any of its predecessors of the same name, however, and while it was as lively and as fast as most of these it ran with exceptional quietness; indeed its maker's slogan was "The Silent Sports Car" (which was not factually correct but was effective in publicity). Yet the original intention had been to produce a sporting car that was noisy in the contemporary fashion.

It had been thought necessary to make any new car as unlike current Rolls-Royce models as possible. Quiet running was unimportant, and to emphasise the sporting nature of the car (and to remind potential buyers of the competition activities and successes of earlier Bentleys) supercharging was to be an engine feature. At the time Rolls-Royce were experimenting with a smaller version of the 20/25 model, code-named Peregrine, which had a 2.3-litre., 6-cylinder engine. The latter was chosen for supercharger trials, but it objected to forced induction in various ways, and as time was short and the list of impatient potential customers long, a quick solution to the problems of providing sufficient and reliable power had to be found. Someone – it may have been Ernest Hives, the resourceful, practically-minded head of the Experimental Department at Derby at the time – suggested trying a prototype $3^1/_2$ litre 20/25 engine instead. It fitted into the Peregrine chassis without difficulty and the combination was so promising that all thought of supercharging was dropped. A period of intensive development followed, and in October, 1933 the $3^1/_2$-litre Bentley was introduced.

One of the earliest customers for the Derby Bentley was the late Duke of Kent (H.R.H. Prince George), whose 1934, AE-series 3¹/₂-litre had a Barker body. It looked – and it was – a Sports Saloon but, most unusually, it sported a division between front and rear seats.

Although its engine was basically similar in design to the current 20/25 it had a much more effective induction system, with twin S.U. carburettors and a water-heated manifold, and with slightly raised compression it produced about 105 bhp. unsilenced, which was about 20% more than the output of its Rolls-Royce touring counterpart. It was in unit with its maker's superb synchromesh gearbox, with right-hand change, – an almost unsurpassable combination at that time. The chassis was of the double-dropped type and was carried on long, flat semi-elliptic springs, controlled by Rolls-Royce hydraulic shock-dampers. In the manner of the period suspension was firm, but very careful attention to the phasing of seat-springs and padding resulted in above-average comfort for driver and passengers. By later standards, however, ride was on the hard side, and on really bad surfaces a reduction in speed was considered prudent by most owners.

In production form the 3¹/₂ had a top speed above 90 mph., with 34, 54 and 75 mph. available at 4,500 rpm. (the recommended limit) in the indirect gears, and its acceleration was very good for its day, 0 to 70 mph., for example, averaging 27 sec. In spite of its very high top gear ratio – 4.10 to 1, which gave 22 mph. at 1,000 rpm. – it

was extremely flexible and would accelerate from 10 to 30 mph. in "high" in less than 9 seconds. The excellence of its performance was matched by the power and quality of its Rolls-Royce servo-operated brakes, and because of its exceptional roadholding, full use could be made of its sprightliness by the enterprising driver.

It was a very economical car as well; 18 mpg. was easily attainable and above 20 mpg. could be reached on long runs. The low weight, high gearing and high overall mechanical efficiency of the car were largely responsible. It was also economical in the long term, with an almost

E.R. Hall and his potent 3¹/₂ as they were in 1934, the first year of semi-official involvement in racing by Bentley Motors (1931) Ltd. The step was a satisfactory substitute for a door on the driver's side.

Above: **Barker & Co. described the body of this 1934 3¹/₂-litre Bentley as a Sunshine saloon, presumably because it had a sliding, or sunshine, roof.**

Opposite page top: **Marshal Pilsudski, of Poland, ordered this impressive Tourer, on a late 1934, AMS-series, Phantom II chassis, from Barker & Co.**

unequalled record for reliability and durability. Flexibility was a feature of the chassis of the first few hundred cars built, between 1933 and the end of 1934, and this caused some problems for bodybuilders. The cure was a stiffening of the front end and the adoption of the harmonic-stabilising type of front bumper that was popular during the second half of the 'thirties. Roadholding and ride benefited, and cracked windscreen pillars (particularly on drophead coupés) became a thing of the past, which was all to the good. In the writer's experience, however, the modified cars are slightly less agreeable to drive.

But this was a matter of degree, only; few cars have given more driver satisfaction overall with their real quietness of running at all speeds, their quick response, their smoothness, their delicacy of control, their complete lack of temperament and their ability to cover hundreds of miles in a day without effort. There was nothing unconven-

The H.R. Owen 'Design for A MOTOR CAR, the predominating material being metal' was officially registered on December 12, 1932. Fortunately bodies built to what sounded such a prosaic description were usually of exceptionally good appearance, a fact demonstrated in this 1933 H.R. Owen Sedanca drophead built by Gurney Nutting Ltd., on a 20/25 chassis.

Another racing Bentley – the 3½ developed to such a high state of liveliness by the late Lord Ebury and now part of Lord Moray's unique collection of high-grade sporting cars based on the Doune Motor Museum in Scotland. It is still in regular road use.

tional about the design of the Bentley as made by Rolls-Royce; like all other motor-cars it was a compromise, but it was a particularly successful one. Its balance of qualities was just about perfect for its day; it was among the fastest of its contemporaries, it was better made than any and more durable, therefore; it had a precision of control possibly only excelled by Bugatti and a standard of appearance that reached the highest levels on occasion.

It arrived on the motoring scene at a time when the open sports car was still popular but for some reason the number of bodies of this type fitted to Bentley chassis was quite small. The best-looking was the original Vanden Plas tourer – a classic of its type and period, with its cutaway doors and fine proportions. Dropheads, especially those designed and built by Barker and by Park Ward suited this chassis well, and here the Owen sedanca coupé must be singled out for special commendation.

Sports saloons were in the majority, however, and of these by far the greater number was designed and manufacturered by Park Ward, whose success in developing an all-steel coachbuilt body that was boom- and rattle-free (and did not suffer from problems of corrosion in the manner of some of its post-war successors)

was quite unique. On the 3½-litre chassis their handsome product was catalogued at £1,510 – a price maintained until 1939 although the larger-engined 4¼-litre chassis introduced in April, 1936 cost £1,150 – £50 more than its predecessor. In its final development this excellent body acquired curves of somewhat greater complexity, but it was still well-proportioned and distinctive in appearance and served as the model, not only for the catalogued saloon on the B5 chassis of the

A 1934 3½-litre Barker Foursome Coupé de Ville – not a true drophead, in fact; its "head" is fixed and its "irons" are dummies.

late summer of 1939 but for the post-war "standard steel" body made by Pressed Steel for the Mark VI Bentley.

The 4¼-litre engine was offered as an option, to cope with the old, old problem of owners who sought increasingly weighty luxury, yet complained when performance suffered. After its introduction, in fact, there was no further demand for the 3½-litre engine. With about 20 extra bhp acceleration and hill-climbing were improved substantially, but top speed remained between 90 and 95 mph. Unlike the broadly similar 25/30 Rolls-Royce unit offered as an alternative to the 20/25 at that time the Bentley engine was unchanged in design, apart from the increase in its bore and the provision of a much larger air-cleaner and silencer to deal with its improved "breathing" capabilities. A special high ratio axle was offered as an option.

The final development of the conventionally sprung model appeared towards the end of the 1938. It had larger section tyres and Marles steering, and its gearbox reverted to much earlier Rolls-Royce practice, with a geared-up top. Greater controllability was claimed as a result of the changes in tyre size and steering that was

lighter (but lower geared) than before, and an even higher degree of mechanical ease was due to the overdrive, which gave 26 mph. per 1,000 rpm. In use this car was outstanding for its quietness, its span of speed and its liveliness. Even in overdrive, the ratio of which was 3.64 to 1, it was possible to accelerate from 10 to 30 mph. in fractionally more than 9 seconds. From a standstill to 70 mph. took 24 seconds. Under normal conditions top speed remained much as before but on long downhill stretches it could be pushed beyond 100 mph. without reaching the safe engine limit of 4,500 rpm. Absolute maxima in the indirects were 38, 60 and 89 mph. and third, which was direct drive in fact, could be used up to quite high speeds as a normal top.

The overdrive 4¼ was the ultimate development of its type. It was well suited for high-speed work on the German *autobahnen* and Italian *autostrada* – those temptations to excessive indulgence in speed which had been the cause of a good deal of bearing trouble on the early 4¼ engines because thoughtless owners drove at the maximum for unreasonable distances. With the new gearing it was practically impossible to over-drive these cars, cruising at

80 mph., for example, representing little more than 3,000 rpm. Engine life was greatly increased and there was a small improvement in fuel consumption.

But with further development work even more was possible in terms of speed and economy. In its issue of February 17, 1939 *The Autocar* described tests that had been carried out in France and Germany with a specially bodied $4^{1}/_{4}$, created for the Greek racing driver, N.S. Embiricos, by the manager of the Paris branch of Rolls-Royce Ltd., Walter Sleator. The chassis was standard but the engine had raised compression (8 to 1 against the normal 6.4 to 1, special pistons and larger carburettors. Its output was around 140 bhp; with gear ratios of 8 to 1, 5 to 1, 3.41 (direct) and 2.87 to 1 the car could reach speeds of approximately 50, 80, 115 and 120 mph.

Its body (built by Vanvooren) was designed by Monsieur Paulin, in consultation with Rolls-Royce, and a model was wind-tunnel tested. Much use was made of light alloys in its construction – Duralumin being one – and overall weight, at a little over 31 cwt., was 3 cwt. lower than average. It was a good looking car in a rather tough sort of way but not readily identifiable as a Bentley because its radiator was cowled over as part of the process of wind reduction.

The effectiveness of these departures from standard was considerable. In Germany a speed of 118 mph. was reached on the road and extremely high averages were sustained with an astonishing lack of effort. Fuel consumption was vastly

A sports saloon (with division) on Phantom III chassis, no. 3 AZ-43 – the first V-12 to be supplied to a private owner (in this case HRH The Duke of Kent), in the summer of 1936. The Barker body featured a chrome-plated instrument panel.

Right: A 1937 Park Ward standard Steel Sports saloon on a $4^{1}/_{4}$-litre Bentley chassis.

improved, earlier tests producing such impressive figures as 26 mpg. at a steady 60 mph., 21 mpg. at a steady 80, and 17 mpg. at a maintained 90. As a matter of interest the post-war Bentley Continen-

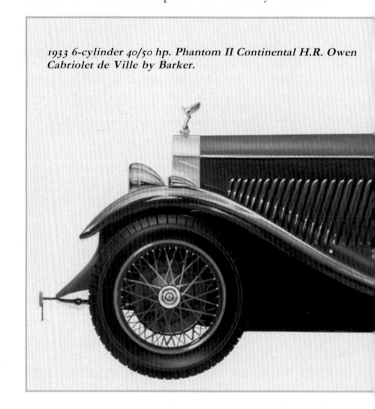

1933 6-cylinder 40/50 hp. Phantom II Continental H.R. Owen Cabriolet de Ville by Barker.

tal, which was a direct successor of the 1939 car, had the same top speed, weighed 33½ cwt, had an engine of 4½-litre capacity, and averaged 24 mpg. at 60 mph., 20.2 mpg. at 80 and 16.5 mpg. at 90.

In July, 1939 the Embiricos car was taken to Brooklands track and there Captain G.E.T. Eyston drove it round and round for an hour, during which time it covered 114.6 miles. In the previous month two specially prepared V-12 Lagondas had taken third and fourth places in the Le Mans race. The Brooklands demonstration by Bentley Motors was staged as a reminder of the capabilities of their cars in terms of high speed and reliability.

In 1949, in 1950 and again in 1951, this streamlined and apparently immortal machine competed in the Le Mans 24-hour race with distinction. Against brand new rivals it averaged 73.5 mph. in 1949, in the hands of its owner, H.S.F. Hay, and the motoring writer, T.H. Wisdom. In 1950 it was 14th, at an average of

78.6 mph., driven by Hay and Hunter, and in 1951, with Hay driving again, it was 23rd. In the 1950 event another historic Bentley took part, this being E.R. Hall's 1933/ 1936 4¼-litre Tourist Trophy car, which was eighth, averaging 82.9 mph. in the charge of its owner and T.G. Clarke.

Although Rolls-Royce had given up competitive motoring well before the first World War and it found no part of the scheme of things as far as Bentley Motors (1931) Ltd. were concerned, Hall managed to persuade the latter concern to help him to prepare his 3½ for the 1934 Tourist Trophy race, which was held on the Ards circuit in Northern Ireland, near Belfast. As far as the public knew at that time his was a private entry,

Captain G.E.T. Eyston's name was seldom out of the motoring news throughout the 'thirties, the making and breaking of records of various kinds being almost a full-time occupation. His normal road car was this sleek and unassuming 3½-litre.

and it was not until well after the war that Bentley support for the project was publicised in any way. Hall's chassis (35 AE) was rebodied for the race, with a certain concern for drag reduction and the saving of weight. Its engine had raised compression (7.35 to 1) and a straight-through exhaust system that conformed to regulations, and developed 131 bhp. The rear-axle ratio was raised to 3.75 to 1; as a result the car could rush up to 50 mph., in first gear and in top it could reach about 110 mph.

Its normal hydraulic shock-dampers were supplemented by friction Hartfords (in the manner of early Continental Phantom IIs), an extra oil tank was fitted and the petrol tank capacity was raised to 26 gallons. The car was ready well ahead of the race and its engine had successfully survived a 12 hour endurance test

One of the most covetable of all 'thirties cars – a 1935 3¹/₂ with H.R. Owen Fixed Head, Foursome Sedanca Coupé body of utmost style and elegance.

beforehand. On a course that did not favour the larger sort of car at all the big Bentley ran extremely well. Tyre wear was a good deal higher than had been estimated and a seized wheel nut during the second pit stop for wheel changing and refuelling led to a delay of more than 5 minutes. Hall's driving was so spirited, however, that he finished second on handicap to Dodson's little M.G., at an average speed for 478 miles of 78.4 mph., and broke the lap record with a circuit at 81.15 mph.

For 1935 power was increased, to 152 bhp., by raising compression to 8.35 to 1, and increasing the size of the inlet valves, carburettors and induction manifold. Again Hall took second place on handicap, finishing only 13 seconds behind Dixon's nimble Riley. In 1934 he had successfully dealt with strong opposition from a team of three 4¹/₂-litre Lagondas, three Ford V-8s and two 4¹/₂-litre Invictas. In 1935 he was up against two Lagondas and three 8-cylinder, 3.3-litre Bugattis, and disposed of this powerful opposition in no

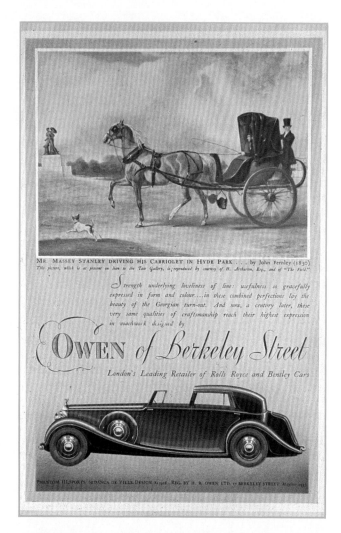

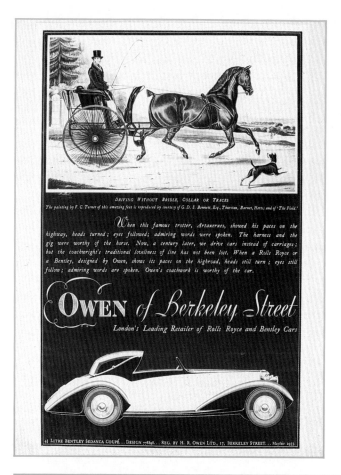

Above, left and right: **H.R. Owen Ltd., the London retailers, issued a series of most attractive colour advertisements in the The Field and Country Life magazines. They linked stylish horse-drawn vehicles of the past with Owen's newest body designs for Bentley and Rolls-Royce chassis.**

Opposite page top: **Silver Ghost shares the Edinburgh showroom of John Croall & Sons, the local retailers, with brand new Hooper bodied Mark VI Bentleys – an early example of the use of this historic car for promotional purposes. November, 1950.**

mean fashion, completing the race 3 minutes ahead of the best-paced Bugatti – that driven by Earl Howe.

In 1936 Hall reappeared, with the same car. Its engine, now a 4¼-litre, had been endurance tested for 24 hours at full throttle in anticipation of an appearance at Le Mans that year. Political troubles in France stopped the event, however, and Hall had to be content with yet another second place on handicap in the T.T. Once more

1934 6-cylinder 20/25 hp. Brougham de Ville by Park Ward.

130

James Young, the long-established Bromley coachbuilders, were responsible for this pillarless body on a 1938 4¹/₄ chassis. It appears that the front doors were carried on the parallel-links system used by this concern on occasion.

he had to give best to Dixon (and Dodson) in a Riley, but his race average was 80.81 mph. and he dealt with three rival Lagondas, a solitary Bugatti and six 3¹/₂-litre Delahayes, no less, in most convincing fashion. He finished one minute behind the winning Riley – and almost nine minutes in front of the second car in the over-3-litre class, Fairfield's 4¹/₂-litre Lagonda.

According to W.A. Robotham, who was unofficial chief development engineer of the car section at Derby at the time (and much involved in preparatory work on the 3¹/₂-litre Bentley) the success of Hall's car in the T.T. was a real help to sales. But there was no attempt to enter competitive motoring, either then or at any subsequent date. With the discreetest of factory support a private owner had publicly and conclusively demonstrated the speed and stamina of the "Silent Sports Car" – just as Northey and Rolls had done, with the Light Twenty more than 25 years before.

The one-hour run in 1939 was not the first event of its kind to be staged by the Company at Brooklands; in 1908, it will be remembered, two of the seventy hp cars had been driven round the track at speed, and in 1911, after the successful conclusion of the top-gear London to Edinburgh trial, the car concerned was slightly tuned, fitted with a higher rear-axle ratio and a wind-cheating body of minimal dimensions and dispatched to the Track, where it exceeded 100 mph.

When Rolls-Royce Ltd. acquired the assets of the old Bentley concern in 1931 they took over W.O. Bentley as well, his service contract having some time to run. According to his own account he played no part at all in design; he was involved only in development testing of contemporary Rolls-Royce models and of the 3¹/₂ Bentley. In 1935 he left, to join Lagonda as technical director, and until his ideas for new models of up-to-date design could be implemented he developed and refined the current 4¹/₂-litre car, which was more powerful and less costly than the Bentley. In 1937, as we know, his revised 6-cylinder and a new 12-cylinder model appeared with i.f.s, which gave them a decided sales advantage. But it was not until well on in 1939 that Bentley answered back, with the B5 (or Mark V) model. It had independent front-wheel suspension (by coil springs) and a very much stiffer, x-braced frame that was deeper in section than its predecessors. It was two inches shorter in wheelbase (10 ft. 4 in. instead of 10 ft. 6 in.) but because its engine had been moved forward to a noticeable extent there was additional passenger space and a flat floor for those seated at the rear, a divided propeller-shaft helping in this latter respect.

Apart from a re-arrangement of certain auxiliaries the engine was unchanged but altered mountings were part of an overall scheme further to reduce sound and to improve already high standards of smoothness of running, much advantage being taken of intensive development work carried out on the Rollys-Royce Wraith. The Mark V was to have been marketed in two forms. The standard chassis was intended for spacious saloon bodywork and had much the same performance as earlier models. But its suspension was softer, its ride a good deal better, its "feel" much more in accord with the most up-to-date ideas. The second model, the Corniche, was designed to carry aerodynamic coachwork and to reach speeds in excess of 110 mph. A prototype began endurance testing in France in the summer of 1939 and was much too fast for its tyres. It carried one of the least comely bodies ever fitted to a Bentley chassis and was destroyed at Dieppe at the beginning of the war.

Whatever the sentimentalists may say and write, the take-over of the Bentley name and assets in 1931 was a matter of well-considered commercial wisdom. At one stroke it eliminated possibly damaging competition from two quarters; the 8-litre Bentley was not revived and Napier were kept out of the luxury-car market. When the Derby-designed Bentley appeared it was as an entirely distinctive car of the best possible quality, with high performance and low running costs. It was as quick as a short-chassis Phantom II, could travel almost twice as far on a gallon of petrol, and cost two-thirds as much. It was very quick and very quiet, and it successfully realised its maker's stated aims.

"There is at the present time an ever increasing demand for a car of moderate size which can carry in comfort up to four passengers and, at the same time, maintain a high average speed. Such a car

A Van Vooren pillarless saloon on a 4¼-litre overdrive chassis. In spite of the absence of central, standing-pillars, its body is quite remarkably free from rattles.

A 1951-model Mark VI, with Hooper bodywork, on display in John Croall & Sons Edinburgh premises in November, 1950.

A Hooper Drophead coupé on a 1952 Silver Wraith chassis, its long, flowing front wing line and enclosed rear wheels characteristic of this coachbuilder during most of the 'fifties.

The two-colour scheme of this splendid c.1958 Hooper Sports saloon, on a Silver Wraith chassis, combines with its superb finish to epitomise the highest grade of luxury car.

In 1958 Silver Ghost was back in Scotland on yet another sales promotion, and is seen at the head of a procession of the latest Bentley and Rolls-Royce cars, in Glasgow.

must combine the seemingly incompatible qualities of high engine-power and low chassis weight with silence and good riding qualities."

So began the first catalogue. Its introduction concluded – "The $3\frac{1}{2}$-litre Bentley . . . has been produced to meet the demands referred to above, and its arrival has proved that Performance and Peace can now be reconciled . . . in its docility and absence of fuss . . . it is without a rival amongst sporting cars."

The swiftest pre-1940 Bentley was the Embiricos $4\frac{1}{4}$, seen here at Brooklands Track in 1939, when it covered more than 114 miles in the hour. Its body design influenced later design thinking to quite an extent.

The original Corniche Bentley began endurance trials in France just before the outbreak of war in 1939. The lines of its Van Vooren body anticipated those of the "tin meringues" of the early 'fifties – but from all accounts this prototype went extremely well.

Chapter 5
Maintaining Standards

While Rolls-Royce aero-engines were making a tremendously important contribution to the winning of the war in the air between 1939 and 1945, car engines of a kind different in many ways from the 6- and 12-cylinder units made at Derby before 1940 were being exhaustively tried at ground level. Although work had begun on these in 1938, and prototypes had been installed in one or two chassis of a new design, the coming of war in September 1939 had cut short the normal programme of endurance testing in France. An enormous amount of road experience was subsequently gained, however, because W.A. Robotham (who had been effectively in charge of motor-car development since 1936, when Ernest Hives moved from the Experimental Department to become Works General Manager) was able to ensure that his experimental cars were used by Company officials and others for essential journeys throughout the war.

By the time the Silver Wraith and the Bentley Mark VI were introduced in 1946 (in April and May respectively) they had been more thoroughly road tested than any previous Rolls-Royce productions. They were the visible results of a scheme of simplification and standardisation that Robotham had initiated some eight years earlier, and they marked a return to the one-model policy sustained between 1908 and 1922 with such notable success in terms of profit and prestige.

It should be explained at this stage that those first post-war Rolls-Royce and Bentley models were almost identical, mechanically speaking, with a high degree of "commonisation" of parts. In appearance they retained separate identities, just as their predecessors had done before the war. Only with the introduction of the Silver Cloud and S-series Bentley in 1955 did the makes became totally alike, differing externally only in name, badges and radiator shape.

But in 1938 for example, there had been two entirely different Rolls-Royce chassis in production and the 4¼-litre Bentley. While the latter had an engine of the same size and overall design as that of the 25/30 Rolls, the similarities between them from a manufacturing and spares-keeping point of view were few indeed. From the customer's side the range of choice was a good and sufficient one, no doubt. For the Company though, it may not have been the most economic to make and market.

From readily accessible records it is difficult to determine exact production figures for any particular year and those that follow must be taken as approximate, at best. 1936 was the year when Phantom III deliveries began (200 at least), when the 20/25 gave way to the 25/30 (50 perhaps, and 600), and when the 3½-litre Bentley was replaced by the 4¼ (90 and 530, respectively). The total was around 1,500 – a very high figure for such costly cars at a time when the fact that our home economic situation was improving had to be set against growing political tension and uncertainties throughout Europe.

By 1937 it was down to 1,000, and in 1938 and 1939 it levelled off at about 700, Phantom III sales plunging in the latter year. Since 1936 the average annual sales of the smaller Rolls-Royce just failed to reach 500 (which was more than double the V-12 figure until 1938). The Bentley total

Above: **John Sword's 1948 Silver Wraith alongside his 1908 40/50 Barker-bodied Roi-des-Belges, at the end of a Rally.**

Opposite page top: **The facia of a 1977 Silver Shadow II.**

Below: **A Camargue on the move in 1975.**

1938 V-12-cylinder Phantom III Sedanca de Ville by Park Ward.

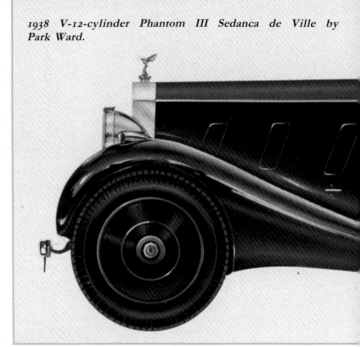

The first post-war Hooper design was handsome and was well suited to this kind of two-colour treatment. The late John Sword, a Scottish collector of motor-cars on the truly grand scale, owned this 1948 Silver Wraith.

steadied at 400 in 1937, fell inexplicably to 100 in 1938 (if the records are to be believed), then rose to 200 for the period between October 1938 and September 1939.

A drop of 100% in sales in less than 4 years was serious, but suitable measures had been put in hand early in 1938, despite the fact that Rolls-Royce Limited were preoccupied with an urgent and enormous expansion of their aero-engine business as part of the British rearmament programme. By then W.O. Bentley was snapping at Rolls-Royce heels again; history was repeating itself with strong competition from his LG6 Lagonda, which had been introduced in late 1937. This was a good example of prudent planning for economical production, with a very up-to-date chassis and handsome standardised coachwork, and the option of a conventional, but well-tried, 6-cylinder Meadows engine or an entirely new, short-stroke V-12 of high output and turbine-like smoothness.

There were three lengths of chassis, and the short-wheelbase 12-cylinder Lagonda-bodied sports saloon, which could sweep up to 100 mph. and more with ease, and combined fine roadholding with real comfort, sold at around £1,500. This was at least £350 less than the chassis cost of a Phantom III and half the price of a complete car. How the situation would have developed if war had not ended production of both makes is a subject of considerable speculative interest. The chances are that production of the big Rolls-Royce would have been stopped before long in any case; it was much too costly to build, for one thing, and for another the sudden drop in demand in late 1938 was a clear indication that its market was a fast-disappearing one. The V-12 Lagonda (the XJ-12 of its time) might have survived on merit and because it was such fine value for money.

As far as the largest American cars of this period were concerned the sheer scale of their production was such that they could be made and marketed at half the cost – or less – of European contemporaries. Yet they were neither cheap nor nasty; their quality of running and the luxuriousness of their bodywork (whether standard or custom-built) reached high levels, as anyone familiar with Cadillacs or the largest Packards of the late 'thirties will know.

Even in America though, the demand for luxury cars was falling. The day had been saved for Packard, for example, some years earlier, with the providential introduction of a simple, sturdy straight-eight – the famous Model 120 – that sold in impressive numbers at around $1,000. It is scarcely possible that Robotham and his colleagues were thinking in terms of a high-volume, low-cost automobile of that kind, but they were certainly most anxious to secure a much higher, more stable annual rate of sales than the one then prevailing. It is an acknowledged fact that they were much influenced by the small Packard when design and development of the post-war chassis did begin.

140

Standardisation and a return to simpler mechanisms that would be less difficult and less costly to construct, to service and to repair, seemed to be the answer. Rolls-Royce history was about to repeat itself in another way; common parts were on their way back again. So too was the valve layout of the first Royce engines – those "F-heads", with their overhead-inlets and side-exhausts, that were made in ever-decreasing numbers until 1907, when the side-valve 40/50 replaced them all.

This arrangement reduced engine length, which was important because one of the new range was to be a straight-eight. It made for a shorter, therefore stiffer crankshaft, allowed for the use of much larger inlet valves (with better

"breathing" as a consequence), and enabled a high compression-ratio to be safely employed, even when low-octane fuel was the only kind available, as was to be the case in Britain for some years after the war.

As in the earliest years there were to be variations on a basic design. At first, work was concentrated on in-line 6- and 8-cylinder units, the former of about 120 bhp. and intended for the normal Rolls-Royce and Bentley models, the latter for a long-wheelbase chassis suitable for carrying the larger kind of limousine body. Its output was to be in the region of 180 bhp. and it was intended to replace the complex V-12.

In other respects – in transmission, in suspension, in braking and in general chassis design – the new cars were to follow the pattern set by the forthcoming Wraith. Towards the middle of 1939 a Bentley 6-cylinder prototype – the original Corniche – and a Rolls-Royce 8-cylinder – the

Good vision for its occupants was a notable feature of this 1948 Mark VI James Young Sports Saloon – one of the four body types catalogued by Bentley Motors in the late 'forties.

celebrated "Big Bertha" – were ready for proving trials, and in France they proved the soundness of their concept in no uncertain way. The smaller Bentley was the more agile, obviously, but was unable to sustain its very high speed potential because the tyres of the day could not stand up to maintained 100 mph. running. The large (and rather unlovely) limousine, on the other hand, held a steady 90 mph. without trouble.

"Rippletto" – which had extremely flexible engine mountings for maximum quietness and smoothness, and because it was substantially smaller and lighter than the standard Bentley it was quite lively. But not as nimble as "Scalded Cat" – an 8-cylinder engined Bentley of the new type that was far from handsome but excited all who drove it because of its quite outstanding top-gear performance.

After all this change-ringing, however, the 6-cylinder engine and the short chassis were selected for initial production at Crewe, where the car factory was now situated. Differences bet-

At a later date – but well before the end of the war – experimental running was carried out with a 4-cylinder engine of the same type, and it was resumed in 1945, in a slightly scaled-down version of the Mark VI Bentley that was to appear in the following year. This prototype (code-named "Myth") came to nothing, which was just as well, according to Robotham, because its performance was so poor, and in any case the Crewe factory was pressed to the limit to cope with orders for the Silver Wraith and Mark VI after their introduction.

There was one more experimental 4-cylinder –

Although the proportions of this circa 1950 Freestone and Webb Drophead are not altogether satisfactory the individuality and visual interest of the car are considerable.

ween the Silver Wraith and the Mark VI mainly showed on the outside, as we have already learned. Mechanically speaking the main differences between their engines were in the induction systems. The Rolls had a single carburettor – a dual downdraught Stromberg – that gave extremely smooth and regular low-speed running, while the more mettlesome Bentley had twin S.U. instruments. According to the description of the Silver Wraith that appeared in *The Autocar* of April 5 1946, its engine developed about 137 bhp. with open exhaust and 122 bhp. silenced and installed in the chassis. In the latter state the Bentley engine probably produced about 130 bhp.

Both cars were available in chassis form for those customers who preferred to go to one or other of the surviving coachbuilders. Certain styles of body were catalogued in the pre-war manner but for the first time ever a standard steel saloon was available direct from Bentley Motors. It was made by the Pressed Steel Company but

strong emphasis placed on export in post-war Britain. It was a high car and quite a heavy car – yet it was a lively and very fast car, with a maximum above 90 mph. It was economical too, unless full advantage were taken of its accelerative powers and its ability to cruise in the seventies or eighties without stress. It was very high geared in the manner of all its forebears, 70 mph., for example, being reached at little more

1950 H.J.Mulliner Sportsman's Sedanca de Ville. The running-boards so characteristic of pre-war designs are still there, but hidden behind the extra-deep doors.

trimmed and painted at Crewe (to very high standards), and apart from the fact that it was of good and distinctive appearance it was much more spacious than any of its predecessors. Its design (for which John Blatchley and Ivor Evernden were responsible) was a development of a Park Ward sports saloon originally created for the short-lived Mark V of 1939.

The standard steel was an immediate success. It was a car of much wider appeal than its sporting forebears; roomier, more comfortably sprung, even quieter and with greater ground clearance – the latter an important selling point in view of the

than 3,000 rpm. Yet its top gear spread of speed was every bit as wide.

The Silver Wraith was also high geared, but because it was larger and weightier than the Bentley it was less lively and about 10 mph. slower. In fact acceleration was inferior in some respects to that of the 1939 Wraith and the earlier 25/30. Its owners were not stop-watch holders, however; the extra space, the luxury, the comfort and the extremely quiet running that the Silver Wraith provided was greatly to their liking. There were still sufficient craftsmen to build bodies for them to traditional levels of quality, and although Barker & Co. had gone out of business in 1938 most of the other leading coachbuilders were still active in 1946. They were to remain so, in gradually decreasing numbers, however, for much of the next decade.

The post-war cars were designed to run for 100,000 miles without need for rebore or major overhaul. Most did. There was a certain amount of excessive wear in some early production engines that was quickly cured by an alteration in cylinder bore materials and surface treatment, and occasional big-end bearing failures were stopped by changing from a by-pass to a full-flow oil filtration system. The "F-head" unit then proved to be at least as reliable and durable as any of the pre-war engines.

The writer ran a 1951 Mark VI for over 50,000 miles of most enjoyable and economical motoring. Overall it averaged 18 mpg. and its oil consumption did not rise above 1,600 mpg. It ran 20,000 miles or so on a pair of tyres and required little in the way of replacements – sparking-plugs, a set of points, a pair of petrol-pumps, a brake master cylinder and a rear silencer being the only items necessary. When the car was sold, at 108,000 miles and after more than 17 years of use, its indirect gears were no noisier than they had been when the car was new, and there was no significant decrease in performance or increase in engine audibility apart from a characteristic, subdued clatter from the little-end bearings at idling speeds.

Another Sword-owned Silver Wraith. It appeared to be a standard H.J. Mulliner Sedanca but in fact it carried a great deal of armour plating and the window glass was inch-thick. Legend has it that the car was ordered by the late Eva Peron but not delivered.

In its original form this engine was of $4^1/4$ litres capacity. In 1951 it was enlarged, to $4^1/2$-litres, and its power output raised to something like 150 bhp. This gave it more life and more top speed without sacrifice of quietness or drastic fall in economy. The Bentley – the "big bore" as it was known unofficially – became a 100 mph. machine, and the Silver Wraith could reach 90 mph. under suitable conditions. More important than top speed as such was the ability of these cars to hold high cruising rates abroad without fear of mechanical failure; more and more motorways were coming into use in Europe in the early 'fifties, and reliability of this kind was an essential mechanical feature. So too, were braking and suspension systems capable of coping with the extra demands made upon them by fast driving that was often over surfaces of indifferent quality.

In these respects the cars did well. With independent front-wheel suspension their ability to tackle rough roads at speed was far superior to that of their normally sprung predecessors which, like most contemporaries, had had to be slowed down when surfaces deteriorated. In braking power, progressiveness, consistency and freedom from fade these cars had no rivals, yet Royce's mechanically-operated servo system of 1924 was still in use. It had been modified in some respects for the post-war cars and the operation of the front brakes was no longer via a complicated, cunningly laid-out set of rods and linkages – beautiful to look at but costly to make and assemble – but by "hydraulic means." The rear brakes were still actuated mechanically by rods instead of the cables used pre-war.

It was the best system of drum braking in its day, and this was one that lasted a very long time as far as the normal Rolls-Royce and Bentley models were concerned. It was not dropped until 1965, in fact, when the "Silver Shadow" and T series cars were introduced, with hydraulically-operated disc brakes all round. But for the largest post-war Rolls-Royce model, the Phantom V, it was retained, and is a feature of the Phantom VI, which is a very large, heavy and speedy machine.

It was not until 1950 that an 8-cylinder chassis comparable in size and carrying capacity with the big pre-war chassis appeared. Until then the standard 10ft. 7in. wheelbase Silver Wraith was the only one available, whether the buyer wanted a finely proportioned and relatively compact sports-saloon or convertible to seat 4 or 5 in style or a tall and imposing limousine that would carry five in utmost luxury in its rear compartment. Many handsome cars of the former type were made but the number of good-looking limousines was small indeed. The "razor-edge" treatment that had worked so well before the war was less successful after it, when used for the larger kind of body, and it was not until designers had longer chassis to work on that they managed to restore some degree of elegance. The introduction of a long wheelbase alternative to the Silver Wraith, in 1951, was a great help in this respect, the extra 6 inches being warmly welcomed all round.

For the favoured few the new straight-8 Phantom IV, with its 12ft. 1in. wheelbase, was to give exceptional opportunities. Production was severely limited. Less than 20 cars were made between 1950 and 1956, and sales were made only to Rulers; with characteristic diplomacy Rolls-Royce made no distinction between Royals and Republicans, as long as they were Heads of State. The first was built for our present Queen, when she was Princess Elizabeth, and for her husband, the Duke of Edinburgh, who had sampled the manifold attractions of "Scalded Cat" some years before and, it is said, was extremely reluctant to part with it.

Their new car was fitted with a sumptuously appointed limousine body by H.J. Mulliner, with extra-large window and windscreen areas to enable its occupants to see, and to be seen in turn, on State occasions. It was built and finished to the very highest standards, and apart from anything else it was a most valuable and important reminder that this country still held a comfortable lead in "bespoke" or "custom-built" coachwork. Overall the appearance of this massive motor-car was restrained, perfectly suited to its special function.

It was not the first Rolls-Royce to be owned by a member of our Royal Family. The late Duke of Windsor had at least one 40/50 of the Silver Ghost type in the early 'twenties, and a Phantom I, and his brothers, the late Duke of Kent and the late Duke of Gloucester, were Phantom III and Wraith owners, respectively. But it was not until after Princess Elizabeth succeeded to the British

Rolls-Royce: the best car in the World

Throne in 1953 that Royal Daimlers gave way to Royal Rolls-Royces.

Other regal Phantom IV owners included the Aga Khan, the Shah of Persia, the Shah of Kuwait, the Prince Regent of Iraq, King Faisal, and the late Duke of Gloucester. General Franco had two of these cars, a distinction shared with our present Queen whose second Phantom IV carried a Hooper Landaulette body. Princess Margaret was another owner.

Cars of this size were not intended for owner driving, but the Rolls-Royce Silver Dawn built between 1949 and 1955 was cleverly aimed at this sector of the market. It was an export-only car at first, designed to attract overseas buyers who sought Rolls-Royce quality but did not necessarily want to be chauffeur driven. and as it had a potentially large market in North America a left-hand drive option was offered, with steering-column change. The right-hand drive cars had the traditional floor-mounted gear lever on the driver's right.

The Silver Dawn was the first catalogued Rolls-Royce with a standard steel saloon body. It was, of course, a Mark VI with a Rolls radiator, names and badges. It had a single carburettor and as a result its performance was a good deal below that of the contemporary Bentley. When it was fitted with the 4,566 cc. engine in 1951, it became a brisker car and in its final form, with automatic transmission (optional in 1952 and standard equipment from 1953) and the large boot that was the main visible difference between the Mark VI

Ivan Evernden and John Blatchley were largely involved in the design of the Standard Steel Saloon for the Mark VI. The rear view showed it off to particular advantage. 1951 4¹/₄-litre.

and its successor, the R-type, it was a most attractive vehicle. At the time of its introductin, in 1949, its price in Toronto was quoted as $14,000, or £3,500 in British money. In 1953, when it became available on the home market, its cost, with automatic transmission, was a few old-fashioned shillings over £4,704. For those who preferred to have a body of their choice fitted the Dawn chassis was available for £3,429. Some especially attractive dropheads were fitted, notably by Freestone & Webb, H.J. Mulliner, and Park Ward. More than 750 Silver Dawns were sold.

The practical potential of automatic transmis-

In 1952 a modified, long-tail Standard Steel body was introduced, on the R-type Bentley. It was also used on the "Silver Dawn", a 1954 example of which compares interestingly with the earlier Mark VI.

sion had been well demonstrated in the United States before the war, and the engineers at Derby, and then at Crewe, had been keeping a close watch on developments there. As early as 1945 Robotham had arranged for it to be incorporated in the design of the projected limousine chassis and in the following year he went over to General Motors to acquire licensing rights to manufacture their Hydramatic gearbox. In 1952 the latter was offered as optional equipment on all export chassis and in 1953 it was available on the home market as well. Although the manual gearbox that had been fitted to these cars since the early 'thirties was the best of the synchromesh type made, with its noiseless gears, its short, swift and sensually satisfying movement to and fro in a visible gate, and its lack of physical effort, the practical advantages of the automatic were already making themselves apparent.

Despite all the post-war problems of materials supply and quality, coal and power shortages, labour difficulties and a generally hostile attitude on the part of Government, the British motor industry had gradually pushed up production to a high level by the early 'fifties. Traffic densities were rising swiftly and in the ever-increasing clutter of vehicular congestion anything that would ease the motorist's task was welcome. The elimination of gear changing under such circumstances was a major factor in this respect.

In the case of the Rolls-Royce or Bentley owner he had a choice, until 1955, that is to say. During the previous two years the majority of buyers had specified automatic transmission, and when the new S-series models were announced in April, there was no option. The passing of the superb manual gearbox was a pity, but it was inevitable.

Rolls-Royce were the second British manufacturers to introduce synchromesh, in 1932, the year after it was made available here by Vauxhall. Twenty one years later they were the first in Britain to offer their own make of automatic transmission as alternative equipment on home market cars. The fact that it was American in origin worried only the diehards – descendants, no doubt, of those who had called the Twenty an expensive Buick in 1922.

After the first war the export of our motor-cars was not a matter of great importance or urgency, but after the second it was of enormous economic significance. For some considerable time, indeed, two-thirds of output had to go abroad, and manufacturers who failed to reach this target were in real danger of having supplies cut off. It was a necessary but unhappy state of affairs that was not without certain short- and long-term benefits, a most important one being the eventual dropping of the much-disliked system of taxation by horsepower (the latter calculated on the quite out-of-date R.A.C. formula), which had discouraged development of the larger kind of engine in this country as long as it was in force. Another was the greatly increased attention that had to be given to suspension on the one hand, and to heating, dustproofing and ventilating on the other.

Rolls-Royce had been exporting since 1907, in a serious way, and were well aware of the problems of making cars sturdy enough to stand up to the most trying conditions of climate and terrain. An important reason for their partial switch to all-steel coachwork from 1946 onwards was its suitability for truly universal use, the alternative, traditional system of composite construction (wood frame and metal cladding) producing problems in extremes of heat or cold increasingly difficult to solve under post-war circumstances.

The North American market was their most promising one immediately after the war. Another was the Middle East, where the number of Rulers and Heads of State who were potential customers was still large – a state of affairs no longer prevailing farther East, in India, where the disturbed political situation actively threatened the future of the ruling-Prince class.

If sales were to be increased, more and more attention had to be paid to local needs in other countries. Automatic transmission, for example, was commonplace in top-grade American cars soon after the war, and its eventual adoption by Rolls-Royce was essential, not only to make their cars acceptable on the United States market but elsewhere also, wherever they might be in direct competition with Cadillac, Chrysler or Packard, for example.

Another commonplace item in American cars were efficient heating and ventilating systems, which had, of course, to deal with great extremes of temperature. Intensive development work in this respect did not begin in Britain until the late 'forties and it was to be a long time before a heater – let alone ventilating and demisting facilities – became standard equipment. From 1946 onwards this was not the case with Rolls-Royce and Bentley, the systems of which gradually increased in complexity and efficiency.

Although most American States had strict speed limits in force – and still have, for that matter – power and speed were made much of in automobile publicity in the 'fifties, until common sense prevailed. Before then, however, the cars from Crewe had to be reasonably competitive in this respect, and while bhp figures were seldom given directly (but could be divined by perspicacious persons like the late L.H. Pomeroy, for example) their performance potential was well publicised, when appropriate.

The 4½-litre Mark VI was capable of 100 mph., which made it one of the fastest luxury-cars in the world in 1951-52. For those who sought something even swifter and were prepared to sacrifice space and the trappings of extreme luxury to some extent to obtain it, a very special Bentley was introduced in February, 1952. This was the "Continental" – one of the really great cars of its time and one of the most expensive. In a sense it was a latter-day "London-Edinburgh", a show-car to prove that the quiet could be quick, reliable and economical. Napier was no longer challenging, but Jaguar was; the current 3.4-litre Mark VII saloon was slightly faster than the 4½-litre Mark VI and its acceleration was better. People took note of such things. They also saw that the Jaguar was extremely well-equipped and many wondered how its home price, including Purchase Tax, could be held down to £1,693. At that time the Bentley cost £4,473, and if space were available it would be very much easier to explain why it was so expensive than to detail the reasons for the cheapness of the Mark VII.

The performance of the Continental was, perhaps, used to remind the keener type of motorist that Bentleys had a speed reserve not normally exploited. The new model was about 3cwt. lighter than the standard car and its sleek H.J. Mulliner body was long and low and quite distinctive in appearance. It was panelled in light alloy, it had only two wide doors and its interior was stylish and functional. The engine was modified slightly, with higher compression, and induction and exhaust changed from standard, and its gear ratios were raised appreciably. Without Purchase Tax its basic cost was £4,890, which meant that it sold abroad for upwards of £7,000, once shipping charges, local import duties, insurance and so on had been paid. By 1953, when it was available on the home market, its price here was £6,928, with Purchase Tax.

It was fast. Top speed was around 120 mph. and third could take the big car up to 100 in a tremendously exciting sweep; almost 80 was possible in second and as much as 44 in first. Yet there was nothing fierce or noisy in its running, early road tests making much of the fact that it was so quiet and so completely effortless at any speed. Its lightly stressed engine, its high gearing and its low-drag body combined to give it quite exceptionally low fuel consumption. 20 mpg. was easily achieved without special restraint being observed, and even at a constant 90 a figure in the region of 16 mpg. was returned.

It was a pity that the original design plan was

The high standard of appearance design, so characteristic a feature of H.J. Mulliner bodies, was well maintained in post-war years as is proved by this circa 1951 Touring Limousine. The long line of the front wing is particularly successful.

The sleek H.J. Mulliner Bentley Continental in its early form was a car of great distinction of appearance – a true classic of its time. Although its body was shaped to cleave the air with minimum effort its occupants were cradled in spacious comfort.

not followed through; in time customer demand for even greater internal luxury gradually pushed weight up and pulled performance down, until the gap between the Continental and its fellows was much reduced. Slightly more than 200 were built between 1951 and 1955 and the only major change during that period was the enlargement of the engine capacity, in 1954, to 4,887 cc. A year later this larger unit was standardised for the new Silver Cloud and S-series cars.

These had been under development for some years; now there were no mechanical differences between Rolls-Royce and Bentley, and no difference in performance or fuel consumption. The Bentley cost a little less because its radiator was much easier to make. The new cars were lower and longer and somewhat heavier than their predecessors but their 4.8-litre engine was powerful enough to take them up to an easy 100 mph. There was still a chassis, with revised front suspension and braking to take care of the extra speed, and it was still possible to have specialist coachwork fitted if the standard body did not meet customer needs. In fact the coming of this model was to lead in time to the going of the custom-built car as an important element in the luxury class. As will be seen, however, there was a successful revival some years ago, initiated at Crewe, and sales of the Corniche and Camargue have been substantial ever since their respective introductions.

The S-series cars were extremely good value for money – a fact quickly realised by prospective buyers, who practically queued up to pay £4,796 for the Silver Cloud or £4,669 for the Bentley. By 1955 a special-bodied Silver Wraith cost around

£8,000; even so there was sufficient demand to keep this chassis in production until 1959, when it was replaced by the much larger and costlier Phantom V – now available to commoners as well as kings, and fitted with the new V-8 engine and automatic transmission.

The six-cylinder Cloud and SI were current from 1955 until 1959, during which time the relentless, traditional processes of development and improvement continued. In 1956 "because of increasing sales to hot countries" an internal refrigeration system was offered as an extra on all models except the S-series Continental.

Another option on export cars was power-assisted steering, and with the addition of these features (so long taken for granted on many American cars) Rolls-Royce were in a far stronger position than ever before to increase their sales.

The new models had already found wider acceptance. During 1956, for instance, the value of exports to the U.S.A. was almost twice as high as that of the best previous postwar year, and in 1957 and 1958 a most carefully devised publicity programme extended awareness of the Company and its products right across the country. Apart from road cavalcades (including a most spectacular procession from Fort Worth to Dallas, Texas, that showed off 23 new cars from Crewe, led by the Company's own 1905 two-cylinder) there was an exceptionally clever press advertising campaign, created by David Ogilvy, of Ogilvy, Benson and Mather Inc., a rather special New York agency. It was not only clever – it was extremely successful. According to a report in the

Sunday Times in May, 1959 it caused Americans to go out and buy Rolls-Royces "in droves". Sales in the last eight months of 1958 were 300% higher than they had been in the first four.

In spite of all the problems of making and marketing expensive motor cars in postwar Britain, Rolls-Royce were expanding production. Robotham's estimate of 2,000 annual sales had not yet been reached, but it was certainly within sight. The *Financial Times* was a bit optimistic in suggesting in its issue of October 18, 1957 that output of all models was about 2,500 per year – that figure was not to be reached until a good deal later in fact. It was said that private sales since the war had averaged about one-third, the rest being to Company Chairmen and other business eminences. About 50% of production was exported and about 20% went to the United States. Although executives were inclined to buy Bentleys because they thought them less ostentatious, perhaps, firms with really important overseas clients tended to collect them from airports in Rolls-Royces.

In 1959 the six-cylinder in-line engine was replaced by a new, over-square aluminium V-8 of 6,230 cc. capacity – quite the largest unit made since the prewar V-12 yet 10lbs. lighter than its immediate predecessor. It had overhead-valves (another reversion to prewar practice) and these were of the "self-adjusting" type, as in the V-12.

A late-fifties design project from James Young for the Silver Cloud chassis. Bodies of broadly similar type were designed and built both before and after the war.

Opulence – but in the best possible taste. Front and rear compartments of a Silver Spirit, designed and finished to the highest standards.

Stretched Silver Cloud – this 1957 long-wheelbase car had a division and was marketed as a dual-purpose model, to be chauffeur-driven during the business week and owner-driven at week-ends or on holiday.

This unit replaced the big six-cylinder in 1936 largely because the latter had reached the end of its practical development, and for much the same reason the new and compact V-8 took the place of the postwar i.o.e. unit. In its final form the latter produced about 180 bhp. as installed.

The V-8 was also used in the new Phantom V, along with power-steering. It was by a long way the largest and most expensive car on the home market, if not in the world, and in spite of its size and weight it could exceed 100 mph. in level flight. Power-steering was now standardised on the Silver Cloud II and SII, a fact reflected in raised prices, and weight. In 1959 the former cost £5,802, the latter £5,660. Air-conditioning – a more suitable term, surely, taking note of the British climate, than refrigeration – was an extra £389. Possibly the next most costly car sold here

A focus for attention at the 1957 London Motor Show was this Freestone and Webb Drophead, on an S-series Bentley chassis. Its hooded headlamps, its concave sides and its extended fins were controversial, to say the least.

at that time was the only surviving large-capacity French luxury car, the Facel Vega, at £4,700 or so.

The final development of the Cloud appeared in 1962. The SIII cars were instantly recognisable, with their paired-headlamps and noticeably falling bonnet top. They had 7% more power and were about as fast as the early Continental, upwards of 120 mph. being possible without effort. Once again prices were up, the standard Cloud III costing £6,277, its Bentley equivalent £151 less. A typical Phantom V price, for a limousine, that is, was around £10,000. By then there were only three firms left to make special bodies on this chassis or for that of the SIII – James Young, of Bromley, Kent, H.J. Mulliner & Co., of Chiswick, and Park Ward & Co., of Willesden. Rolls-Royce had taken over the latter in 1939 and twenty years later had acquired Mulliner. In 1961 they united them and H.J. Mulliner Park Ward Ltd. shared what was left of a once-large market with the Kent firm until it closed down in 1967. Before it did, however, it had built some handsome bodies on the Phantom V chassis.

By the early 'sixties it was obvious that there was unlikely to be any significant revival as far as specialist coachwork was concerned, but on the other hand demand was likely to remain at a certain level. Very wisely Rolls-Royce kept their largest chassis in production, and even after the introduction of the far more up-to-date Silver Shadow in 1965 – the first chassisless car the Company had ever made – sales were maintained at a satisfactory level. In 1968 the Phantom VI appeared, with the latest Shadow engine and with air-conditioning as standard, but with little different otherwise from the previous model. It is still in production on a very limited scale – not surprising since its basic price is well over £200,000 nowadays – almost, but not quite, the last car with a separate chassis made in England. Tradition, intelligently preserved, as in this case, is no bad thing.

Although the overall concept of the Silver Shadow marked a turning away on the part of its maker from traditional design practices, mechanically speaking, it was still unmistakably a Rolls-Royce or Bentley. There were positive links with the past, ancient and recent; Crewe standards of construction were retained, with the excellent workmanship and close attention to fit and finish

Another coachbuilder who managed the enormously difficult task of designing large-scale bodywork that compromised successfully between the traditional and the up-to-date was James Young. This 1961 Phantom V Sedanca de Ville is a fine example of the firm's capabilities.

The clean and simple lines of the Camargue make an interesting contrast with its architectural background.

Opposite page top: 1981 Camargue.

that have distinguished its products from most others, decade after decade, for much of this century.

The automatic transmission system and the excellent V-8 engine of the Cloud III were retained but the new model was of the monocoque, or chassisless type, with separate front and rear sub-frames to carry engine, transmission, steering, suspension and wheel assemblies; independent suspension for all four wheels (with automatic height control); disc brakes operated by a high-pressure hydraulic system, with two independent circuits, that provided 78% of the necessary effort, plus an ordinary hydraulic system to supply the balance of 22%, and a new kind of power steering. Gear selection was by a lever-controlled electric motor and, typically, a tommy-bar was provided for manual operation in the unlikely event of electrical mal-function.

1939 6-cylinder Wraith Sports Saloon by Freestone and Webb.

158

THE ROLLS-ROYCE SILVER CLOUD II—$15,655 P.O.E.

Should every corporation buy its president a Rolls-Royce?

There is much to be said for it. It is a prudent investment. It enhances the public image of the company. And rank is entitled to its rewards.

A GREAT MANY of the Rolls-Royce and Bentley cars sold in England are sold to companies for the use of their top executives. "Take a Rolls-Royce or Bentley into partnership," is a saying well observed by British businessmen.

What makes the Rolls-Royce the best *executive* car in the world? Consider these facts:

Longest guarantee

The Rolls-Royce chassis is guaranteed for *three years*—the longest warranty by far of any motor car.

A good part of the cost can often be written off in five years or less. The car will then be in the infancy of its usefulness. You can sell it for a good price or drive it for many more years.

The Rolls-Royce obviates the extravagant practice of trading in cars frequently for later models. This costs you money each time a change is made. With the money that is wasted in a few such transactions, the company could have bought a Rolls-Royce.

No "planned obsolescence"

The owner of a Rolls-Royce is not threatened by annual style changes. Only an expert can tell whether it was bought yesterday or five years ago. The Rolls-Royce people do not practice a cynical and self-serving policy of "planned obsolescence."

Maintenance is minimal. With

Rolls-Royce dealers throughout the country, service is no problem.

Your president will live longer

Send the Rolls-Royce to fetch your president from his home every morning; he will reach the office in better shape. During the day, emancipate him from waiting for taxis on street corners. At night, send him home in the Rolls-Royce—he can do his homework, or take a nap. Do these things, and your president will be a *better* president. He will also live longer.

A *safe* car

On bad roads, or in heavy traffic, the Rolls-Royce can be handled like a sports car. It will not normally be so driven. But such driving shows the great ability of the vehicle to cope with critical circumstances.

The brakes have no equal in the world. There are *three independent linkages*. Should one fail (an unlikely event), the others will keep the car under control. "We would never produce a car that would outperform its brakes," says a Rolls-Royce engineer.

Free from exhibitionism

An executive's car, like his office, undoubtedly influences public opinion toward his company. The Rolls-Royce implies taste, conservatism and a re-

gard for quality. Of all luxury cars, it is the least exhibitionistic.

A source of contentment

There is satisfaction in owning such an exquisite piece of machinery. To handle a Rolls-Royce, to look at it, even to smell its leather, are pleasures which the executive of a successful company should not be denied.

Those presidents who feel diffident about driving a Rolls-Royce can be provided with a Bentley. It is exactly the same car, except for the radiator. It costs $300 less.

If you would like to try driving a Rolls-Royce or Bentley, write or telephone to one of the dealers listed on page 60, or to Rolls-Royce, Inc., 30 Rockefeller Plaza, New York 20, CIrcle 5-1144.

Two other models for executive use:

Long wheelbase Silver Cloud II with division, $19,185 P.O.E.

Phantom V, 7-passenger limousine, $25,895 P.O.E.

Rolls-Royce, Inc., of New York, chose their advertising agent with extreme care and the results were spectacular, to say the least. Yet the advertisements themselves were of restrained appearance. 1961.

The new model was shorter, lower and narrower than its predecessors but its driver still sat in a commanding position, with a splendid all-round view. Interior space was in no way reduced. It was a less aggressive looking car than before – a little bit less noticeable, even; but this was no bad thing, as time has proved, for the Silver Shadow (and the T-series Bentley) remained in full production until autumn, 1980, little changed externally, except in detail, yet in no way out of fashion. Unlike the S range cars, which have dated to some extent, their successors have the timeless quality of good design.

But if these cars looked much the same on the outside, at a superficial glance, detail changes to further improve them during 15 years of production were numerous. One of the most important was made in 1968, when the four-speed gearbox of home market cars was replaced by a superior three-speed unit which had been standard equipment on all left-hand drive cars since 1965. Another was the changeover to Burman rack-and-pinion steering that coincided with the introduction of Silver Shadow II in 1977.

In spite of small but steady increases in power over the years the Shadow and its derivatives remained among the quietest cars made. The writer vividly remembers a drive in a Corniche convertible during which the speedometer needle held steady at 120 mph. for a considerable distance. The driver himself, a man of much experience in fast cars, was quite unaware of how rapidly the car was moving until a rear seat

1966 Silver Shadow Standard Steel Saloon. After more than a decade in production Wordsworth's lines are apt – "The form remains, the Function never dies."

Above: **A Bentley Mulsanne in France, in 1981.**

The 'painted-in' radiator shell of the Mulsanne is very effective in enhancing the reticence of its appearance.

1950 8-cylinder Phantom IV Enclosed Drive Limousine by H.J. Mulliner (for H.M. Queen Elizabeth when Princess Elizabeth).

passenger asked how fast it was going. In that case the hood was up; had it been down the rush of air would have indicated speed more positively.

Since 1970 the V-8 has been of 6.7-litres capacity. It has been modified in some respects to meet American exhaust emission regulations, with lower compression to allow the use of low lead content fuel, for example, Lucas electronic ignition, a dual exhaust system (with six silencers, no less) and so on. For its size and power (however much that may be above 200 bhp.) and taking into account all that it has to do in normal service, it is not a thirsty engine. The sensitive driver might expect 15 mpg. in mixed running.

The present-day Rolls-Royce is a far more complicated machine than any of its forerunners and its mechanism is not of the kind to tinker

Opposite page top: **1973 T-series Bentley – lower, wider, sleeker than its predecessors and still in fashion although its shape was finalised in the early 'sixties.**

Opposite page bottom: **From 1973 Rolls-Royce cars exported to the United States (by then the Company's largest single overseas market), were fitted with energy absorbing bumpers, designed to give complete protection from damage in 5 mph. impacts.**

with on fine summer afternoons. But it is right for its time, as its selling success across the world has proved. In 15 years 32,300 Shadows and Bentleys were sold. 17,000 of these were exported. Impressive figures when it is recalled that the world oil crisis happened during that period and was followed by a worldwide economic recession that is still with us to a certain extent.

Visual changes to the Silver Shadow have been few in number. Pierced disc wheels and side-flashers are the only differences of any importance between this 1973 car and its forerunners.

In the circumstances it was either very courageous, or very foolish of Rolls-Royce to introduce two special models during the 'seventies. In 1971 the Corniche made its first appearance, and was followed, four years later, by the much more costly Camargue. The Corniche was available in two-door saloon form, at a price of £12,829; as a Bentley it cost £12,758, and the convertible version was about £600 dearer. The Camargue was described by David Plaistow, the Managing Director of Rolls-Royce at the time, as "the ultimate personal car". In March, 1975 its price in this country was £29,250, all taxes paid, which was almost enough to pay for two standard Silver Shadow saloons.

Its high price did not deter potential customers, however, and in no time at all a waiting list existed. Initial production was a car a week, with a build-time, it was said, of almost six months. The year before, when the Corniche cost just over £16,000, there was a three-year waiting list. As much as £28,000 was being paid for

Rolls-Royce: the best car in the World

second-hand examples and Rolls-Royce and their official retailers in this country were greatly concerned at a situation not of their making and not all to their liking. Some owners whose cars had been on long-term order were accepting delivery in the normal course, taking an immediate and very substantial profit right away by selling, then promptly placing an order for another Corniche.

A Mulsanne Turbo in its element, at speed on a long, straight, tree-lined French highway.

Its exclusiveness and consequent scarcity had much to do with that unfortunate state of affairs (which did not last, however). A building time of four months was quoted, much of which was given to the assembly, finishing and fitting-out of the distinctive looking coachwork. In the first place the main steel pressings, along with

A Corniche Convertible in a stormy setting, below the Golden Gate Bridge, at San Francisco.

166

The Corniche Convertible has catered very successfully for lovers of open-air motoring ever since its introduction in 1971. Its body is specially made by H.J. Mulliner Park Ward.

aluminium doors, boot lid and bonnet top, were put together at the London works of H.J. Mulliner Park Ward; in the second this unit was sent up to Crewe, for priming, painting and mechanical assembly, and in the third it went all the way back to London for interior trimming and final finishing. The Camargue was built in the same manner.

Each of these models was based on the Silver Shadow platform and running gear, as part of a continuing programme of rationalised produc-

The interior of the Rolls-Royce Camargue has something of an aeronautical air.

tion. They were intended to serve as engineering and style leaders for the normal cars but there was nothing experimental or untried in any respect. They shared the same engine, the 6.75-litre unit, with 10% more power than standard, and much the same top speed of about 120 mph. But the Camargue featured an altogether new, fully-automatic, air-conditioning system of tremendous complexity. Its intricacies were out of sight, however, and only three controls were visible – two temperature selectors for face- and foot-level and a mode switch that could be left on automatic or could be over-ridden. In practice it was a matter of "set and forget"; meanwhile invisibly and almost inaudibly, the electronics and the far-from-rude mechanicals worked their miracles. In 1977 this supremely effective system became standard on the new Shadow II and T-2 models.

And it still remains a feature of the current range, which has been on the market since October, 1980. These cars, though bearing a

Camargue flight-deck. The walnut veneer of the fascia is applied directly to impact absorbing aluminium sheet; another safety factor is the recessing of switches to minimise injury in the case of accident.

strong family resemblance to their forebears, have a completely new body-shell and chassis unit (such as it is), and incorporate the revised rear suspension first seen on the two-door models in 1979, which was designed to reduce transmitted road noise even further and to improve, by subtle means, both ride and handling. Engine and transmission were left very much as they were; it was the appearance of the Silver Spirit and its sister Bentley Mulsanne and the longer Silver Spur, inside as well as out, that changed.

The former emphasis on the standard cars as four-seaters was maintained. Externally, and from the front, there is more than a suggestion of the Pininfarina-designed Camargue, but the proportions are better; the treatment of the twin-headlamp clusters more satisfying. In profile or in three-quarter view the new car is not so different from the old, but from the front its more massive look gives it greater presence, and in a very subtle manner, a look of greater authority. As driving cars the current model and its variants are detectably superior; the balance between good ride and good handling is a better one; levels of quietness of the mechanicals and wind noise have been improved.

Above: **State of the art – a Bentley and a fine new office building in Texas.**

Right: **The main identifying feature of the Silver Spur, the long wheelbase version of the Silver Spirit, is its vinyl roof covering.**

Below: **A good market for Rolls-Royce products has been established in the Middle East in recent years. A Silver Spirit at home in a desert setting.**

Below right: **Modern technologies in an ancient country – a Silver Spirit in a somewhat uncharacteristic Middle East landscape.**

Project 90 was a full-scale styling mock-up of a two-door coupé. It was an all-British design by John Hefferman and Ken Greenley.

What the next full-scale model change will produce is the most open of questions. There has been talk over the years of lighter cars, with smaller engines, but when these will materialise is a matter of conjecture still. Reductions in size in no way lead to reductions in first cost, and it has to be remembered that the typical owner probably has no wish to own a car of less impressive look. The one certainty is that Company attitudes towards quality will not alter. They remain immutable.

Development of the current cars was an eight-year long process. The Bentley Mulsanne Turbo that was announced in March, 1982 was the result of intensive work over a seven-year period, and because of its superior performance in terms of acceleration and heightened top speed it could be considered as a natural successor to the celebrated Continental. The Turbo was for the owner who appreciated the excitements of a truly spirited large car that could rush up to an effortless 135 mph., where that was possible and

legal, and jump from a standstill to 60 mph. in little more than seven seconds. Yet fuel consumption was reduced by 5%.

There was no change in engine size or type; the 6.75-litre V-8 got its 50% increase in output – to 300 bhp. approximately – with the aid of a Garrett AiResearch turbocharger, driven by exhaust gases from both exhaust manifold feeds into a Solex downdraught carburettor, along with a good deal of detail change elsewhere. A higher rear-axle reduced engine revolutions and was an important contributory cause in the reduction of fuel consumption. 21 mpg. was the official 56 mph. figure (18.1 was quoted for the standard car), and the overall figure was given as 15.5 against 14.9. With no increase in engine capacity a 50% gain in power had been achieved. Was that an early indication of things to come from Crewe?

Chapter 6
See how they look

Its reflection in large plate-glass windows was always good to glimpse. As an aid to credit-rating or social status it might have had its uses. In wet weather, however, it leaked, and to be caught short, as it were, in a rainstorm with the hood down meant 15 minutes struggling in the wet to put it fully up. In dry weather, on the other hand, it rattled. It was sold, eventually (and somewhat reluctantly despite its bodily failings), on an autumn day that was neither wet nor dry.

The semi-Weymann sports saloon, also mounted on a 20/25 hp. chassis, held together for twenty-six years. Increasingly the driver's door, on the off-side, sagged on its hinges but before rectification could take place it dropped off: fortunately this happened in a car-park and little damage was caused. Driving home was a draughty business, however.

The subtly-shaped H.J. Mulliner limousine body gave no trouble; it had no rattles whatsoever: no leaks: no draughts. It was mounted on the sub-frame that Ivan Evernden had devised for the Phantom II as a means of reducing customers' waiting time for their completed cars, and this seemed to provide an extra-strong foundation for coachwork. A later Phantom III all-weather, without the sub-frame, was not rattle-free and suffered badly from visible scuttle-shake on rough surfaces taken fast.

Soundness was a feature, also, of a 1934 Hooper sports-saloon, remembered for the comparative austerity of its interior and the super-fine quality of its brown leather upholstery. No fault could be found, either, with a 1935 H.J. Mulliner sports-saloon on a 3^1/$_2$-litre Bentley

chassis, or with a 1937 Park Ward standard-steel saloon on a 4^1/$_4$. Their respective freedom from rattling was unexpected; in particular the 3^1/$_2$, with its fairly flexible frame, might have been a major source of din and dither.

As far as the all-steel Mark VI Bentley was concerned there was a good deal of wind noise if a side-window was open at speed or if the large-area sliding roof were fully back. Of rattles or boom or road noise there was nothing. But there was rust.

Body corrosion in the bodywork of that model became a noticeable feature quite early in the life of some cars, and it was blamed largely on the quality of steel available to the Pressed Steel Company, its makers, in the early post-war years. That was not the whole truth, of course; to some extent design deficiencies were a contributory cause, and as mentioned elsewhere in this book, problems of corrosion remained a worrying feature of the Cloud standard-steel bodywork throughout production. According to an *Autocar* guide for second-hand buyers, which had obviously been well researched, prospective purchasers of Silver Clouds or S-series Bentleys were wise to take as close a look as possible at the chassis where it swept up and over the rear axle. Signs of rusting there could have really serious consequences if ignored.

That state of affairs ceased, to all intents and purposes, with the introduction of the Shadow series; intensive study of the manifold problems involved led to the use of highly effective methods of protection, and while the sight of a rusted Cloud was far from uncommon, signs of

Above: **A Corniche Convertible** – the perfect car for crossing counties, countries or continents.

Opposite page top: 1982 Camargue. Each of its four headlamps, it will be noted, has a wiper.

Below: One feature of the Silver Spirit is the strong horizontal emphasis in its body design. Another is the attractive appearance of its wheels.

1953 6-cylinder Silver Wraith 4-door Drophead Coupé by Hooper.

corrosion anywhere on a Shadow are extremely rare.

With coachbuilt bodywork it does not do to let physical damage remain unrepaired; below the superbly shaped and finished metal, more often than not, there is a substantial wooden frame that is, however, vulnerable to damp and susceptible to wet- or dry-rot. Because this framework is normally out of sight, trouble can develop invisibly until a stage of dissolution, so to speak, can become so advanced that something gives way (as in the case of the door that fell off the writer's 20/25). Then, and only then, is the owner alerted, by which time the trouble may have reached a chronic stage.

It will be seen, therefore, that the steel body is not the only kind to pose problems. Composite construction – aluminium panelling on a wood frame in the case of Rolls-Royce and Bentley cars – has its own special set of ailments. In the writer's experience with his own cars and from observations of many others, over a long period, corrosion of aluminium on a serious scale was uncommon. He had body frame trouble with the aforementioned 20/25 and with the drophead coupé to which reference is made at the beginning of this chapter. In the first case wet-rot developed

The look of this 1936 20/25 Thrupp and Maberley Drophead Coupe, once owned by the author, drew much of its inspiration from the patented H.R. Owen design of 1932 but was somewhat less elegant.

in a front door pillar because water got into it through a cracked windscreen pillar; in the second the sheer weight of a door gradually weakened its standing pillar, until a stage was reached at which the hinge-retaining screws pulled clear away. Satisfactory repairs were possible.

For the coachbuilder who concentrated on production of "one-off" or limited-run bodies aluminium had numerous advantages. Apart from its lightness it was easily worked, without need of costly, specialised machinery, and it was readily available. With appropriate treatment it served as a first-class base for the finest kinds of paint finish. Rolls-Royce specify its use for bonnet-tops, boot-lids and doors to this day,

largely as a weight-reducing measure, and if forecasts of lighter cars from Crewe in the future are anywhere near correct it is possible that we may see much greater use of aluminium in years to come.

As early as 1899 its potential value in carriage building was spelled out at the twelfth annual conference of the Institute of British Carriage Manufacturers by Mr. P.W. Northey, (who may very well have been the same Northey who joined Rolls-Royce in the early years in a rather vaguely

Other days . . . other ways: in 1962 the author paid £210 for this handsome 1935 H.J. Mulliner 3½ in good condition. In spite of a high mileage its body was still completely rattle-and draught-free.

Rolls-Royce: the best car in the World

defined capacity, and did so much to enhance the reputation of his company). In the same year we hear of Charles Rolls specifying aluminium for the body of his new Panhard. A year later The *Autocar* reported that Mr. H.J. Mulliner, who had just founded the coachbuilding firm of H.J. Mulliner & Co., had plans for the entire construction of car bodies in aluminium.

But it was the long-established firm of Barker & Co. – it had been founded in 1720 by a Guards officer and built largely for the aristocracy and for the Royal Family – that was the first to become officially involved in the design and construction of bodies for Rolls-Royce chassis, once deliveries began from Cooke Street. C.S. Rolls & Co. – Rolls and Johnson, in other words – had a very high opinion of Barker's work and in their first catalogue stated that "All Rolls-Royce cars will be fitted with Barker bodies". In practice that was not to be so – or not for long at any rate; apart from anything else a single coachbuilder would not have been able to cope with the demand.

Soon Hooper bodywork was to appear on the 40/50 hp. chassis, designed and built by one of the most highly respected firms in the industry:

founded in 1807 and granted the Royal Warrant in 1830 and to be involved in the supply successively of coaches, carriages and motor-car bodies to our Royal Family for well over 100 years. Hooper bodywork was also popular with the rulers of many other countries and because of this, perhaps, it tended to have a rather majestic look. So, it may be said, did some Barker bodywork sold to the same sort of client.

During their long involvement with the luxury-car these concerns maintained a consistently high level as far as attention to, and satisfaction of, customer needs, workmanship and finish, and the choice and use of best, most appropriate materials were concerned. From an aesthetic standpoint their achievements were more uneven; to paraphrase the well-known nursery rhyme:
"When they were good they were very, very good:
When they were bad they were horrid."
The critic must tread warily here, however; for

A coachbuilder's 'visual' of the kind used to illustrate the earliest Rolls-Royce catalogues.

one thing he has his own set of standards, which may not be shared by all. For another he has little or no idea, as a rule, of how much what he considers to be a bad-looking body was due to the coachbuilder's design department and how much to the client. As an example – an extreme one certainly – the late Nubar Gulbenkian had a major say in the look of bodies built to his order, and one has only to examine the photographs of his Hooper Sedanca-de-Ville, on a Silver Wraith chassis, on page 87 of *Rolls-Royce, The Elegance Continues* to see what could happen. This car is not only bad, it is positively horrid. And yet . . . it reflected the taste and to some extent the personality of its owner and is of some interest from that point of view.

Ordering a coachbuilt body was rather like ordering a house. General requirements had to be outlined in the first place – the type and size of body, the number of people to be accommodated, interior equipment and trim, colour schemes, luggage provision and so on. A suitable foundation – in this case the chassis – had to be selected. In certain instances the coachbuilder would have stock designs available for consideration (before the war, for example, Hooper had a

basic scheme for a sports-saloon for the 20/25 chassis; after it, the Teviot, for the Silver Wraith; in the late thirties Park Ward's standard steel sports-saloon or their drophead-coupé, for the Bentley, could be 'bought off the peg', like a ready-made suit, but alterations and additions, in moderation, could be made as long as the customer was prepared to pay for them). Possibly one or other of these might serve as a basis, to be adapted as necessary. Or an entirely new design might be asked for, and in that case the design department would prepare a "visual" (what an architect would call a "rendering"), which gave a general impression, in two- or three-dimensions, of how the finished car would look. It was supported, usually, by general arrangement drawings, to show seating arrangements, dimensions and other relevant information.

Once everything had been settled, the order placed and the deposit paid, the customer might have a long wait before delivery. Framing up the

In the early 'fifties the chassis and Barker body of this 1912 40/50 were reduced to their component parts, necessary repairs and renewals were carried out and the car (one of sixteen Rolls-Royces in the collection of John Sword, in Scotland) was often seen on the road thereafter.

Rolls-Royce: the best car in the World

body was not too lengthy a job; it was tackled by a gang of highly skilled craftsmen, under the direction of a leader who had previously negotiated an all-in price for this first, essential part of the building operation. Clothing it, so to speak, took rather longer. The panelling – the outer shell of the body – had to be cut from the "white metal" (aluminium sheet normally), shaped on simple machinery, joined to other parts where necessary and gradually fitted over the wooden framework. Meanwhile, elsewhere in the works, the trim-shop craftsmen were getting on with their tasks – building up the seats, with particular attention to their springing and padding, and covering them with chosen materials (leather for the front ones almost always: leather or cloth, of one kind or another, for the rear); making the trim to cover door interiors and other parts of the body inside, not forgetting the tricky to cut-and-fit headlining; selecting, cutting and shaping the woodwork, then finishing it to the highest possible standard; cutting and laying floor-coverings, and so on.

Then there was the putting-together of the interior trim and furnishings; the priming and painting and final-finishing of the body; and with the great amount of preparatory work and laborious laying of coat upon coat of paint, plus necessary waiting between operations this last stage could take up a lot of time. But the final result was worth the wait. It was not uncommon for the customer concerned to pay occasional visits to watch the progress of work; historical precedents for so doing were numerous; Mr.

A Bentley and sundry Rolls-Royce 'in the white' at the Bromley works of James Young Ltd., a concern founded in 1863. At that stage of production there was still a great deal to do before the extended painting process and final finishing could get under way.

There is quite a difference between the 1905 Barker visual and this early 'sixties design scheme for a Bentley 'S', by James Young of Bromley.

Pepys called on his coachmaker, for example, as did King Edward the Seventh.

Coachbuilding of that kind has disappeared completely. One of the things that it provided was an almost unlimited range of choice – of type and shape and size of body as well as colour and final finish, equipment and interior furnishings. It provided service of a very special kind; offered the resources of a concern staffed by designers of consequence, at best, and craftsmen of highest skills, working with materials of the finest and most appropriate kind. Post-war economics gradually reduced the number of concerns involved and while it was possible to order a special body for a Silver Cloud chassis until production ended in 1965, H.J. Mulliner Park Ward Ltd., and James Young Ltd. were by then the only survivors of once-important industry, of international reputation and standing, capable of building it.

The Mulliner/Park Ward amalgamation took place in 1961, under Rolls-Royce ownership; by 1965 it had been responsible for an extremely handsome drophead on the Silver Cloud III chasss; for a neat-looking two-door, fixed-head version; for a development of the H.J. Mulliner Flying Spur design previously used on the Bentley Continental chassis; for some really impressive bodywork on the very large Phantom V; and for distinctive two-door saloon and drophead derivatives from the standard Silver Shadow.

Before closing down in 1967 James Young adapted fifty Shadows – at considerable cost,

doubtless – turning them into two-door saloons (at a later date H.J. Mulliner, Park Ward were to concentrate on production of Rolls-Royce and Bentley cars of this specialised kind, in the form of the Corniche and Camargue). The Bromley firm was also responsible for some good work on the Silver Wraith and on the Mark VI – it should be remembered that the latter was available in chassis form for the owner who wanted to fit his own kind of body. And when the long, flowing front wing was fashionable, through much of the 'fifties, its designers made better use of it than most of their contemporaries. Youngs built quite a number of special bodies on the Cloud chassis and were particularly successful with the big Phantom V, as study of the appropriate Dalton Watson picture books will confirm.

Much of the work carried out on Rolls-Royce chassis before the war was of indifferent quality, visually speaking, but by 1939 (perhaps after the arrival of a new designer?) some very well-proportioned, distinctive, and handsome Young bodywork was being built on Wraith and Phantom III chassis. Razor-edge styling was especially well handled by this company.

Park Ward was founded in 1919 and quickly became most active in the design and building of bodies on Rolls-Royce chassis. Its principals worked in close collaboration with Ivan Evernden, for example; their willingness to try new methods and materials was not at all common in the trade at that time and had attracted the attention of Royce himself, at a quite early stage in the life of the new concern. A most interesting account of Park Ward development and developments in the between-wars period was written by Charles Ward, whose father, C.W. Ward, had joined with W.M. Park to establish the company, and this copiously illustrated history appeared in the magazine, *Motor Body* between 1959 and 1960.

An early activity was the rebodying of Rolls-Royce cars that had been used on war service. A major achievement in the thirties was

1935 3½-litre Drophead Coupé by Park Ward Ltd. This standardised body was handsome and, because of intelligent production methods, not at all costly by contemporary standards.

the design and development for batch-production of an all-steel coachbuilt body for the 3½-litre Bentley, with Rolls-Royce collaboration. Unusually it featured a steel frame, instead of the conventional wooden one, and this led to a great number of practical problems at the experimental stage, when welding techniques were being tried out. In production, according to Mr. Ward, aluminium panels were substituted for many of the steel ones, but he does not explain why: a likely explanation would seem to be that this was a weight-saving measure. Although it was built down to a price it was a well-made, well-finished, well-equipped body, and it was a handsome one, moreover. A companion drophead-coupé (Park Ward called it a Single Coupé-de-Ville) used many common components in the interests of economical and speedy production.

Along with many of their contemporaries Park

The 'streamline saloon' of 1934–35 was a passing fashion; it was seldom any faster than more conventional looking cars and rear seat occupants had limited headroom. This 3¹/₂ litre Bentley, with Trupp & Maberly body, was shown at Olympia in 1934.

Ward produced a few "streamlined" bodies around 1934, the most successful, aesthetically and practically speaking, being an "Airflow" two-door saloon on a 3¹/₂-litre Bentley chassis, that was built to the special order of Sir Roy Fedden, of the Bristol Aeroplane Company. With such a knowledgeable client the incorporation of his ideas was inevitable: the practical result, in terms of increased performance and superior handling, was impressive.

Although a production version did appear, and one or two bodies of similar type were built on Phantom II chassis (resulting in aesthetic near-disaster and frightening handling problems, apparently), the style went out of fashion very quickly indeed as far as the custom coachbuilder was concerned. His clients, on the whole, much preferred the conventional kind of body.

Some of the best-looking Park Ward bodies were built in the early 'thirties; by far the worst appeared after the war when their designers seemed to lose any sense of proportion they might once have possessed. In that respect they were far from alone; Hooper scored few

successes, apart from some early sports-saloons on short-wheelbase Silver Wraiths and one or two very striking drophead coupés on the long-wheelbase versions. In general their later work was notably ugly and ostentatious. As might have been expected from their past record H.J. Mulliner maintained a much higher and more consistent level of good appearance during that period but even their design staff found it almost impossible to create satisfying limousine shapes for the Silver Wraith chassis.

But let it never be forgotten that Mulliner (*the* Mulliner, not the Northampton one), was responsible in part for the first Bentley Continental (in conjunction with Ivan Evernden and John Blatchley, of Rolls-Royce), a classic design of all time. To some extent it was a later development of the Park Ward Airflow fast-back of almost twenty years earlier but it was a much more practical and exciting-looking machine.

Another post-war survivor was Freestone & Webb, a company that had built a considerable number of bodies on Rolls-Royce chassis before the war (and some for the Bentley, also) and was to go on doing so until 1958. As a minor fashion for "razor-edge" treatment developed in the late 'thirties this company took it up with some success and their "top-hat" body – a close-coupled, two-light coupé as a rule – was a particularly pleasing example of how effective the use of sharp edges and subtle curves could be. Apart from anything else this return to restraint was an overdue reaction to the excessive use of the compound curve that had had its origins in the United States.

Quite a few post-war Freestone & Webb bodies retained excellence of proportion and even when they went astray their excesses were seldom as extreme as some of their rivals.

In a book of this kind and length it is impossible to go into detail, even on a subject as important and fascinating as coachbuilding. In earlier chapters mention has been made of a number of bodybuilders active between the wars – firms like Gurney Nutting, for example, which set a high standard and was responsible for so many of those beautiful H.R. Owen dropheads on the large and small Rolls-Royce chassis. That design, which was registered towards the end of 1932, is in its way, timeless; it has a rare unity even though its luggage "boot" is a separate unit right at the rear; its proportions are superb; it has style of a most thoroughly satisfying kind.

As may have been gathered no high opinion is held of Arthur Mulliner design, which was in general workmanlike but uninspired. Windovers produced some attractive work during the 'twenties and some decidedly unattractive work in the next decade – perhaps their good designer left. Vanden Plas, again, were uneven; as might be expected from a firm with Bentley connections going back to the early 'twenties they were very good with open bodies, of sporting aspect, and also managed drophead coupés neatly and well. And, finally, of the English coachbuilders (for the acknowledged leaders were mainly located in the London area) Thrupp & Maberly may be mentioned; their sense of proportion was consistent – until the mid-thirties certainly, – and from time to time they produced an exceptional-looking design.

Of the American bodybuilders Brewster is the best remembered, and for the best of reasons; their bodies were handsome, often extremely well-proportioned and excellent in shape; very well furnished and very well made. A personal

Top hatted Bentley – a 1938 4¼, with razor edge coachwork (possibly by Freestone and Webb) – and top-hatted Humphrey Metcalfe go well together.

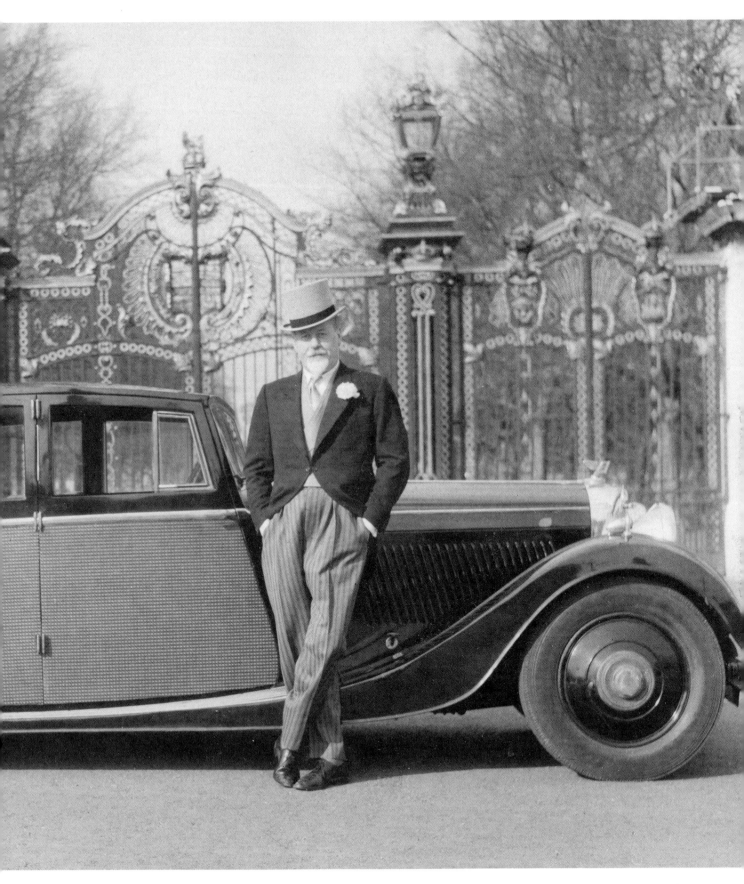

favourite is the "Henley" roadster: another of those rare designs difficult to date accurately.

Of the French firms Binder built some distinctive bodies on both the large and the small chassis – and distinguished, (perhaps disgraced), themselves with a design for an open Phantom III so disliked by Rolls-Royce that it had to be withdrawn from the Paris Salon. Franay were better-mannered; their bodies are remembered for their restraint and good proportions, as are those made by Van Vooren. The Paris firm of Weymann made its name with the patented type of construction that it introduced in the early 'twenties and which had such a vogue for about a decade.

Pininfarina designed one or two bodies on Rolls-Royce and Bentley chassis before the war and as we have already learned, that extremely important concern was credited with the Camargue. It is not, in the writer's opinion, a totally satisfactory design; its proportions lack the subtlety one expects from what was arguably one of the greatest car appearance design organisations in the world at the time.

No attempt has been made in this chapter to provide a guide to the different types of body fitted over a very long period to Rolls-Royce chassis or, over a somewhat shorter one, to its sister Bentley. While it is relatively easy to distinguish between a saloon and a sports-saloon, a limousine and a landaulette, for example, problems begin to arise as soon as one begins to consider what their builders called them. Sports-saloons become touring-limousines; even become saloon limousines; all weathers become convertibles, or vice versa; sedanca-de-villes become sedanca coupés, and so it goes on. Let the interested reader lay hands on the invaluable Dalton Watson books of photographs of hundreds and hundreds of bodies and try to puzzle it all out for himself or herself. Interest – even excitement at times – can be guaranteed.

Chapter 7
See how they run

Early in 1953 the writer had a rare chance to make comparisons between two kinds of Rolls-Royce within the space of a single day. He had been asked by what was then the Montagu Motor Museum (and is now the National Motor Museum) to inspect and road test a 1909 40/50 located at Reston, near Berwick-Upon-Tweed, then report on its condition and suitability for purchase, and on casually mentioning this fact to his friend, Mr. W.P. Dale, he was immediately invited to make the journey necessary in the latter's newly restored Phantom I touring car.

The day, when it came, was very special. On the one hand it allowed a closer acquaintanceship with the 1927 car that Mr. Dale, aided by a small group of knowledgeable friends, had rescued, then removed from a farm barn situated well within the Edinburgh city boundary some months previously (and had then driven home, after working clearance had been restored to the valves, with such dexterity and dash that modern support cars were unable to keep up); on the other it afforded an opportunity to drive a really early Rolls-Royce on empty roads.

The journey south from Dunbar was much too quick; the big black and primrose, barrel-sided tourer swept along almost traffic-free stretches of the Great North Road with the needle of its black-faced A.T. speedometer rock-steady on the 60 mark, riding firmly yet comfortably and running quietly, with the expected feeling of stability and solidity. Mr. Dale's generosity extended to the handing over of control for much of the journey southwards and the writer, whose everyday transport was a singularly lively 20/25

sports-saloon, was soon conscious of the quite different feel of the larger car. It gained speed, it appeared, more deliberately, and moved with all the dignity appropriate to its kind, its class and its make. By normal large car standards its steering was light (and very direct), as was the operation of its clutch and brake pedals and tall gear lever, but it was not the sort of car, one felt, to drive near its limits on narrow, bending and unfamiliar roads. It was very large, after all, it was heavy and it belonged to someone else.

At Reston, where the 1909 car awaited trial, sudden rain of a force and ferocity unusual even by Scottish standards, made the change of cars a damp and messy matter. Fortunately the ritual of starting passed off with traditional ease and speed, the big side-valve engine responding at once to a half turn of the handle, and after the ascent to the cab – all that remained of the original body – the clutch was "taken out" and first gear engaged.

By force of circumstance the test run had to be brief and because of the prevailing conditions most attention had to be concentrated on navigation, for there was no screen-wiper and forward visibility was practically non-existent. Furthermore one was handling a kind of vehicle not previously driven any great distance, with controls in unlikely places and a gear change of legendary difficulty. Over-riding all such considerations, however, was awareness of the significance and importance of the occasion and a powerful feeling of excitement.

The lasting impression was of a large car that felt and behaved like a very good small one; of a

Rolls-Royce: the best car in the World

machine enormously responsive and manageable and one, moreover, that would encourage fast driving, either on straight or twisting roads. In comparison with the Phantom I it felt like a sports-car, but an untypically quiet one. At a crawl its startlingly direct steering was heavy but as soon as speed was gained the car could be directed with as little real effort as a top-grade cycle, any necessary changes of course being achieved mostly by wrist movements. On winding roads, therefore, its handling was quite delightful; it was real fun to drive in such conditions and could be hustled along without much conscious attention, whereas the Phantom asked for somewhat more concentration and physical effort.

It has to be said at this stage that in terms of weight the older did have a substantial advantage. Its bodywork stopped, abruptly, just behind the bench-type front seat, with only a pair of plywood mudwings fitted temporarily over the

Retrieval of a 1927 Phantom I from a barn where it had stood for many years.

On the road again; Mr. W.P. Dale stands beside his splendid 'Phantom I' in appropriate period dress.

rear wheels to make the vehicle legally roadworthy. It was, moreover, an early, light-weight chassis without front wheel brakes; consequently its steering – as so often with those pre-first war 40/50s – was superbly light, positive and accurate.

At a later date that car was driven the length of England, from the Border to Beaulieu, in Hampshire, within two days and without me-chanical hitch of any kind, the fact that it had been standing, unused and uncared for, in a field for at least two years before purchase (and had been in active use for the best part of forty years before that) affecting in no discernible way either

its performance or the manner of its going. It used much petrol and engine oil on the long journey south, but no more than it would have done in 1909. When Mr. Maddocks, from the Rolls-Royce London Service Depot, inspected the car the only fault he found was in its magneto; the shellac in the windings had melted and these had to be renewed. But the engine still started and ran very well on the trembler-coil side of the ignition system.

The chance to drive a 1909 car for several hundred miles is one that seldom comes the way of the motoring historian, and when the car in question happens to be a Rolls-Royce of especial historical importance because of its early date the interest and value of such a journey cannot be over estimated. Although one had previous experience of the 40/50 on the road the prospect of driving so far, in a vehicle whose mechanical provenance was completely unknown, might have had its darker side. In the event, however, there were no problems at all.

Three years use of an early 20/25, the gearbox of which was of the plain, or "crash" type, gave one confidence when changing speed was necessary, and the knack of pulling the gear lever sideways to clear it of its retaining notches before moving it to another position in the gate, was quickly learned. In fact the greater part of running was carried out in direct drive. The greatest driving excitement of all occurred south of Oxford, where the prospect of a long and traffic-free stretch of road encouraged selection of the fourth speed, the famous or notorious "sprinting gear". The lever was pulled slightly sideways, to the right, to ready it for the move rearwards, then, as engine speed gradually fell, it was eased towards position 4 in the gate. There was no grating of gear wheel teeth; by chance more than anything else the move had been perfectly timed; the lever was moved firmly to the left, into its retaining notch, and the clutch pedal gently released. With light pressure on the accelerator speed was gained, not swiftly but steadily, and for the next few miles one enjoyed a very special driving experience. The big Elliot speedometer was not working and in the circumstances one could only guess at the speed attained. Probably it was little more than 60 mph. but telegraph poles, trees and the surrounding landscape all appeared to flash past very swiftly indeed.

Utmost velocity was not the point, of course; it was the manner of its achievement that was so thrilling. The old car ran straight and true, its steering rock-steady, its roadholding exemplary, its suspension almost sports-car firm yet very comfortable in an absolute sense. There was the faintest of screams from the indirect drive that the winds of passage practically concealed; nothing else of a mechanical nature was heard or felt so that the sensation of flying was vivid. Ahead the engine was turning over at no more than a fast tickover. Under proper conditions, it was clear,

the car could maintain this kind of utterly effortless progress as long as required. In present times the ideal area of the British Isles for full enjoyment of such a Rolls-Royce would be Aberdeenshire (or should it now be Grampian?), with its almost always empty, beautifully surfaced roads.

Any knowledgeable enthusiast would expect a side-valve engine of seven-litres capacity to combine flexibility with a total lack of fuss. He might be surprised, however, to find similar qualities in engines of much smaller size, and in the case of the 10 and 15 hp. Rolls-Royces the general use of their ratings under the old R.A.C. formula could be deceptive. Between the wars, certainly, quiet, easy and adequate performance was not a widespread characteristic of the majority of cars in the 10 hp. class, and it was only towards the end of the 'thirties that the best examples (Austin, Morris, Rover and Wolseley in particular) acquired mechanical refinement. In fairness, however, it must be said that engine capacities were then in the 1- to 1.3-litre range.

The 10 hp. Rolls-Royce had only two cylinders, but the capacity of each was around 900 cc., in the case of the early cars, and 1-litre in the case of the later ones. It was not an engine of the high-speed type, like the contemporary De Dion, for example, and "gave off" its power at low revolutions.

The chance to drive a 10 hp. car — in fact the oldest known Rolls-Royce in existence – was offered by its then-owner, the late Mr. Oliver Langton, in 1964, immediately after a fast and exhilarating drive from Glasgow to Leeds in the writer's Mark VI Bentley. But the sheer excitement of that occasion made one forget to make comparisons. They came later, when normal thinking had been resumed. A first impression was of the smallness of the car; from the driving seat one looked down on a short, flat-sided, pitched-top bonnet, with a brass radiator cap of familiar shape and proportions at its far end, and after so much experience of later and much larger Rolls-Royces there was an initial feeling of being in charge of a toy.

But what a toy! With 10 hp. in mind a lack of liveliness was anticipated. It was not forthcoming, however; the little car moved off with surprising willingness and had so much torque that the highest speed, third, was gained within a matter of yards. Though the change was of the unfamiliar quadrant type no particular difficulty was found in its management. Another surprise was the sound produced in first and second gears. For all the world one might have been driving a 40/50, so close was the similarity of sound and volume.

The smaller engine had a quite different feel and sound, naturally. It could be heard and it could be felt, but it was in no way noisy, in no way rough, and it ran without any kind of mechanical fuss. Whether or not its maker's claim, made in their first, 1905, catalogue, that the 10 hp. was "The most silent two-cylinder car in the world" was true is a matter impossible now to determine. What can be said, from a continuing

acquaintanceship with the car, is that the existence of its engine can very easily be forgotten when out on the road.

Because the word "silent" has been used endlessly in connection with the running of Rolls-Royce cars since their earliest days many interested people without actual experience must have gained a false idea of this matter. An anonymous writer in *The Autocar* made the point indirectly in a road test of a secondhand 20/25 in 1933:

". . . the expected standard was reached in all respects. It is really rather unfair to this make that

In April, 1954 the author drove a 1909 40/50 from Berwickshire, in Scotland to the Montagu Motor Museum at Beaulieu. Here it is during a lunch stop in Alnwick.

almost too much is expected in advance by most people, so that the thrill of realisation may be lessened."

The observant reader will be aware that up to now the words "silent" and "silence" have not been used by the author anywhere in this book. Silence, according to the dictionary, is the absence of sound. At best, under normal conditions on earth, it can only be relative. "Quiet" or "quietness' are much more accurate and sensible words to use, surely.

Of the 15 hp., three-cylinder car its makers said that it was the ideal lady's carriage for use in town and country and that it was "silent and vibrationless". In general one would agree: the only known surviving car of this type is as easily

Driving the only known 15 hp. car is not difficult; its controls are few, their action positive, their effect immediate, moreover the torque of its 3-litre engine allows most running to be carried out on top speed. The spare tyre is mounted on a Stepney detachable rim of very early pattern.

managed as the smaller 10 hp. and its 3-litre engine makes light of any demands made. It is so quiet, in actual fact, that one has to strain to hear it running from the front seat, and to rear seat passengers it is utterly inaudible; indeed the only sounds they hear when on the move are the rush of passing air and a low-pitched hum from the final drive.

As impressive is the comfort of the suspension, at both front and rear, yet this is not gained at the expense of stability. The platform type of suspension of the rear axle might be expected in theory to allow roll but in practice it does not. The driver is especially favoured. He sits high, in a commanding position, and all controls really are readily to hand. The operation of the clutch is an immediate delight for it is light and smooth-acting, and gear changing, even though it is of the quadrant type, presents no problems. The run-up through the gears can be swift; with so much low speed torque available little running time need be spent in first and second; one eases out the clutch,

squeezes the ratchet on the gear lever that retains it in each speed and lets it fall forwards into the next position. In top there is a feeling of great liveliness that makes driving a particular pleasure yet the engine gives no evidence, by sound or feel, that it is under any kind of strain. With the governor (the equivalent, to some extent, of present day speed controls) the indolent driver can delegate regulation of speed, within the limits of power available, to this efficient, unseen servant; at any given setting it will maintain road speed at a constant figure, almost regardless of road conditions.

The surviving three-cylinder is a remarkable machine, with a quite remarkable history. It was sold secondhand, after the death of its first owner in 1907, and a year later, passed into the hands of Douglas Dick, a Kilmarnock garage owner. When, after years of service as official hack, he decreed that it should be scrapped, his son Adam hid it, and twelve years later in 1933, it featured in the historical car section of that year's Scottish Motor Show. Thereafter it was tucked away in the comparative obscurity of the Dick Institute in Kilmarnock until Mr. Dick – a man of most resolute character, to say the very least – determined to restore it completely. That this was effected eventually, by Mr. C.W. Morton and a specially selected team of helpers of exceptional tenacity and ability, explains in full the reason for the present excellence of this car which was left by its rescuer to the Royal Scottish Automobile Club and is out on the road still, from time to time.

Perhaps the Light Twenty Rolls-Royce was the most attractive of the early models. Without driving experience it is impossible to say, but from contemporary accounts and from the opinions so gracefully expressed by Mr. Kent Karslake some years ago (and to which reference was made in Chapter 1) it is clear that it was an exceptionally appealing vehicle. Its competition involvements and its successes therein tend to obscure the fact that it was a thoroughly practical touring car in standard form, with the nice balance of qualities already recognised as being characteristic of its make by 1905.

It was quiet and smooth running, it had great flexiblity and a good performance and, obviously (and importantly) it had a special kind of charm. Some day, perhaps, Mr. Stanley Sears, whose restoration of a Twenty a good many years ago must rank of one of the great achievements in that field, may be persuaded to tell us of its road behaviour. At the same time he might let us know about the running of the only known surviving 30 hp. six-cylinder car, which he brought back from Australia as a pile of pieces and gradually turned into a most impressive motor-car.

Again one cannot speak of the running of this model from experience but when an early example took part in the "Battle of the cylinders" in 1906, with a four-cylinder Martini as opponent, it generated a good deal of favourable comment. Its six-litre engine was scarcely troublefree in practice but provided the quietness, the flexibility and the performance by then expected of an expensive, top quality car. That 37 chassis were sold during its short production span is a measure of its popularity in its day.

Information about the road behaviour of the "Legalimit" and "Invisible Engine" models is even more difficult to come by. It is to be hoped that Sir Alfred Harmsworth, for whom the first car of these scarcely different types was built, to special order, did make notes on its manner of going, and that some day, these may be found. It is hard to believe that someone so deeply involved with the motor-car in its early development and someone, moreover, actively concerned with writing about the subject (among other things he edited the Badminton Library *Motors and Motor Driving,* the first edition of which appeared in 1902 and which is one of the most important and useful source books of its time), should remain silent on such a matter.

As a friend of the Company he may not have wanted to embarrass by public complaint or criticism. The idea of the eight-cylinder model was one of Claude Johnson's in the first place; he imagined that the type was going to compete successfully with the electric broughams still relatively popular (particularly in London) but he was wrong. The interested reader, who wants to learn more about what Anthony Bird called a "Brief flirtation with folly" in *The Rolls-Royce Motorcar,* is advised to refer to that master-work and to the equally authoritative *A History of Rolls-Royce,* for C.W. Morton's fascinating analysis of the V-8 engine, and if he can track down a copy of the Rolls-Royce catalogue of 1906

Above: **A Camargue in Covent Garden.** *Imaginative photography of this kind has been a feature of Rolls-Royce publicity since the early 'fifties.*

Opposite page top: **A Bentley Mulsanne.**

Could anything be more inviting than the driving seat of a Bentley Mulsanne? Perfection of look, fit and finish.

1959 V-8-cylinder Silver Cloud II Standard Steel Saloon.

Percy Northey at the wheel of the Light Twenty that was second in the 1905 Tourist Trophy race. Note that its body is of standard touring type and not of the "wind cheating" kind.

he will find there some eight pages of illustrations and description of considerable interest.

Somewhat out of order, chronologically speaking, the 40/50 side-valve car has already received some mention. Earliest experiences were with two cars then in the Sword Collection, in Scotland – chassis no. 712, which carried a period wagonette body of some elegance, and chassis no. 750, which had formerly belonged to the Marquis of Bute (and had a little brass plate in the driving compartment to confirm the fact) and had a Roi-des-Belges body that was a superb example of Barker's work. From a passenger's point of view the quietness, the impressive flexibility in direct drive and the ease of riding were outstanding features. The Bute car was usually in the charge of Mr. David Frew, a driver of rare skill and sensitivity, who did not believe in always sticking to three of the four speeds available but used fourth (the overdrive) whenever possible. Even with a full load it would slide along well below 20 mph., almost soundless and without snatch.

Another Sword car, a 1910 model that had

been rebodied by Barker soon after the first war, was once driven some distance in a rally and is remembered for three things; although its appearance was archaic, to put it mildly, no one took the least notice of it in busy Glasgow streets, the interior became unbearably warm until the scuttle ventilators were found and opened, and the ride in its dickey-or rumble-seat was hard and uncomfortable.

Of postwar 40/50s one can only speak of the magnificent 1922 Park Ward barrel-sided tourer that Mr. John Sword bought from its first owner in the early 'fifties, in as-new condition and with something like 25,000 miles of running, and which passed at a later date into the discriminating ownership of the late George Milligen. Its engine was especially unobtrusive – so much so, in fact, that once the highest gear was engaged the car appeared to be eternally coasting. In this

196

regard it rivalled the uncanny behaviour of the Company's 1907 car (the original and one and only Silver Ghost). During the course of a recent and much too short drive in this famous English car one was genuinely unaware of the existence of the engine in motion unless an indirect gear was in use and its mellow note indicated that power was being produced.

It has been said that the handling of late-date side valve 40/50s can be ponderous, and this may well be so in the case of those cars overburdened with the kind of closed coachwork in fashion in the first half of the 'twenties. The additional weight of the four-wheel brake system introduced in 1924, towards the end of production, cannot have helped either, especially where the distribution of weight between front and rear axles was an unfavourable one. When that balance is right (as it usually is) these large cars are enjoyable to drive. Of Mr. Dale's Phantom I this can be said from extensive spells behind its steering wheel. Although it is a long and broad machine, as may be seen looking either forwards or backwards, it does not feel so on the move so that one wants to go on and on in the driving seat.

Another Rolls-Royce model that can give comparable satisfaction is the Twenty – the postwar, six-cylinder car, that is. As has been said

already it is not the flier that the 40/50 is, and it was never intended that it should be so; in its day it was the town carriage par excellence and with a comfortable cruising speed around 50 mph, it was excellently suited to long distance touring in this country. For continental motoring it was, perhaps, somewhat slow; quick passages across France, for example, were really the province of the faster 40/50s, which could easily sustain 60 mph. or so over all but the worst of road surfaces and were even better hill climbers.

In urban traffic the Twenty could hold its own very well; its acceleration in the gears was brisk and the change itself swifter and easier than that of the big car. Its high geared steering, stability and powerful braking (even before the four-wheel system was offered, at first as an option, then as a standard fitting), coupled with the excellent all-round visibility insisted upon by its maker, were as valuable for town work as they were for open road driving.

Over the years, in the minds of the ignorant and unthinking, has grown an image of the Twenty as a dull and decidedly dilatory motor-

A catalogue illustration of the V8 'Legalimit' that shows how the shallowness of the engine made possible a very low bonnet and, as a result, excellent forward visibility.

Rolls-Royce: the best car in the World

car. Even when fitted with lightweight
coachwork – with the type of barrel-sided tourer
that Barker and Park Ward designed and built so
well, with one or other of the types of "Doctor's
Coupé" that are in such demand nowadays, or
with a Weymann construction, close-coupled
four-light saloon – it could not compete with a
3-litre Bentley, for example, in speed or accelerative powers. But it was not intended that it
should. Extreme quietness and flexibility of
running, economy all round and excellence of
suspension, roadholding and braking were considered to be of greater importance than an
emphasis on performance with attendant high
levels of noise.

If comparisons must be made the Sunbeam,
certain Daimler models (and, goodness knows,
there were plenty of those from which to choose
all through the 'twenties!) and the better sort of
American car, for instance, must be taken into
account, for quiet running was a feature shared by
all. French, German and Italian cars of comparable class and capacity were not really in direct
competition. At that stage in motor-car development quietness of operation was not an
important consideration as far as their makers
were concerned.

"Fair, and soft, and sweet" wrote Andrew
Marvell, and he might have been writing with the
Twenty in mind . . . When all is well,
mechanically speaking, and the car is in the
charge of a driver temperamentally in tune with
it, travel in a Twenty is a richly rewarding
experience for the connoisseur. The self-effacing
nature of the engine in a good example is matched
by an equal absence of loud noise from the
transmission so that it is difficult to detect when a
change down from top speed is made.

During the early 'fifties half-a-crown ($12\frac{1}{2}$p.
in present day terms) would buy time and travel
in one or other of the numerous Rolls-Royces
that made up the major part of the Edinburgh
taxicab fleet. For anyone anxious to acquire as
much road experience of the make as possible
there was no better, no cheaper way at that time.
The variety of vehicles was considerable, ranging

*A Mulsanne in the right place, with a chateau in the
background and the prospect of high speed motoring on
French roads ahead.*

as it did from three-speed, centre-change Twenties that were close on thirty years old to sleeker looking 20/25 models of the mid-thirties.

Those earlier cars, however archaic looking their bodywork might be, attracted little curiosity of a hostile or mocking kind; they were an everyday feature of city street life, and as such taken for granted. Although the average family car was by then reasonably muted in motion those elderly Rolls-Royces went about their daily business with such quietness that one often suspected pedal, rather than mechanical, propulsion. It was common to all, regardless of age, and was as much a feature of transmission systems as it was of engines. Rear axle gears were soundless and even the knowledgeable ear had to be strained to detect the faintest hum of indirect gears. The unsung designers, fitters, inspectors and road testers at Derby so many years before had indeed carried out their respective duties superbly.

Because of the particularly trying conditions of taxi work in Edinburgh – a quite hilly city, with granite setts as none-too-smooth surfacing for its central thoroughfares – the manner in which those old cars kept going, year after year, was quite astonishing. One or two of the oldest landaulettes did rattle on the worst stretches but in the main the Barker, Hooper or Park Ward bodies had retained their structural integrity, and with it their quietness, to a remarkable degree. Few all-steel bodies of recent times are likely to last to anything like that extent; rusting of a terminal kind will surely develop long before the onset of rattling.

"Tough and Twenty" might be an apt description of that model. Almost 3,000 were made between 1922 and 1929 and the number surviving is positive proof of their eternal popularity and of their exceptional lasting powers.

At almost the same time, towards the end of 1929, the Twenty was replaced by the 20/25, which had half a litre more engine capacity and ten per cent extra developed power, and the Phantom I gave way to the Phantom II, which had a new overhead-valve engine of the same capacity but increased output. The difference that the extra power made on the road was noticeable. In the case of the smaller car it made little change

to the maximum, which is so much a function of engine speed and final-drive ratio. These were unaltered and around 65 mph. was still the normal limit. Acceleration and hill climbing were perceptibly improved, however,.

At first the top speed of the larger model was not significantly increased. It was, perhaps, five mph. higher than that of its predecessor, which could manage 80 mph. with a not too heavy or bulky body. Its gear ratios were better chosen, with the practical result that the indirects could be used to greater effect for acceleration and hill climbing. Although the Phantom I could be pushed to 50 mph. in third gear few drivers bothered to run it up to that speed. Torque characteristics were such that little was to be gained, in accelerative terms, by forcing it so. It was much more sensible – much better driving manners, indeed, – to take top gear before 40 was reached.

For one memorable year the writer owned and used a 1930 Phantom II limousine and a 1936 20/25 drophead for everyday business and pleasure motoring. The smaller car was decidedly feminine in nature; soft and sweet running yet lively, its engine and gears inaudible to rear-seat passengers. It could be a mile burner when required, however, slipping up to 75 mph. easily and readily and cruising without effort at 65. It was most economical, in spite of its "cat's back" carburettor.

The larger car, almost twenty feet long and weighing something like 2¼ tons, was neither wholly masculine nor wholly feminine. There was a lot of it (a dispiriting fact when wash time came round) and it had a great deal of power that one was tempted to use simply because it was so easily delivered. At steady speeds it sailed along with little evidence of engine, but under hard acceleration the latter was heard and felt. As usual the driver was most aware of this fact, largely because of his close connections with mechanism through hands, feet and trousers seat. Again, however, the excellent inherent balance of the engine and its low rate of rotation – with the high ratio axle 70 mph. was reached in top at well under 3,000 rpm., – meant that there was no sense of stress, and this in turn made for fast motoring, or slow, of a totally relaxed kind.

Although the Phantom II was large and heavy,

only at the lowest speeds was its steering at all taxing. The operation of all other controls demanded little physical exertion. In particular the brake pedal responded to very low pressure and was properly sensitive and progressive in action. The clutch, too, was light to operate and exceptionally smooth in taking up the drive. As long as tyre pressures were maintained at the recommended figure, wheels accurately balanced and the oil level in shock-dampers kept to its proper level, suspension, and roadholding were very good indeed.

That car was not so economical to run as its smaller companion. In a full year of mixed running, fast and slow, in town and country, its fuel consumption averaged 11¾ mpg. Because a total mileage of less than 10,000 was covered during that period, tyre life could not be accurately determined but would probably approach 15,000 miles a cover. Tyres were very expensive new but petrol cost around 22p. per gallon in 1958–59 and the Phantom, which was purchased for £75 in the former year, was sold for

£100 twelve months later. It was worth every single penny spent upon it.

A fact well known to any experienced Rolls-Royce owner is the degree of difference that can exist between models of the same type and age. This might be expected of the individually built pre-1940 cars but not of the postwar ones which were assembled in a somewhat more impersonal way. Concentrated trial of a number of different Mark VI Bentleys some years ago proved, however, that individual differences could be every bit as strong, whatever the date of manufacture.

An extreme case occurred during the late 'fifties with one's first-ever drive in a Phantom II. With realisation came deep disappointment. The engine was unbelievably rough and noisy; the car itself was lumpy and lethargic in motion.

Disillusionment did not persist, however. A

Despite the fact that the car was much used, the engine of the late J.P. Smith's 40/50 – the Auld Lady – was always maintained in this state.

1962 V-8-cylinder Phantom V Landaulette by H.J. Mulliner Park Ward (for the Ruler of Bahrein).

The Silver Spirit looks particularly handsome in profile.

Opposite page top: **A Mulsanne Turbo at rest in France.**

second example tried was in proper mechanical order and felt and handled like an oversize 20/25 of the best sort, ran with comparable smoothness and lack of fuss and moved with great fluency. In every respect it reached the expected standard.

Personal knowledge and road experience of the 20/25 model is extensive and because one has driven so many different examples over a period now exceeding 30 years, quite a few bad ones have been encountered. This has been especially so over the past decade – so much so that one began to wonder if remembered pleasure in ownership (and approximately 100,000 miles of driving in 1931, 1934 and 1936 cars between 1950 and 1962) was a matter of long-term self-deception. The cars brought along for appraisal at

203

different times lacked charm, without exception. They lacked refinement also; their engines were rough and noisy by Rolls-Royce standards and lacked life. More often than not braking was poor by any standards and to check progress at all, extremely heavy pressure had to be applied to the pedal, which was most untypical, and the hand brake pulled on for extra aid. Heavy and unresponsive steering was another commonly found feature. Yet the owners concerned seemed satisfied and were not inclined to listen to diplomatically-worded criticism.

A recent encounter with Mr. John Morrison's 1933 20/25 Owen sedanca coupé has redressed the balance most convincingly. One was right, after all, in thinking that the smaller Rolls-Royce, whatever its age, is a car of great subtlety and lasting appeal, with a most useful performance for everyday motoring even now. Obviously it has to be in first-class mechanical condition throughout and in a state of perfect tune before it can give of its best. Tucked in behind the wheel of Mr. Morrison's supremely handsome car one felt totally at one's driving ease. Through the shallow windscreen one looked along the long, familiar bonnet top to the Flying Lady mascot perched on a radiator cap dimensionally similar to that of the earliest cars, to the headlamp tops and to sidelamps clearly in view, along with the sharp curves of the mudwings. Here one was back in well-remembered motoring territory.

The engine responded at once to a touch on the

This well-preserved 1923 Twenty was the oldest of the large fleet of taxis in use in Edinburgh after the last war.

chrome-plated starter button. One advanced the ignition lever a few notches and left the mixture control (also located at the steering wheel centre) where it was, to the right of its quadrant and towards the rich position. Once the engine warmed a little it could be moved back to the centre. The clutch pedal was depressed; nothing amiss there, for its action was light; and first gear engaged. The right-hand lever moved so easily and smoothly and over such a small arc that one gave an involuntary downwards look to see if it had really gone home in the visible gate. It had, of course, and within seconds the clutch was released again and the lever eased back into second, timing all-important now because of the absence of synchromesh. No double declutching

was attempted; from long experience one knew that a slight delay was all that was necessary for a clean and quiet change. From second to third, and from third to top synchromesh of the finest kind took over. Once in the highest gear it was time to take a glance at the speedometer, the needle of which was already closing on the 50 mark. Yet one had not been pushing the car in any deliberate way; the unobtrusive gathering of speed was characteristic.

There was time, too, to consider the steering which was found to be quite excellent, the suspension, which was above average most decidedly and the quietness of the coachwork. Of all bodies in the writer's experience the drophead and the all-weather are the ones most likely to rattle and leak and give trouble in general. The owner of this over-50 year old car did admit that water does get in on occasion and this may well be so; it was not susceptible of proof on a dry summer day. What was perfectly and surprisingly clear was that there were no body rattles whatsoever. Over rough surfaces one or two distant squeaks could be heard if one listened specially hard, and there was a little noise from the hood. On a day of high winds that was scarcely surprising.

That run, brief as it was, completely restored one's belief in the fundamental quality of the 20/25. The long remembered charm was there. The light, firm and direct steering, the precisely-moving hand controls, the shapely, easily seen and easily read instruments, the sensitive yet powerful braking available from very light pressure on the pedal, the superb visibility (except to the rear quarters which were, inevitably, blind) and suspension so efficient, that it seemed, to head off any road irregularities before they reached the occupants. One longed for time to drive this car far and fast.

For a year or two during the early 'sixties the writer had another pair of cars in daily use, one being a 1934 20/25 Hooper sports saloon, the other a 1935 3½-litre Bentley, fitted with a most handsome J. J. Mulliner sports saloon body. He had to make fairly regular journeys to London and used these cars alternately. Although the

Rolls-Royce: the best car in the World

Bentley was 15 mph. faster it was decided that it should be held down to the same cruising speed as the Rolls, which is to say 60-65 mph., and the cars were driven in much the same manner. Over a journey of about 400 miles the Bentley was usually an hour faster, this being attributed largely to its superior acceleration and handiness on the many, many miles of ordinary roads encountered on the chosen route. It was not nearly so comfortable as the 20/25; indeed speed had to be reduced sharply when rough surfaces were approached.

Differences in ride quality are to be expected with the pre-war cars, the first owners of which had been consulted as to the type of springing preferred; soft for urban use, for instance, or firm, for fast touring at home or abroad.

A great deal of trouble was taken to ensure that the balance (and with it, sometimes, the very look of the car) was not upset. This is a matter taken care of in the current cars, of course, by their fine self-levelling suspension. An extreme example from the past may be quoted. The problem for Rolls-Royce was a portly owner-to-be, who chose to sit on the same side of the car as his equally portly driver. With a normal high-grade car so laden there would have been an unsightly lean to the offside. But not with this Rolls-Royce. When it was delivered it had more positive camber on the offside springs and stood higher on that side when empty. When the portly persons were in place nice calculations ensured that all was brought level.

At one period, soon after the last war, there was a feeling (quite strongly held in some quarters) that independent front wheel suspension was unnecessary for the largest kind of car. The briefest of journeys in a Phantom III, however, demonstrated very clearly that its ride comfort is manifestly superior to that of the Phantom II, good as it could be. A short run is all that one has experienced as far as the V12 is concerned but it was enough to reveal the improvements in comfort and roadholding resulting from the adoption of i.f.s. and altered weight distribution made possible by setting the engine forward in the frame.

The mushroom-shaped structures behind the Mulsanne are probably water collectors. A Middle-East scene.

206

It was also sufficient to indicate that the decision to change from a big six-cylinder, in-line engine to a much more compact V-12 had been wise when it was made in the early 'thirties. Acceleration – and what acceleration it was for a large limousine, even in top gear – was no longer accompanied by the tangible thrust of six large pistons, and if one missed the distinctive feel of the six-cylinder engine under load one really preferred the electric motor smoothness and the even swifter pick-up of the twelve.

As contemporary road tests of the Phantom III reveal its performance matched that of its sister car, the 4¼-litre Bentley, despite the fact that it weighed close on three tons (the official weight limit was 59 cwt.) and its aerodynamic efficiency was very low indeed. In no way, however, were these two cars in competition; although they shared such common features as quiet running, high performance, light and delicate controls, high constructional standards and excellent roadworthiness, they were aimed at totally different markets. Laurence Pomeroy, that wittiest, most entertaining and most authoritative of motoring writers, once said that anyone in receipt of £5,000 or more per annum could afford to run a Phantom III. In 1938 he could readily justify that statement, along with his assumption that to use such a car on a 12,000 mile year basis would cost around £500. Almost 50 years later a large multiplication of those figures would be necessary.

In its day the V-12 was lauded by motoring writers, without exception. Its combination of riding comfort and fine roadholding; its speed; its brilliant acceleration; its extreme quietness and smoothness; its superb brakes and its lightness of steering were all singled out for praise; the model inspired some fine writing. A personal favourite is "The acceleration is like the swoop of a bird down the wind". Another that has stayed in memory since 1936 was written by the Earl of Cottenham for "The Sunday Pictorial". He began a most favourable review with "I lay six to four on "Phantom III", an amazing mover by painstakers out of Derby". He went on to make it very clear indeed that the new car had given him much driving satisfaction.

Laurence Pomeroy was one of those who praised the steering of the V-12 for its lightness but in more recent times there has been some diversity of opinion in that regard. Some observers continue to admire its qualities of lightness and accuracy while others speak of heaviness and a detectable lack of rigidity at the front end of the frame. Meanwhile one waits hopefully for an opportunity to find out which faction is right. Incidentally, did Browning, Symons and Hamilton, who drove a Phantom III limousine from London to Nairobi and back in early 1937, complain of heavy steering? One thinks not.

For Rolls-Royce the Phantom III marked the beginning of a swing away from the kind of car that had been built at Derby since 1908. Outside influences on their design (while undoubtedly present) were not particularly obvious until the introduction of the Twenty in 1922, when cries of "Expensive Buick" and other unthinking remarks were bandied about. "When the new 20 hp. car was first announced, a host of armchair critics immediately got busy with their idle pens, and among them were a few who boldly stated that the car was made mainly, if not entirely, in America, at least as regards its components, the assembly alone being completed at Derby . . . Let it be stated and understood that not a single component of the 20 hp. chassis comes from the United States." (*The Motor World*, December 29, 1922).

Modifications made to the American-built 40/50s, both side- and overhead-valve models, had full Derby approval. The new V12 engine puts the 40/50 in the running again in competition with its multi-cylinder American competitors.

By the early 'thirties i.f.s. was being widely developed and introduced by American manufacturers, and there was increasing interest on the part of some European makers as well. In Italy the Lancia Lambda had featured a sliding-pillar system since its introduction in 1922 (as had the English Morgan three-wheeler, since 1910); in Germany, by the early 'thirties, Mercedes-Benz were producing cars with independent suspension all round, and in France, about the same time, the first front-wheel drive Citroens were causing a sensation because of the excellence of their all-independent, torsion-bar springing.

In this country, with its generally good road

surfaces, there was much less need or urgency to adopt the new systems, and this was all very well as far as the ordinary family car was concerned; the number exported was still negligible and there seemed to be no particular effort to raise it. But the matter was taken more seriously by Rolls-Royce; so far their principal European rivals Daimler, Hispano-Suiza, Isotta-Fraschini, for example, showed no sign of changing from their conventional systems. Across the Atlantic, however, i.f.s. was being taken up with great energy an enthusiasm. Interestingly enough it was Maurice Olley, an Englishman and a former Rolls-Royce employee, who played a major part in its development there, and it may well have been through him that his former employers (with whom he had always maintained close relations) negotiated licensing rights for the making of a General Motors coil-and-wishbone or 'knee-action' design at Derby. With Rolls-Royce modifications and refinements, of course.

High-geared steering remained a feature of the better kind of European car for a surprisingly long time, even after the introduction, in the mid-twenties, of the balloon tyre, which had much greater surface contact with the road than its high pressure, narrow section predecessors. The problem of combining high gearing with maintained lightness of operation was not an easy one to solve. There were all manner of side effects arising from the use of the new tyres that also had to be dealt with; but one maker who did so with outstanding success was Hispano-Suiza; another was Rolls-Royce, yet another was Mercedes-Benz.

In the United States, on the other hand, where the needs of the woman driver had been taken into account for a much longer time simply because she existed there in such commerically significant numbers, and where anything that eased the physical aspects of driving was always welcome, low geared steering was taken for granted. The average American driver did not mind turning his or her steering wheel four or five times to make a 360° turn. In time manufacturers in other countries began to follow suit, which was not always a good thing.

Less than a whole revolution of its steering wheel took the 15 hp. Rolls-Royce from lock to lock. By the nineteen-thirties not much more than

two turns were needed for the much larger and heavier 20/25 and 40/50 models. When the 25/30 was introduced in April, 1936, at first as an alternative to the 20/25, the only significant difference between them, apart from the extra power provided by the bored-out engine, was in their steering. This was no longer made at Derby; it was a Marles system and it was lower geared, requiring some three turns from lock to lock. Although it was noticeably lighter in use the writer has never found it easy to adjust to, after so much experience of the earlier, more direct control. He had the same problem whenever he drove overdrive Bentleys, which also had Marles steering. So far he has not had an opportunity to try a Wraith, but has good reason to believe that in its steering and in other aspects of control, suspension and so on it is very similar to its successor, the Silver Wraith.

To some extent the process of distancing the driver from the mechanism in his charge began in the early 'thirties. Steady development of flexible engine mountings made for smoother, quieter running, as did a gradual process of improving crankshaft stiffness. Rolls-Royce made little use of sound damping materials, relying mostly on the muting of noise and the suppression of vibration at source wherever possible. During the second half of that decade, however, more and more attention was given to this important matter, which other English manufacturers – Rover and Wolseley prominent among them – had been taking seriously for some years. One remembers seeing thick layers of felt fitted on the driving compartment side of the engine bulkhead of an 8-litre Bentley serving a double function as insulation from engine sounds and engine heat.

Certainly the $4\frac{1}{4}$-litre Bentley had "Seapak" sound damping material on its toe-board that was used also in the contemporary 25/30, and we know that the Wraith design featured a number of ingenious mechanical methods of suppressing or minimising sound and vibration not only in its engine but in its chassis and running gear as well. Some were used also in the B5 Bentley. Practically speaking the later prewar cars were undoubtedly quieter, though this was very much a matter of degree.

The comfortable cruising speed of a 1931 20/25, driven more than 50,000 miles, was

50 mph. Above that rate one became increasingly aware of the engine although, up to its limit it did not become raucous or rough. Later cars (from late 1932 onwards, that is, after a long overdue power increase) could be driven into the mid-seventies without fuss but because of the significant increase in fuel consumption that fast driving caused, it was best to hold speed at 60 for general touring. A 1934 20/25 once owned did 20 mpg. at a steady 50., 18 mpg. at a steady 60 and 14 mpg. at a steady 70. It was in excellent condition, mechanically, and in proper tune, and it was driven for economy, with gentle acceleration, top gear engagement below 30 mph. as a rule, intelligent use of the mixture control and little resort to the brakes.

After the war, of course, new models of Rolls-Royce and Bentley were introduced, of the rationalised type that Robotham and others had been advocating since the 'thirties. For the first time ever a complete car, the Mark VI Bentley, could be purchased, its body design a matter of close collaboration between H.I.F. Evernden and John Blatchley at Crewe, Conduit Street, Park Ward Ltd. and its eventual makers, the Pressed Steel Company. In feel it was a very different kind of car from its conventionally sprung predecessors, the 3½- and 4¼-litre models. Independent front suspension gave a far softer, more comfortable ride (the difference for rear seat passengers was very noticeable), the controls were even lighter than before and it made far lower physical demands on its driver (again, of course, this was a matter of degree).

It was no longer a sports-car in the old sense; it was much too quiet and comfortable to merit that description any longer, and with its much larger body no longer even looked the part. It appealed as a very fast, effortless and economical car. The writer enjoyed over 50,000 miles in a 1951 model bought secondhand, at 59,000 miles, in the mid-sixties. It made light of a fast journey to Venice and back and its sheer size was reassuring in the cut-and-thrust of driving in Italian cities. On the autostrada its reserves of acceleration and speed, not to speak of its excellent brakes, were put to good use. The roadholding of the Mark VI has often been criticised and one must admit to treating it with care in the first few months of ownership. In some years of driving, in every

kind of weather, no faults were encountered; indeed a safer-feeling car on ice has yet to be tried. One is left with the belief that anyone who got into trouble at the wheel of one of these cars probably deserved to do so.

The ultimate development of the Mark VI was the R-type, which was even better-looking, had improved luggage space and, from all accounts, felt even better balanced. From limited experience, and that in urban driving only, informed comment is not possible. But a general impression is that an R-type in good fettle is one of the most desirable of the early postwar Bentleys, either in manual-or automatic-gearbox form; distinctive to drive, distinctive in appearance.

With its Silver Wraith, Rolls-Royce continued to cater for their traditional market, such as it was in economically difficult postwar times. In general its engine and chassis design very closely resembled that of the companion Bentley, which made excellent sense from a manufacturing point of view. No standard body was offered at first; one ordered one's chassis and went to see one or other of the still-surviving coachbuilders to command the construction of suitable mobile accommodation. This model is remembered for levels of quietness, at all speeds, significantly below those previously encountered, and for a suspension system that provided notable ride comfort and a feeling of great stability. Like its sister Bentley it was a most manageable car, for all its size and weight. Its steering and other hand controls were literally finger-light in operation, as were the pedals, and as an experiment the car could be pulled up smartly with finger pressure only on its brakes. Not the most convenient nor practical thing to do but convincing as a demonstration.

The action of changing gear was everlastingly enjoyable, the short right-hand lever floating from one position to another in its gate under finger-tip control. As an aside it may be said that Rolls-Royce had lost none of their traditional skills in gear-wheel cutting and assembly; only in first gear and in reverse was there any sound and at that it amounted to no more than a low-pitched, tuneful hum. As a matter of interest the indirect gears of the writer's three Bentleys (3½-, 4¼- and Mark VI in turn) were just as quiet at mileages all greatly exceeding 100,000 as they had been when new and much the same could be said of their engines.

As we have learned the days of the superb manual gearbox were nearing their end by the early 'fifties. Ever-increasing traffic densities, worldwide, were hastening the adoption of automatic transmission systems as one way of reducing demands made on drivers. With a great deal more of the world now open to it as a possible source of sales than ever before the Company wasted no time in offering an automatic option, adopting and adapting the General Motors "Hydramatic" design. As installed it had four forward speeds and reverse and was controlled by a typically neat little lever, to the left of, and just below, the steering wheel.

It was used also in the new cars announced in 1955 – the Silver Cloud' and 'S-series Bentley – but by then there was no manual alternative. Rolls-Royce were quite right to make this so on practical grounds. Their American market was of increasing commercial importance and was having more and more influence as far as the Company's design thinking was concerned. One remembers approaching a trial of an early Cloud in critical fashion, as a self-confessed and determined traditionalist. Conversion was swift, and while one missed very much the pleasures of handling the manual change with proper skill the undoubted advantages of the automatic in urban driving, even then, were overwhelmingly obvious.

A year or two later power steering became available as an option and at first one wondered if this were not a gilding of the lily, for the manual system of those cars was pleasantly light and although five turns of the wheel were required to pass from lock to lock response was much more immediate than that figure might suggest. But weights were increasing steadily and in the modern manner a high proportion was carried by front wheels. As with automatic transmission the coming of power steering was inevitable and before long it was standard equipment. Its presence permitted a reduction in lock to lock turning to $4^1/_2$ turns. Insulation from mechanical sound and from the road, from the elements and the world outside, was a striking feature of

Princes Street, Edinburgh in the early 'fifties. Two thirty-year old Twenties on 7-day a week duty – and no-one thought there was anything unusual about that.

the new cars. They were bulkier than their predecessors (apart from certain long-wheelbase Silver Wraiths, with limousine coachwork); more powerful and as quiet, yet faster. Their internal amenities were more numerous and included a new and somewhat complicated heating and ventilating system, which added to all-up weight. When an air-conditioning scheme was offered as an optional extra in 1956 its installation added more to the weight of the car and its compressor required engine power for its drive. Before long, clearly, an increase in output would be necessary, otherwise the extra demands created by power steering and refrigeration plant, for instance, were going to affect performance.

The six-cylinder, in-line engine, which had gone into production in 1946 but was of prewar design, basically, had reached the end of practical development. In its final form its capacity was 4,887 cc. and its bhp. was around 185. It had a splendid reputation for reliability and durability. Its replacement was of greater capacity; it was a 6,230 cc. V8-8, made largely of aluminium, that produced more power – but how much more is a matter for speculation. There was a performance increase, certainly, but whether or not this resulted from stepping-up output to 200 bhp. one does not know. The larger capacity did lead to an increase in torque that made a decided difference to acceleration and yet allowed the use of higher gearing. That, in turn, led to even more relaxed high-speed cruising and an improvement, however slight, in fuel consumption.

In terms of quietness there was little to choose between the new engine and the old, though one or two contemporary road test writers referred to

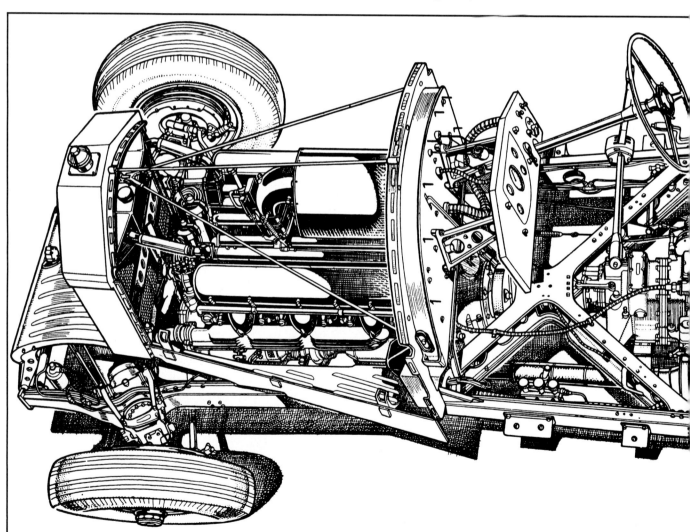

the lumpy slow-running of the V-8. The difference, as far as the driver was concerned, was greater liveliness without increased fuss or higher consumption.

This state of affairs was a feature of the next range of cars from Crewe — the Silver Shadow and T-series Bentley. Although these new models were lower, shorter and narrower, in standard form, than their predecessors their interior space was slightly greater. The traditional chassis and the long-lived servo brake system (still with drums) were finally abandoned; chassisless (or monocoque) construction was now the order of the day, disc brakes were fitted all round and

The Phantom III chassis. This drawing by Clark shows the forward mounting of the radiator and engine made possible by the change to independent suspension of the front wheels.

independent suspension now extended to the rear wheels. As far as engine and transmission were concerned, however, there was no change, except in details; the V-8 and the four-speed gearbox were retained.

On the road the car looked smaller and at the wheel it felt so. Control was now so light that the temptation to call it "touch-sensitive", in the manner of certain present-day camera shutter-releases, is not to be resisted. At first the steering was much too light, and was so lacking in feel of the front wheels that cornering was a matter of slight apprehension until one got used to things. Press reaction to the early cars was not at all favourable. The writer missed driving them during the Press launch in 1965 and was not given a chance for a trial for a year or two afterwards.

The four-speed gearbox had its shortcomings

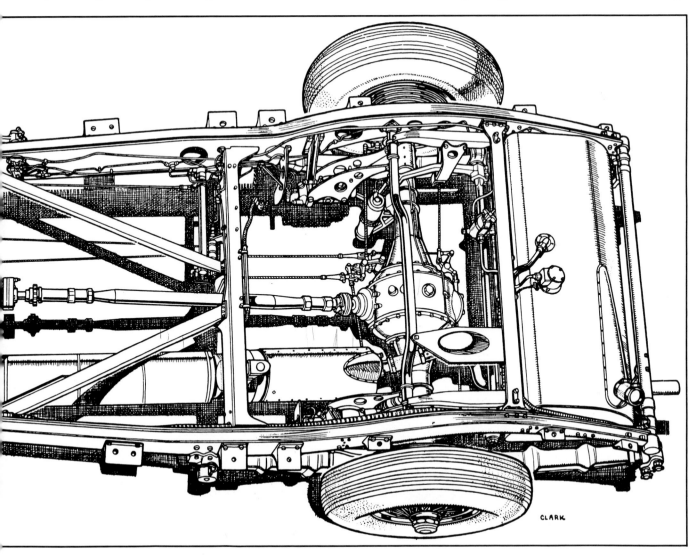

also, though these one felt, were of a relatively unimportant kind. The introduction of the three-speed torque converter transmission in 1968 did make a detectable difference, however. One recalls a first drive in a Shadow so equipped; the way in which it would shoot ahead of other traffic without the slightest feel or sound of engine was impressive, to say the least. That particular car steered well, as did many others tried subsequently, but always one had reservations, until the Shadow II came along in 1977, with a new rack-and-pinion system that was a great improvement. It was no longer finger-light and vague. Now it was firm and precise, so that the driver was properly in touch with the front wheels, but it was by no means heavy.

With the former vagueness of control, directionally speaking, no longer present, management of these cars required much less concentration than before, a point noted in a memorable hour spent in a Corniche convertible in the late 'seventies. If its driver wished to loaf, as it were, the car would loaf also, drifting along almost without sound and moving scarcely at all on its supple springs. On narrow, winding, secondary roads its size was of no consequence; it handled like a good small car (long a characteristic of its make), indeed one was reminded of the first postwar Morris Minor, with its delicacy and immediacy of response). But the side-valve Minor had no "go", whereas the Corniche had an enormous reserve of power, a great reserve of speed for use when necessary, and would idle (or so it seemed) at 70, at 80, at 90, or more, without stress.

Obviously there are other cars as fast, as quiet, as effortless. Some are faster, some may be even quieter. But their look and their shape are not the same. The view from the driving seat is a quite different one, and for many still, this is an enormously important matter. Over the years the length of the bonnet in front has varied to some extent but two things have remained constant, the shape of the radiator and the fact that both front wings remain visible. One is conscious of its width more than anything else in the Camargue; of its length rather than its bulk in the Phantom VI.

In the current cars, the Silver Spirit, the Silver Spur and the Bentley 8 and Mulsanne, one is saturated in luxury, insulated to a remarkable degree from any evidence of engine, of road

The author's Mark VI on its way to Venice in 1964.

surface, of the elements without. Even in the Turbo-R the high-performance model in the present range, there is no fuss. This exceptionally fast car can be drifted through built-up areas in best traditional town-carriage fashion, or flown down motorways, so to speak, with an equal lack of effort.

Of the new 3½-litre Bentley it was written in 1933:

. . . "its arrival has proved that Performance and Peace can now be reconciled . . ."

Much the same might be said of its present-day counterpart which is, however, one-and-a-half times as fast and far, far more luxuriously equipped.

Since 1983, when the foregoing was written, progressive development work has continued at Crewe, a major step forward being made in 1987 with the introduction of petrol-injection and anti-locking brakes as prime features of the Silver Spirit and Silver Spur. With 20% more power than their predecessors the current cars are very noticeably brisker on the move; acceleration is of a truly exciting kind but it is always under total control, for subtle improvements to steering, roadholding and handling overall give the driver an even greater feeling of command than before – which is saying something.

As speed is gained there is a distant, muted growl from the engine that disappears completely at steady speeds, however high, and this is good, especially from the safety angle, because it does remind the driver of the considerable forces that he controls. In all normal driving changes of gear are totally unnoticeable, the smoothness of transmission being strictly comparable with that of the engine. The power-operated, rack and pinion steering is now beautifully balanced; neither too light nor too heavy; precise to a degree and, because there is a little feedback through the wheel, keeping the driver in touch with the road. Insulation from the outside world is at no time so complete that it has a potentially dangerous anaesthetic effect! Although the feel of the anti-lock brakes differs from that of the system previously used the same tremendous, but absolutely smooth and progressive power is available at all times at the touch of a toe.

These remarks – so inadequate to describe the excitements and satisfactions of driving these cars, incidentally, – apply also to the current Bentleys. Fuel injection has raised the already considerable power output of the Turbo R by 10% and improved its fuel consumption (already excellent for such a potent performer) by 18%. Despite its weight and sheer bulk this model can soar from rest to 60 in less than seven seconds, and its previous, artificially restricted top speed of 135 mph. is now in the region of 150, which makes it one of the fastest road cars in the world. Although it is the fastest Bentley ever, it remains one of the most docile, untemperamental, quiet and uniquely comfortable of all high-performance motor cars. The "Performance and Peace" to which reference has already been made now stand at the most exalted of levels.

Chapter 8
See how they last

"She seemed a thing that could not feel
The touch of earthly years"

In an earlier chapter reference was made to the 1909 40/50 hp. cab-and-chassis that the writer drove from the Scottish border to Beaulieu, in 1953. The point was made that the mechanism of that ancient car was a totally unknown quantity at the time. It was driven away with the minimum of preliminary attention. The oil levels were checked, and regulated as necessary, the petrol tank was filled and as the engine seemed to be in proper working order it was decided to take it on trust. If anything were seriously wrong, it would reveal itself during the hundreds of miles ahead. In the event the few tools taken along as wards against trouble were undisturbed.

Although it was known that the car had been standing in a field for at least two years previously, where it had been and what it had been doing before then were unknown factors. There was vague talk of long service in Dundee as a breakdown truck – the way many 40/50 cars ended their useful life. The Motor Museum at Beaulieu (now the National Motor Museum) bought it at the right time, and at the right price, and it has always seemed a pity therefore, that a more convincing-looking period body was not built on what turned out to be such a good and original chassis.

It is known that a number of prospective purchasers of that car refused to believe its age although the chassis number – 1979 – was clear to read, and the gearbox had four forward speeds – another positive dating feature. They could not

see past the taper bonnet (a much later feature) or the Autovac housed beneath it. They had forgotten, if they ever knew, that the modernisation process began at Derby a very long time ago. 1979 had gone back, in 1914 or thereabouts, to be given the latest type of bonnet, which must have involved major surgery to the front end of the original body or a complete change of coachwork. Such things were not unheard of, so swiftly did fashions change in those years.

The matter of what might be called improperly dressed Rolls-Royces is by no means a recent affair. Historical precedents are numerous enough. For many years of its long, long life Mr. Thomas Love's 1904 2-cylinder car was driven about northern England in disguise. A half-round cowl covered the upper part of its little radiator and a curved-top bonnet concealed the original one beneath with its distinctive pitched-roof construction. The curve of the alien bonnet top was carried through to the foot of a shallow windscreen and a body of nondescript type (if that is a proper way to describe it) took up the rest of the chassis space, accommodated the seats and supported the hood. This amateurish attempt to modernisation was rather spoiled by retention of the original large-diameter, wood-spoked artillery wheels and flat-section mudguards.

But Mr. Percy Binns, the owner responsible, made good use of his little car from around 1920, when he received it as a twenty-first birthday present, until 1930, when he laid it up. It was restored to active life during the first half of the 'fifties by the late Mr. Oliver Langton, who carried out a comprehensive rebuild of its mechanicals, and has been in regular use ever since.

Another very early Rolls-Royce was in daily use during much of the 'twenties. In October 1924 a letter from one Captain Haig was published in *The Motor* magazine. It described a 15 hp. 3-cylinder model that the writer had owned since 1919, by which year, according to him, it had completed more than 160,000 miles. In five years or so he had driven over 30,000 miles and the car, he claimed, would still touch 50 mph. and average 33-35 mph. on long runs (not bad going in the days of a universal 20 mph. limit in Great Britain). Like Mr. Binns he, too, had modernised his car. By raising its radiator, lengthening the bonnet, raking the steering column and replacing the original heavy, four-

seat body with a more modern two-seater he had effected a somewhat more successful transformation, as a photograph published in *The Motor* the following week proved. The records have since revealed that Captain Haig's three cylinder was the very car that a group of Old Etonians (Charles Rolls one of their number) had presented to their then-Provost, in 1905.

Much of the fascination of Rolls-Royce cars for those sympathetically inclined rests in the fact that it is so often possible to discover their past history. With records still available, through the

This hearse had been driven from Inverness to Kenmore, Loch Tay 'on duty'. When it was photographed, in 1952, smooth tyres caused little concern. The 40/50 was favoured for conversions of this kind during the between-wars period.

Mr. Percy Binns, a Leeds insurance broker, in the 1904 Rolls-Royce that he 'modernised' in 1920.

Rolls-Royce Enthusiasts' Club, a quite remarkable amount of information about individual cars may be obtained, simply by supplying the chassis number and a modest fee. "Construction and Test" record cards were made out for each new chassis during its lengthy assembly, and these were kept up-to-date with notes of work carried out subsequently. Although the cards themselves carry a certain amount of printed matter much of the information recorded on them was written (often in what used to be called a 'good hand'), with the initials or signature of the person responsible for individual entries. This evidence of human involvement adds greatly to the interest and attractions of these unique documents.

It is also possible, always assuming that the records for a particular chassis are still available, to obtain a photo-copy of the original chassis

order, which makes accurate dating an easy and quite incontrovertible affair. Until 1926 there were fifty cards per chassis but during an economy campaign in that year, according to Mr. John Fasal, ways and means of reducing their number, without reducing the amount of information recorded, were found and put into effect. It may be useful to know that one's 1934 Phantom II had its piston-rings replaced in August 1948 and that the dynamo brushes were renewed a year later. That is the kind of additional information to be found on these cards.

For the buyer, even the knowledgeable one, it can be reassuring to have details of this kind. When the writer bought his first car, a 1931 20/25, in 1950, he was given a note of its mechanical history, which was short. At the time of purchase total mileage covered was 108,215. New piston-rings had been fitted at 71,000 miles and the brakes had been relined (for the first time)

This Twenty was photographed in Edinburgh in 1950, the paintwork of its Windovers Cabriolet body as good as new. The original owner was said to be P. Johnson.

at 89,000 miles. That was all the major work carried out since 1931. Oil consumption remained constant, at 1,000 mpg., for the next 50,000 miles of driving, and when the car was sold, at 159,000 miles or thereabouts, its engine and gearbox were just as quiet as they had been eight years before. One notch of the brake adjustment had been taken up and the friction-lining of the brake-servo replaced – at a cost of $2^{1}/_{2}$p.

In 1950 a new tyre for that model cost about £16 but it was quickly discovered that half-worn covers were readily available from chauffeurs in the Edinburgh area. With 10,000 miles of life left they were an extremely good buy, at £2 each.

Running a prewar Rolls-Royce or Bentley was a much easier affair in those days. They were not treated as objects of a special kind that had to be attended at all times, even when parked, and few owners bothered to remove mascots when they left their cars. For the untrusting, however, a plain radiator cap could still be purchased from Rolls-Royce for 3/6d – $17^{1}/_{2}$p, in modern money. The price of petrol was relatively low, at less than 25p. per gallon and oil still cost shillings a gallon, not pounds. Consumption was a constant 1,000 mpg. for the 20/25 already mentioned and for a 1930 Phantom II owned at a later date. 1934 and 1936 20/25s, driven considerable distances and a 1935 $3^{1}/_{2}$-litre and a 1937 $4^{1}/_{4}$-litre Bentley also much used, had very low oil consumption. Tyre life, on all these cars, was above 20,000 miles per cover rather than below.

One bought carefully, of course, from reliable sources. Perhaps one was lucky, to some extent. The most expensive single item bought for any of four 20/25 hp. cars used extensively over a twelve-year period was a battery, which cost £11 new, in 1951. Apart from decarbonising the engines, which was a necessity at 20,000 mile intervals, the only work carried out was routine servicing, which was easy to do, with the help of the appropriate instruction book. If everything was obviously working properly one left well alone. Points and spark-plug gaps were set at the specified intervals. The more mettlesome $3\frac{1}{2}$-litre Bentley engine went slightly off-tune as the 5,000 mile mark was approached but was immediately restored to vigour by thorough cleaning of its plugs, and re-gapping. Carburation was trouble-free; once correctly adjusted the Royce carburettor could be forgotten, except for filter cleaning. The later "cat's-back", of simpler construction was more difficult to set, it seemed, but once right stayed that way indefinitely and the twin-S.U. carburettors of the Bentleys remained in perfect order and synchronisation for years.

Perhaps all this sounds too good to be true. One is only recording well-remembered facts, however, and similar stories of their experiences could be told by other owners. Quite clearly there is another side to the matter; "rogue" Rolls-Royces and Bentleys do exist, and this one knows from actual experience, as already indicated. Often, however, the rogue element is a human and not a mechanical one, and quite often it is a consequence of ignorance rather than of deception. But not always.

To begin with there is the ignorance of the buyer as far as the standards to be expected are concerned. "Silent" running may be anticipated because of the gross misuse of that adjective over decades. What will be experienced, if all is in reasonable order, is real quietness in the smaller cars and the Phantom III, with great smoothness. 40/50 hp. Silver Ghost engines vary somewhat but by no means are they noisy, even at worst, and the Phantom I is normally very quiet and smooth. The comparative roughness and audibility of the Phantom II has already been mentioned: it is relative. From the prewar Bentleys a little more noise may be expected; again it is relative and the way these cars will run up to high speeds in their gears without fuss, is still impressive. The MR and MX-series overdrive Bentleys of 1938-39 are particularly quiet.

Such sound as those engines produce is noticed principally by the driver. Passengers will be largely unaware of the processes of internal-

combustion taking place, a fact not simply confined to cars of recent date.

Gear noise is noticeable in all the early models: distinctive, unmistakable, pleasing in its quality. With the introduction of the 6-cylinder Twenty sound with a lower pitch was produced by the indirects – so low in most instances that it can be difficult to determine which gear is engaged. The same low levels were characteristic of the Phantom I, of early 20/25 models and of the early Phantom II. With the introduction of syn-

chromesh for third and top speeds came the "silent" third, which made no gear-noise at all. The post-war manual gearboxes produce a low-toned hum in first and the faintest of whines in second, which is hardly heard; third and top should be indistinguishable. Automatics are noiseless, to all intents and purposes.

Between 1904 and 1936 steering ratios were gradually lowered, as was the effort necessary; from less than a whole turn, lock to lock, at the beginning, to about two-and-a-half turns, this figure applying to the Phantom II as well as the 20/25 hp.. At any pace above walking speed the steering of these cars should be light yet firm, subject to a slight degree of road-wheel reaction (through the life of the 20/25 work went on to eliminate this as much as possible, with the

This car, a 1929 model with Thrupp & Maberly Fixed-head Coupé body, was in everyday use when it was photographed in Edinburgh, in 1951. It is still in existence, the second 20/25 to be built.

Much of the history of this 1913 40/50, chassis no. 1-NA, was known before Thomas Love began a lengthy and extremely thorough restoration that included the design and building of a fine closed body. It is seen here at an advanced stage of the work.

practical result that the steering of some of the later cars has a deader feel) and very precise, without wander. Unduly heavy steering can cost a great deal of money to put right.

Light, even delicate operation of the foot brake is a sign that all is well, and braking should be completely progressive. It should also be very powerful. If high pressure has to be used suspect the servo-motor first of all. Worn lining surfaces there can make a great difference and replacing essential parts is not a major expense. To carry out a complete brake re-line is very expensive; it is not a matter of pulling off the drums, removing the worn linings, replacing them with new ones

and putting all back together again. On these cars (the prewar ones, that is) a special spanner has to be used to unlock the road wheels, first of all. Once they have been pulled clear of their splined hubs more special tools come into play, to undo the hub-nut and to remove other securing devices; then the brake drums are drawn off.

At this stage anyone accustomed to the braking systems of other cars may wonder that there is any need to make renewals. With those cars, however, it was design policy to make as certain as possible that linings could not be worn down to their rivets (with the consequent possibility of scored drums). Accordingly the linings were of extra thickness to begin with, and when the last notch of brake adjustment had been taken up there was still a goodly amount of lining material left.

To make sure that perfectly smooth braking was achieved it was also necessary to fit the new linings to the drums, for which purpose special cutters were used at the official service stations. The process of cutting lightly and offering up to the drums mught have to be repeated many times over before a conscientious fitter was satisfied. When it is realised that this operation had to be carried out four times over the time required for a proper job and its consequent cost could be considerable. A 1958 quotation for relining the brakes of a 20/25 was over £100.

Rear-axle gear noise is extremely rare, at any time. After exalted mileages a thrust-race bearing there can begin to make discreet noises and should be replaced – and we all know of the half-shafts that never break – one of the oldest of all the apocryphal tales told about Rolls-Royce cars. If a clonk can be heard at the rear of the car when the drive is taken up there is every chance that wear has developed in the driving dogs.

I-NA on the road! – a passenger's view of one of the many hairpin bends on Amulree Hill, Perthshire, a favourite place for competitive hill-climbing before the first war. On this occasion the car was carrying eight altogether.

The only chassis rattles ever encountered came from shock-absorber linkages. Their ball-joint ends can gradually loosen over long periods of use unless they are checked regularly and their adjustment scrupulously maintained.

As for silencing systems one writes again from past experience. The back silencer of a 1951 Bentley had to be replaced when the car was 15 years old. The 1931 20/25 had to have a new tailpipe in 1951 and in the same year its exhaust-manifold downpipe had to be welded. In 1958 some welding had to be carried out on the main silencer of a 1930 Phantom II. In each case the original system was still in use. The silencer of a 1913 40/50 known to the writer is the original one yet the car in question has been used for something like 50 years.

In a previous chapter passing reference was made to Rolls-Royces driven in recent times that lacked the magical running qualities remembered from earlier years. The all-round improvement in sound reduction in motor-cars has to be taken into account when one is making comparisons, and it is a complicating factor that has to be put

into its proper place. A prewar Rolls engine should be quiet and smooth and it should respond immediately to the accelerator, picking up speed swiftly, with absolutely no trace of hesitation. Because of the general absence of effort it is as well to keep an eye on the speedometer to get a more positive idea of the rate of acceleration. In good condition these cars slip up to 60 mph. or more most unobtrusively. They should run with equal lack of fuss at very low speeds, even in top gear, and be able to pull away cleanly and crisply.

A late 20/25 tried some years ago had no life whatsoever. Its acceleration to all intents and purposes, was non-existent. The usual checks of carburettor settings, spark-plug cleanliness and gap measurements, and contact-breaker points revealed nothing amiss. The source of the trouble was soon traced, however. The piston in the carburettor had seized in its guide and as a result the engine could not breathe. Once the piston was freed the running was transformed. It is worth remembering that the carburettors of these cars are fine instruments and should be handled with appropriate respect and care. Rough treatment can lead to rough running.

So far Rolls-Royces, and prewar ones in the main, have been discussed. What applies to them applies largely, to their sister Bentleys – those subtle sports cars that combined quickness with quietness and notable economy and reliability with longevity. As far as quality of running is concerned it is very much the same as that of the contemporary 20/25 and 25/30 models but there should be a good deal more life and speed, with little extra noise. At tickover one can expect slight vibration – the torque reaction of a vigorous engine in effect. It can be reduced by retarding the ignition. With the hand throttle set down its quadrant, on the left-hand side of the steering wheel boss and the ignition lever on the right, also set well down towards full retard, engine revolutions can be reduced to little more than 200 per minute. Moving both levers up their respective quadrants sends the needle of the large-diameter rev. counter spinning its dial.

Those Bentleys were not built down to a price; in fact they were extremely well made as anyone who has ever taken one to pieces will know. But they were more lightly built in certain respects than the sister 20/25 and one or two components have a shorter life than the corresponding ones on that chassis. The steering swivel-pins are one example. Another, if memory serves, is the rear-axle thrust-race bearing. A shorter interval between rebores was to be expected and until improved bearing materials were introduced the mains had a life of 60 – 70,000 miles under normal driving conditions. With the improved materials this was raised by about 20,000 miles, perhaps even more on the overdrive chassis.

Chapter 9
Rolls-Royce and Bentley in words

Before the war the number of books largely concerned with Rolls-Royce was small. The first considerable one appeared in 1926, produced by Cambridge University Press and not for public sale. Its sponsor was Rolls-Royce Limited and it was distributed to favoured associates and friends of the Company. The author, H. Massac Buist, had long and extensive connections with the make and its makers, with Conduit Street and with Derby, and in *Rolls-Royce Memories* he spoke with all the authority of first-hand knowledge and experience. Buist was a most able writer, whose clear partiality for his subject did not lead him into partisanship. His book was to become a useful, often unacknowledged, source of material for later writers. Nowadays the original edition is one of the rarest of all motoring books but because of the initiative of the Rolls-Royce Enthusiasts' Club a facsimile reprint is available. *Rolls-Royce Memories* has considerable interest and value as a primary source.

In *Seven Pillars of Wisdom*, T.E. Lawrence made passing reference to the worth of the Rolls-Royce armoured-cars and tenders that he had been able to use from time to time in his very successful hit-and-run operations against Turkish Forces in Arabia towards the end of the First World War. A closer look at the work of the nine Rolls-Royce vehicles under Colonel Lawrence's charge was given by S.C. Rolls, one of the drivers concerned, in his *Steel Chariots in the Desert*, which was published by Jonathan Cape in 1937.

Very much earlier, soon after the end of the First World War in fact, the Company had published booklets describing and illustrating

wartime uses of its cars for the transportation of senior officers on various fronts, and something of the fighting record of its armoured cars. In 1972 these publications were bound-in with two others of the same kind and period that dealt with Rolls-Royce engined aeroplanes and flying-boats, and disturbed by Bronte-Hill Publications.

Within a year of the death of Sir Henry Royce in 1933, an illustrated biography by his friend, Sir Max Pemberton, was published. Although it is a most agreeable and readable book it is of comparatively little value to the serious researcher. Its author did not go into great detail about his subject, his associates or his cars. At a later date a smaller version, without illustrations, was issued in Jonathan Cape's attractively-produced Florin Library.

Patrick Balfour's *Grand Tour*, which was written in 1934, begins with a light-hearted account of a car journey overland, from London to Quetta in North-West India, that the author, along with some other adventurous spirits, had made sometime before. The instigator and leader of the trip was a member of the Indian Civil Service, (named "Colonel Christmas" by the author) who had purchased a second-hand Rolls Royce to take back to India for use, and who proposed that, if a sufficient number of extra passengers could be found to make the journey with him, his wife and two others, a second car would be purchased to carry them. The advertised cost per seat, for a drive of several thousand miles, was £34.

Christmas attracted his extra passengers and bought another Rolls, for £300. The cars, as the

Rolls-Royce: the best car in the World

Previous page: **Two sorts of British engineering excellence – a Corniche Convertible and the Forth railway bridge.**

illustrations reveal, were four-wheel brake 40/50s, one a late Silver Ghost, the other an early Phantom I. In what is, basically, a travel book (and an extremely well-written one, at that) people and places are dealt with in greater detail than cars. Recommended, nevertheless.

At the Wheel, Ashore and Afloat, which was published in 1935, is an extended account of its author's exploits on land and sea that is well worth reading. Commander Montagu Grahame White earned a very good living both before and after the First World War as a boat-hirer. But his boats, like himself, were somewhat out of the ordinary; in fact they were steam-yachts. It is scarcely surprising to learn he became involved with Rolls-Royce at a very early stage. He moved in the same social circles as Rolls and Johnson and knew many of the same prosperous people. Grahame White had strong views on the design of motor-car bodywork, which he was able to put over to the partners, and towards the end of 1905 he contracted to supply C.S. Rolls & Co, with schemes for a variety of different types of body, at an agreed fee of £75 per design. Barker & Co. were the chosen builders. They were to work within strictly defined weight limits and Grahame White was to supervise construction. Each design was to be registered on submission.

Complete drawings and specifications for limousines, a "Pullman", a town coupé, a sports 4-seat tourer and a speed-model 2-seater were prepared and delivered. Grahame White designed the Pullman* (a top-heavy, clumsy-looking vehicle) for a 12' 6" wheelbase chassis, which Royce did not make and when Claude Johnson refused to sanction the enlargement of the standard 40/50 hp. a rapid re-design had to take place. From pictorial evidence it is clear that Grahame White was in no way a body designer of exceptional aesthetic sensibilities. On the other hand he was a most interesting and colourful character.

The Magic of a Name was the first comprehensive survey of Rolls-Royce history. Its author, the late Harold Nockolds, once told the writer that he spent a fortnight at the Company's guest house in Derby in 1938, researching and writing the book,

and for that not inconsiderable feat he ultimately received a fee of £1,000. Whatever the truth of the matter he produced an extremely readable work, which is still a useful general introduction to its subject. It was brought up to date in 1949 and re-issued, in a second edition, with rather second-rate colour illustrations by the author's brother, Roy. There was a third edition in 1972.

In 1939 *Two Roads to Africa,* by H.E. Symons, was published, with illustrations of professional quality. It dealt with four separate car journeys, made between 1935 and 1939 in, respectively, a Morris Ten, a Morris Twenty Five, a Rolls-Royce Phantom III limousine and a much-modified Wolseley 18/85. The large limousine was driven from London to Nairobi and back in the early part of 1937, with a double crossing of the Sahara Desert for added interest, and coped admirably with the manifold problems presented by such a journey over such varied and difficult terrain. For his own reasons Symons wrote a rather one-sided account and the reader who would like to know more is advised to consult John Oldham's *Ghosts, Spectres and Phantoms.* His meticulously researched description presents the other side of the story in detail of the most fascinating kind, seen in proper perspective a long time after the event.

So much for the principal pre-war works. The diligent reader will come across references to the make elsewhere, of course. Once his plays began to bring in substantial royalties Noel Coward bought a second-hand Rolls, about which he wrote in waspish terms in his autobiography, *Present Indicative.* His first choice, obviously, had not been a wise one but he did not forsake the marque. In numerous, lightweight tales dealing with the adventures of Berry and his friends between the wars Dornford Yates gave them Rolls-Royces for fast travelling on dangerous missions but did not grant the make the cachet accorded to Hispano-Suiza by Michael Arlen, in his widely known novel, *The Green Hat.* Miss Dorothy Sayers, in a number of well-written, well-researched detective stories of the 'thirties provided her aristocratic hero, Lord Peter Wimsey, with a Daimler of high performance and great size, rather than with a Rolls.

For further mention of Rolls-Royce in literature the interested reader is advised to consult the

incidentally a royalty had to be paid to the Pullman Company for the use of their name.

feature, *Cars in Books,* that William Boddy has contributed to his magazine, *Motor Sport,* for many years past. But the largest source of information and comment until the post-war boom in Rolls Royce books began still remains in contemporary newspapers and magazines. Access is not necessarily easy unless one lives within reasonable distance of a major reference library, the National Motor Museum at Beaulieu or, specifically for Rolls-Royce and Bentley material, the Rolls-Royce Enthusiasts' Club Library at its headquarters at Paulerspury, in Northamptonshire.

The writer began his own researches by combing the pages of *The Autocar* from 1904 onwards: then started to go through bound volumes of *The Motor, Motor World, Cars Illustrated, The Automotor Journal* and many, many more. He turned his attention to such weeklies as *The Illustrated London News, The Sphere, The Tatler, The Field* and *Country Life,* for example — sources of much interesting material in their editorial pages and in advertisements. He discovered that one motoring correspondent at least, did not follow the universal practice of passing comment but not writing constructive criticism, where justified, and that was the anonymous author of road test reports in *The Times.* Even when he wrote of Rolls-Royces he passed judgement on various points of design and criticised aspects of control or road behaviour that did not altogether please him. In that respect he differed from all his contemporaries.

Nowadays standards of writing, in general, are not nearly so high as they were then but the quality of criticism is of a better kind. To *Motor Sport* and its Editor, William Boddy, most of the credit is due for this important change in attitude which makes it so much easier now for the average reader to discover what a particular car is really like to drive and to live with. On the other hand the knowledgeable motorist, who had learned how to interpret the older sort of road-test, no longer has the fun of determining what the writer was implying when he omitted any mention of suspension of referred casually to "a slight degree of road-wheel reaction through the steering".

In the 'twenties and 'thirties *The Autocar* and

The Motor tests were never more than two pages long and provided limited information on performance and the specification of the car. Nowadays they extend to many pages and supply a multitude of facts (and opinions); usefully, one feels, comparisons with other cars of the same kind and class are featured. One need not agree with them, after all.

It was in 1964 that the first definitive work on Rolls-Royce was published, by B.T. Batsford Ltd., whose motoring books editor at the time was Anthony Harding. It is still in print, many editions later, and has been kept up to date with each new one. Its authors, the late Anthony Bird and Ian Hallows, brought splendid qualifications to their task. Bird took to it a very personal, very well-informed, usefully detached view (his own motor-car obsession was with the Lanchester) while Ian Hallows possessed formidable resources of technical knowledge and information. The combination of Bird, Hallows, Harding and Batsford led to a publishing triumph. *The Rolls-Royce Motor Car* is an immensely readable, enjoyable, informative, sometimes controversial book that will stand for all time as a major work in its field.

A book of comparable quality is *A History of Rolls-Royce Motor Cars,* by C.W. Morton, which was also published in 1964 by G.T. Foulis. It covers the cars from 1903 to 1907 in the most thorough manner possible. Indeed it is most unlikely that anything better of its kind will ever be done. Morton joined the Company in the early 'twenties and became its unofficial historian about thirty years later, uniquely qualified because of a wide theoretical and practical knowledge of engineering, long experience in various capacities at the Derby works, time spent teaching at the London School of Driving Instruction, an innate sense of history and of proportion, an enquiring mind, an unbiased view of his subject and special powers of comparative analysis. The well written text of his book is supported by excellent photographs and drawings. This was the first volume of a projected series of three covering Rolls-Royce car history from 1903 to 1939. The second was to deal with the 40/50 Silver Ghost model in the same detailed manner but for various reasons it is most unlikely ever to appear. This can only be

Above: **Power on the leash – but the modern Bentley is fierce neither in appearance nor in the manner of its going.**

The sumptuous interior of a Corniche Convertible.

Below: **All controls fall 'nicely to hand' in the modern Bentley or Rolls-Royce. A 1982 facia.**

1976 V-8-cylinder Silver Shadow Standard Steel Saloon.

described as a tragedy. The third was to describe the Twenty and other, later models.

A shorter, less ambitious work *The Rolls-Royce Phantoms*, was the third top-class publication on the make to appear in 1964. It was *A Hamish Hamilton Monograph* one of a small, select series of square-format books on a variety of interesting subjects *(The Camel Fighter*, for example, *Early Victorian Furniture, Patrick Stirling's Locomotives* and so on). D.B. Tubbs was its author, which was an automatic guarantee of stylish, but never mannered, writing, accuracy of fact and authority of opinion, thoroughness of research, wherever appropriate and a fair comparison between the Phantoms and their contemporaries in the same class. The illustrations of this book and, indeed, its whole appearance are of high quality.

In the three major works just considered, text and pictures are complementary. In the Dalton Watson volumes dealing exclusively with coachwork on Rolls-Royce chassis, *Those Elegant Rolls-Royce, The Elegance Continues* and *Coachwork on Rolls-Royce, 1906-39,* the pictures are of overwhelming interest and value. John Webb de Campi's *Rolls-Royce in America* is also very well illustrated; furthermore it has a useful, though brief, text and its captions are helpfully informative. Raymond Gentile's *The Rolls-Royce Phantom II Continental,* also from the same publisher, tells its tale incompletely and in a plodding manner (what it could do with is a touch of the Tubbs, to lighten it). Another Dalton Watson book *Bentley, Fifty Years of the Marque* is also to be recommended for its extensive variety of pictures.

One of the biggest problems for anyone considering the preparation of any book about these cars is to find as many previously unpublished photographs as possible. Although new sources continue to be found their number dwindles, year by year. One excellent showcase during its too-brief existence, was a little, landscape-format monthly called *The Rolls-Royce Owner* that was edited and published by Jeremy Bacon. The latter was able to seek out and publish a great variety of photographs, from all periods in Company history and had a knack of finding hitherto unknown, – or at worst seldom seen – examples. The few issues of this magazine

that appeared between August 1963 and April 1964 are well worth looking for nowadays.

Another most useful publication was the Company's own *Rolls-Royce Bulletin,* an expensively and beautifully produced journal that concentrated on photographs of its cars and Rolls-Royce engined aircraft, in all parts of the world but also regularly carried one lengthy article of specialised interest. In the January 1954 issue, for example there appeared twelve pages of text and pictures dealing with The Continental, from pre-First World War 40/50 chassis with such modifications as higher radiators and extensively louvered bonnet sides to the sleek, Bentley H.J. Mulliner bodied model of 1952. At the end of that same year, in December, the Bulletin had an eleven page long feature on Sir Henry Royce, with a most interesting mixture of pictures for illustration.

The *Bulletin* was issued free, to owners between 1920 and 1958, when publication ceased almost certainly because the costs of production and distribution became unrealistic. In Tom Clarke's very useful compilation, *An Index to Rolls-Royce and Bentley Periodicals,* first issued in 1972 by Transport Bookman Publications, it is suggested that the *Bulletin* may have been begun as far back as 1908.

A much shorter lived, much less ambitious journal, was *Early and Late,* edited for the Rolls-Royce Section of the Vintage Sports Car Club by the late Jimmy Skinner in the first place; then for a time by Commander Stead and, finally, by Michael Sapsford. Small as it was, much valuable material appeared initially on its pages, including first-hand accounts from Ivan Evernden of his development work on C.J.'s Sports Cars (the high-performance Phantom I short-wheelbase models. It was thought that these models might appeal to speed-happy Maharajahs – though Rolls-Royce did not say so in so many words) and of his collaboration with Royce in the creation of the first Phantom II Continental.

Since 1985 the Company has been distributing 'Queste', a periodical of the highest quality that is the natural successor to *Rolls-Royce Bulletin.* The quality of its articles, illustrations and production could scarcely be better.

For a fairly full list of other relevant periodicals T.C. Clarke's *Index* should be consulted. But from personal knowledge *Flying Lady,* the well-illustrated, well-documented journal of the Rolls-Royce Owners' Club Inc. (of America) and the Rolls-Royce Enthusiasts' *Club Bulletin,* which has maintained a consistently high standard of editorial matter, illustrations and presentation since 1960, may be especially recommended for their sheer quality and thoroughness of research.

It is a pity that so many of the more recent books on Rolls-Royce do not reach the same levels of responsible writing and factual accuracy. To compensate however, the last decade has seen the appearance of the late John Oldham's unique *Ghosts, Phantoms and Spectres,* which deals with the 40/50 hp. models in great detail and is packed with previously unpublished facts of every possible kind. It is illustrated with all manner of new photographs, but careless production and poor reproduction on the whole rather spoil their effect and lessen their impact. The quality of writing might not rate a high mark in examination (and some facts are suspect) but this is of no real matter; the author's knowledge of, and enormous enthusiasm for his subject carry the reader along irresistibly. It is such an interesting book that one finds oneself going back, again and again, to re-read and enjoy especially favoured passages.

The same can be said of the second significant book of this decade, John Fasal's *The Rolls-Royce Twenty,* another large and extremely heavy volume crammed with every possible kind of verbal and visual information that is frequently consulted for sheer pleasure, for it is a first-class example of its kind and by far the best history yet to appear solely concerned with one specific Rolls-Royce model. It is well-written. It is well-illustrated. The amount of information given about the model and its makers is enormously wide-ranging yet never in any way boring. The quality of research and standards of factual accuracy attained reach the highest levels.

In 1966 and 1967 Profile Publications issued short illustrated monographs dealing with the 15 hp. three-cylinder, the Silver Ghost, the Phantom I and 3½- and 4-litre Bentleys, and, in 1973, with the Phantom II. Anthony Bird was responsible for the Ghost. During the past year or so longer monographs on the Silver Cloud and

the Silver Shadow have been published by other concerns and may be useful for the concentration of facts and pictures that they provide.

In 1963 Kenneth Ullyett's *The Book of the Silver Ghost* was published by Max Parrish and a year later was followed by the same compiler's *Book of the Phantoms.* The former had an interesting assortment of illustrations and a short and superficial text; its selling point presumably, was the facsimile of a complete, illustrated 1909 40/50 hp. instruction book that it contained. The latter was along the same lines but covered a forty-year long period; text poor, pictures good and varied. The facsimiles this time were of a random selection of pages from many of the instruction books produced for different models between 1925 and 1963.

Very much more interesting and valuable to the serious enthusiast are *The Book of the British Rolls* and *The Book of the American Rolls* for which Dan R. Post Publications, of Arcadia, California, were responsible, in the early 'fifties. These are first-class of their kind; very well produced in large format (their page size is 10½" x 8½", or 280 x 210 mm.) and making proper use of Company promotional material issued between 1907 and 1952. The *Album of sales and institutional literature* that deals with the British cars has such intriguing items as complete reproductions of a special sales catalogue prepared for America in 1907 and another, for more general use, issued in 1914. Their concern is with the 40/50 hp. model and each abounds in words and pictures. All three pre-war Phantoms are represented and one is reminded that Rolls-Royce set a disappointing standard as far as catalogue illustrations were concerned during the 'twenties. They made much use of not-very-good photographs that were then retouched rather clumsily, whether they were to be reproduced in colour (as in the case of the Twenty catalogues and those for the 40/50 cars) or in black and white, as in the case of the 20/25 and 25/30 models.

Fortunately someone was wise enough to realise that the appearance of the pages of technical information would be greatly improved by the use of good line drawings. These were an outstanding feature of the later 20/25, 25/30, Wraith, and Phantoms II and III catalogues.

1977 V-8-cylinder Corniche Convertible by H.J. Mulliner Park Ward.

*Left: **A Silver Spirit on a splendid stretch of rippled sand.***   *Above: **A Scottish hillside is the setting for this Silver Spur.***

Since 1946, as a matter of interest, Rolls-Royce have so much improved the overall standard of design, artwork and photography in their catalogues and other forms of publicity that they have maintained a leading position in this field for many years.

High-quality illustrations, for use in Press advertisements, are a notable feature of *The Book of The American Rolls.* Its concern is with the Springfield-built cars: with the side-valve 40/50 models and the overhead-valve Phantom I: with the ways in which the extremely difficult task of selling long-lived automobiles of the highest quality and first cost was attempted to motorists conditioned to buying off the showroom floor and changing cars quite frequently. The advertisements in no way resemble those created for use in the British Press. There it seemed enough to quote from an owner's letter or from a particularly favourable and cleverly written road test report and present it in a layout of superfine typographical quality. At a later date, in this country, it was considered sufficient to reproduce a good photograph of a Rolls-Royce, with the slogan "The best car in the world" and the maker's name and London address.

But that would not have worked in the United States in the 'twenties or early 'thirties. Selling had to be forceful and to the point. Much was made of the exclusiveness of the make. Its reputation for exceptional reliability and longevity was emphasised. Its snob appeal was certainly not minimised. Apart from the carefully planned, cunningly calculated Press advertising for which Rolls-Royce of America was responsible, there were technically informative booklets that explained and justified Derby and Springfield design philosophies and manufacturing methods. These, presumably, were intended for engineers who might become owners.

Subsequently these first-class books were published together, in a much smaller format, under the title of *Rolls-Royce; The Living Legend.* Whether between two covers or one this stands among the best source books.

Productions of that kind, which may incorporate much material still in copyright, are not easy to do without close co-operation and friendly help from the manufacturer concerned and, at times, from the appropriate one-make Club – in that case the Rolls-Royce Owners' Club Inc. In 1961 the latter was involved also in the reprinting of the 1906 Rolls-Royce catalogue, a key work in any collection of the literature of the make. That handsome little landscape-format book is crammed with information and pictures and reflects in no uncertain manner the quite forceful techniques of persuasion developed by Rolls and Johnson. Testimonials (many from titled owners) and quotations from Press reports abound. There are lengthy specifications and poorly-drawn bodybuilder's "visuals" of the range of styles on offer (some of which do not even represent Rolls-Royce cars . . .) price lists, road contour diagrams to emphasise the hill-climbing powers of the make, letters from owners and Editor's opinions. The hundred pages of this beautifully produced facsimile are crammed with items of

period interest; almost the only thing missing is any reference to Frederick Henry Royce.

Another first-rate facsimile is one issued by the Company in 1974 and so well done that it has been mistaken for the original, which was produced for C.S. Rolls & Co. in 1905. This charming little catalogue printed, like the 1906 example, in red and black, is so realistic that even the steel staples holding its twenty pages together were pre-rusted. Or so one has been told . . . The effectiveness of one selling point is still open to doubt over 80 years after it was written. What did the prospective buyer think when he read that: "C.S. Rolls & Co. have aimed at producing a car that "A fool can drive"?

Brooklands Books have issued a number of collections of contemporary road tests, new model descriptions and other material of interest covering various periods from the early 'twenties to the present time. They are well compiled and well illustrated, though it must be said that the quality of reproduction of photographs is not high. These large-format paperbacks are still good value and are recommended reading.

Rolls-Royce, The Story of The Best Car in the World first appeared in 1977 as an *Autocar* Special, the fifth in a series of portfolios of contemporary road tests, new model descriptions, drawings and photographs from the pages of that authoritative journal. Its cover is wide, from a first mention of the new, all-British car shown at the 1904 Paris Salon to road impressions of the then-new Silver Shadow II published in 1977. Of its kind it is excellent. In 1978 the original paperback edition was supplemented by another, a hardback, published by Hamlyn.

The balance of first-class pictures and text in that book is well contrived. In its *Royal Silver Jubilee Souvenir 1977,* by Colin Hughes, with R.J. Gibbs as Editor, the Rolls-Royce Enthusiasts' Club produced a most attractive pictorial record of a great occasion, concentrating on photographs, however, and keeping text to the minimum. Another Club publication worthy of mention is *Rolls-Royce Small Horsepower Engines,* by R. Haynes and M.A. Grigsby, which deals with the overhaul of 20 hp., 20/25 hp. and 25/30 hp. and Wraith engines and with Bentley $3\frac{1}{2}$, $4\frac{1}{4}$-litre and Mark V units. In addition the R.R.E.C. has been directly responsible for the production of many different technical manuals and other material concerned with maintenance and repair.

Each of the principals most intimately involved in the creation of the Company has been dealt with at book length; Royce first, as we have learned, then Rolls, in *Rolls of Rolls-Royce,* by Lord Montagu and Michael Sedgwick, which Cassell published in 1966, and, finally, Claude Johnson, in *The Hyphen in Rolls-Royce,* a Foulis title written, most interestingly by John Oldham.

An insider's view of the cars and the Company was given by W.A. Robotham in *Silver Ghosts and Silver Dawn.* Its author's name has appeared already in these pages; he was a key figure in keeping his employers in automobile manufacture and, along with his former chief, Ernest Hives, surely deserves a book to himself. The one he wrote after retiring is in no way an exercise in hagiography; "Rb" had strong views about the kind of car he thought Rolls-Royce should be making by the late 'thirties and was not afraid to say so. This is a book with real bite and character.

Rolls-Royce by L.J.K. Setright, originally published in New York, by Ballantine, in 1971, appeared in this country in 1975 over the Haynes imprint, and there were second and third impressions in 1976 and 1979. The author's respect for the putting together of words is, perhaps, somewhat stronger than his regard for his subject or, in some instances, for factual accuracy, and certain illustrations are incorrectly captioned. Because it presents a particular point of view, and that strongly at times, Setright's book stands apart. But it is highly readable; its writing is stylish and the opinions it expresses have been carefully considered. This is a book to irritate some enthusiasts for the make and for that reason alone it should have a place in any Rolls-Royce collection.

Another general survey to be recommended is *Rolls-Royce: 75 years of motoring excellence,* by Edward Eves, whose regular contributions on veteran and vintage cars have added greatly to the attractions of *Autocar* in recent years. If it breaks no new ground it is still a comprehensive, well-documented and well-illustrated account, and by far the best book of its kind to appear in the past several years.

In 1976 the Mowbray Company, of Provi-dence, Rhode Island, published *the american Rolls-Royce,* by Arthur Soutter. Its author joined Rolls-Royce of America Inc. in 1920, as a tool designer, before production began, and ended his service as General Maintenance Manager, in 1936. This is another of the select few of real value: certainly the better of the two studies of the Springfield cars so far written. It is large and handsome, beautifully produced, illustrated with all manner of period photographs, drawings and diagrams, as well as contemporary adver-tisements. Its text is most readable and well balanced (for Soutter was able to distance himself from his subject, somewhat unusually), and – an important point – it goes into the financial affairs of the American operation in much detail.

This, of course, is an important and significant feature of Ian Lloyd's absorbing three-volume commercial history of the Company, written originally as a degree thesis but not published, for a variety of reasons, until more than twenty years later. It is still the one and only full-scale, thoroughly researched study of a side of Rolls-Royce activities little noticed in other histories of the make and its makers so far.

In spite of the number of books, good, bad or indifferent, that publishers have squeezed onto the market in recent years there is still room for more of originality and high literary quality. A full-scale biography of Royce is in preparation at the time of writing. Who is to replace Morton to write with full knowledge and authority about the Silver Ghost? Could Mr. John Fasal be persuaded to deal with other Rolls-Royces in the same exhaustive (but never exhausting) manner as he has treated the Twenty and, more recently, the Rolls-Royces and Bentleys of the Indian Maharajahs? Will Mr. Warren Allport expand the excellent study of Phantom III development that he made for *Autocar,* some time ago? It would make a truly interesting monograph. But Mr. Harvey-Bailey has now done proper justice to the Derby Bentleys and Mr. Ian Rimmer's account of the Experimental Cars is the most thorough work on this subject ever to appear. With the concentration of the Rolls-Royce and Bentley archive material at Paulerspury a vast amount of information is now available and accessible to the researcher of serious intent. It is to be hoped that it will be properly used.

In the summer of 1987 HM Queen Elizabeth took delivery of this impressive Phantom VI Limousine, its body built by Mulliner Park Ward, the Coachbuilding Division of Rolls-Royce.